## More Praise for *The Future of Freedom*

"Zakaria's provocative and wide-ranging book is eminently worth reading. . . . His book displays a kind of argumentation, grounded in history and political philosophy, of which there is precious little these days, particularly among opinion columnists."                    —*Foreign Affairs*

"Zakaria is a serious enough thinker and has produced a serious enough book to require serious attention."

—Gary Hart, *The Washington Monthly*

"Brilliant. . . . Some books are too short. . . . Oh that *The Future of Freedom* had a seventh chapter."                    —*National Review*

"*The Future of Freedom* is one of the most important books on global political trends to appear in the past decade. Its sobering analysis has vital lessons for all of us concerned with freedom's future in the world."

—Samuel Huntington

"At once provocative and illuminating."                    —Bernard Lewis

"Fareed Zakaria, one of the most brilliant young writers, has produced a fascinating and thought-provoking book on the impact of Western constitutional principles on the global order."                    —Henry Kissinger

"In this incisive book, Fareed Zakaria asks searching questions and offers provocative answers. *The Future of Freedom* is an impressive contribution to our understanding of the crises of democracy that lie darkly ahead."

—Arthur M. Schlesinger, Jr.

"Compelling. . . . An intelligent study on the compromises necessary to reach liberal democracy, and on the perils of maintaining it."

—*Christian Science Monitor*

"A book with immense relevance for the immediate future of the Middle East." —*Salon Magazine*

"Thought-provoking and timely." —*Publishers Weekly*

"Fareed Zakaria covers an immense amount of ground in this eloquent examination of the varieties of freedom and democracy. Mastering the nuances of every corner of the world, discussing the critical (and virtually unexamined) problem of 'illiberal democracy,' analyzing what he correctly calls 'the Great Exception' of Islam, Zakaria forces us to think in new ways about values that Americans take for granted." —Richard Holbrooke

"This is a very thoughtful and intelligent book that is important for all Americans and for those who would make American policy. After all, what is more important than the real meaning of freedom and democracy? The book could not appear at a more appropriate time." —Peter Jennings

"Fareed Zakaria's *The Future of Freedom* is a learned, tough-minded, and intellectually courageous warning that easy bromides about democracy, if taken as a literal guide to policy, could make the world a more dangerous and less pleasant place." —Nicholas Lemann

"Our role is to help you think for yourselves. So I won't tell you whether I think Zakaria is right. . . . Just let me suggest that you read the book." —Richard Levin, President, Yale
Freshman Address, Fall 2003

# THE FUTURE OF
# Freedom

Illiberal Democracy at Home and Abroad

FAREED ZAKARIA

W. W. NORTON & COMPANY

NEW YORK LONDON

Manufacturing by Courier Westford
Book design by Chris Welch
Production manager: Devon Zahn


Library of Congress Cataloging-in-Publication Data
Zakaria, Fareed.
The future of freedom : illiberal democracy at home and abroad /
Fareed Zakaria.—1st ed.
p. cm.
Includes bibliographical references and index.
ISBN 0-393-04764-4
1. Democracy.  2. Liberty.  3. Political science—Philosophy.  I. Title.
JC423 .Z35 2003
321.8–dc21                    2002153051


ISBN 978-0-393-33152-3 pbk.


W. W. Norton & Company, Inc., 500 Fifth Avenue, New York, N.Y. 10110
www.wwnorton.com

W. W. Norton & Company Ltd., Castle House, 75/76 Wells Street,
London W1T 3QT


1 2 3 4 5 6 7 8 9 0

For Paula

The Sirens were sea-nymphs who had the power of charming by their song all who heard them, so that the unhappy mariners were irresistibly impelled to cast themselves into the sea to their destruction. Circe directed Ulysses to fill the ears of his seamen with wax, so that they should not hear the strain; and to cause himself to be bound to the mast, and his people to be strictly enjoined, whatever he might say or do, by no means to release him till they should have passed the Sirens' island.

Ulysses obeyed these directions. He filled the ears of his people with wax, and suffered them to bind him with cords firmly to the mast. As they approached the Sirens' island, the sea was calm, and over the waters came the notes of music so ravishing and attractive that Ulysses struggled to get loose, and by cries and signs to his people begged to be released; but they, obedient to his previous orders, sprang forward and bound him still faster. They held on their course, and the music grew fainter till it ceased to be heard, when with joy Ulysses gave his companions the signal to unseal their ears, and they relieved him from his bonds.

—Thomas Bulfinch, *The Age of Fable or Stories of Gods and Heroes*

# Contents

# THE FUTURE OF
# Freedom

# The Democratic Age

W<small>E LIVE IN</small> a democratic age. Over the last century the world has been shaped by one trend above all others— the rise of democracy. In 1900 not a single country had what we would today consider a democracy: a government created by elections in which every adult citizen could vote. Today 119 do, comprising 62 percent of all countries in the world. What was once a peculiar practice of a handful of states around the North Atlantic has become the standard form of government for humankind. Monarchies are antique, fascism and communism utterly discredited. Even Islamic theocracy appeals only to a fanatical few. For the vast majority of the world, democracy is the sole surviving source of political legitimacy. Dictators such as Egypt's Hosni Mubarak and Zimbabwe's Robert Mugabe go to great effort and expense to organize national elections—which, of course, they win handily. When the enemies of democracy mouth its rhetoric and ape its rituals, you know it has won the war.

We live in a democratic age in an even broader sense. From its Greek root, "democracy" means "the rule of the people." And everywhere we are witnessing the shift of power downward. I call this "democratization," even though it goes far beyond politics, because the process is similar: hierarchies are breaking down, closed systems are opening up, and pressures from the masses are now the primary engine of social change. Democracy has gone from being a form of government to a way of life.

Consider the economic realm. What is truly distinctive and new about today's capitalism is not that it is global or information-rich or technologically driven—all that has been true at earlier points in history—but rather that it is *democratic*. Over the last half-century economic growth has enriched hundreds of millions in the industrial world, turning consumption, saving, and investing into a mass phenomenon. This has forced the social structures of societies to adapt. Economic power, which was for centuries held by small groups of businessmen, bankers, and bureaucrats has, as a result, been shifting downward. Today most companies—indeed most countries—woo not the handful that are rich but the many that are middle class. And rightly so, for the assets of the most exclusive investment group are dwarfed by those of a fund of workers' pensions.

Culture has also been democratized. What was once called "high culture" continues to flourish, of course, but as a niche product for the elderly set, no longer at the center of society's cultural life, which is now defined and dominated by popular music, blockbuster movies, and prime-time television. Those three make up the canon of the modern age, the set of cultural references with which everyone in society is familiar. The democratic revolution coursing through society has changed our very definition of culture. The key to the reputation of, say, a singer in an old order would have been *who* liked her. The key to fame today is *how many* like her. And by that yardstick Madonna will always trump Jessye Norman. Quantity has become quality.

What has produced this dramatic shift? As with any large-scale social phenomenon, many forces have helped produce the democratic wave—a technological revolution, growing middle-class wealth, and the collapse of alternative systems and ideologies that organized society. To these grand systemic causes add another: America. The rise and dominance of America—a country whose politics and culture are deeply democratic—has made democratization seem inevitable. Whatever its causes, the democratic wave is having predictable effects in every area. It is breaking down hierarchies, empowering individuals, and transforming societies well beyond their politics. Indeed much of what is distinctive about the world we live in is a consequence of the democratic idea.

We often read during the roaring 1990s that technology and information had been democratized. This is a relatively new phenomenon. In the past, technology helped reinforce centralization and hierarchy. For example, the last great information revolution—in the 1920s involving radio, television, movies, megaphones—had a centralizing effect. It gave the person or group with access to that technology the power to reach the rest of society. That's why the first step in a twentieth-century coup or revolution was always to take control of the country's television or radio station. But today's information revolution has produced thousands of outlets for news that make central control impossible and dissent easy. The Internet has taken this process another huge step forward, being a system where, in the columnist Thomas Friedman's words, "everyone is connected but no one is in control."

The democratization of technology and information means that most anyone can get his hands on anything. Like weapons of mass destruction. We now know that Osama bin Laden was working on a serious biological-weapons program during the 1990s. But what is most astonishing is that the scientific information and manuals found in Al Qaeda's Kabul safe houses were not secrets stolen from government laboratories. They were documents downloaded from the Internet. Today if you want to find sources for anthrax, recipes for poison, or methods to weaponize chemicals, all you need is a good search engine. These same open sources will, unfortunately, soon help someone build a dirty bomb. The components are easier to get than ever before. Mostly what you need is knowledge, and that has been widely disseminated over the last decade. Even nuclear technology is now commonly available. It is, after all, fifty-year-old know-how, part of the world of AM radios and black-and-white television. Call it the democratization of violence.

It's more than a catchy phrase. The democratization of violence is one of the fundamental—and terrifying—features of the world today. For centuries the state has had a monopoly over the legitimate use of force in human societies. This inequality of power between the state and the citizen created order and was part of the glue that held modern civilization together. But over the last few decades the state's advantage has been weakened; now small groups of people can do dreadful things. And while terrorism is the most serious blow to state authority, central governments have been under siege in other ways as well. Capital markets, private businesses, local governments, nongovernmental organizations have all been gaining strength, sapping the authority of the state. The illegal flow of people, drugs, money, and weapons rising around the world attests to its weakness. This diffusion of power will continue because it is fueled by broad technological, social, and economic changes. In the post–September 11 world the state has returned, with renewed power and legitimacy. This too will endure. The age of terror will thus be marked by a tension, between the forces that drive the democratization of authority on the one hand and the state on the other.

To discuss these problems is not to say that democracy is a bad thing. Overwhelmingly it has had wonderful consequences. Who among us would want to go back to an age with fewer choices and less individual power and autonomy? But like any broad transformation, democracy has its dark sides. Yet we rarely speak about them. To do so would be to provoke instant criticism that you are "out of sync" with the times. But this means that we never really stop to understand these times. Silenced by fears of being branded "antidemocratic" we have no way to understand what might be troubling about the ever-increasing democratization of our lives. We assume that no problem could ever be caused by democracy, so when we see social, political, and economic maladies we shift blame here and there, deflecting problems, avoiding answers, but never talking about the great transformation that is at the center of our political, economic, and social lives.

## Democracy and Liberty

"Suppose elections are free and fair and those elected are racists, fascists, separatists," said the American diplomat Richard Holbrooke about Yugoslavia in the 1990s. "That is the dilemma." Indeed it is, and not merely in Yugoslavia's past but in the world's present. Consider, for example, the challenge we face across the Islamic world. We recognize the need for democracy in those often-repressive countries. But what if democracy produces an Islamic theocracy or something like it? It is not an idle concern. Across the globe, democratically elected regimes, often ones that have been re-elected or reaffirmed through referenda, are routinely ignoring constitutional limits on their power and depriving their citizens of basic rights. This disturbing phenomenon—visible from Peru to the Palestinian territories, from Ghana to Venezuela—could be called "illiberal democracy."

For people in the West, democracy means "liberal democracy": a political system marked not only by free and fair elections but also by the rule of law, a separation of powers, and the protection of basic liberties of speech, assembly, religion, and property. But this bundle of freedoms—what might be termed "constitutional liberalism"—has nothing intrinsically to do with democracy and the two have not always gone together, even in the West. After all, Adolf Hitler became chancellor of Germany via free elections. Over the last half-century in the West, democracy and liberty have merged. But today the two strands of liberal democracy, interwoven in the Western political fabric, are coming apart across the globe. Democracy is flourishing; liberty is not.

In some places, such as Central Asia, elections have paved the way for dictatorships. In others, they have exacerbated group conflict and ethnic tensions. Both Yugoslavia and Indonesia, for example, were far more tolerant and secular when they were ruled by strongmen (Tito and Suharto, respectively) than they are now as democracies. And in many nondemocracies, elections would not improve matters much. Across the Arab world elections held tomorrow would probably bring to power regimes that are more intolerant, reactionary, anti-Western, and anti-Semitic than the dictatorships currently in place.

In a world that is increasingly democratic, regimes that resist the trend produce dysfunctional societies—as in the Arab world. Their people sense the deprivation of liberty more strongly than ever before because they know the alternatives; they can see them on CNN, BBC, and Al-Jazeera. But yet, newly democratic countries too often become sham democracies, which produces disenchantment, disarray, violence, and new forms of tyranny. Look at Iran and Venezuela. This is not a reason to stop holding elections, of course, but surely it should make us ask, What is at the root of this troubling development? Why do so many developing countries have so much difficulty creating stable, genuinely democratic societies? Were we to embark on the vast challenge of building democracy in Iraq, how would we make sure that we succeed?

First, let's be clear what we mean by political democracy. From the time of Herodotus it has been defined, first and foremost, as the rule of the people. This definition of democracy as a process of selecting governments is now widely used by scholars. In *The Third Wave*, the eminent political scientist Samuel P. Huntington explains why:

> Elections, open, free and fair, are the essence of democracy, the inescapable sine qua non. Governments produced by elections may be inefficient, corrupt, shortsighted, irresponsible, dominated by special interests, and incapable of adopting policies demanded by the public good. These qualities make such governments undesirable but they do not make them undemocratic. Democracy is one public

virtue, not the only one, and the relation of democracy to other public virtues and vices can only be understood if democracy is clearly
distinguished from the other characteristics of political systems.

This definition also accords with the commonsense view of the
term. If a country holds competitive, multiparty elections, we call it
"democratic." When public participation in a country's politics is
increased—for example, through the enfranchisement of women—
that country is seen as having become more democratic. Of course
elections must be open and fair, and this requires some protections
for the freedom of speech and assembly. But to go beyond this mini-
mal requirement and label a country democratic only if it guarantees
a particular catalog of social, political, economic, and religious
rights—which will vary with every observer—makes the word
"democracy" meaningless. After all, Sweden has an economic system
that many argue curtails individual property rights, France until
recently had a state monopoly on television, and Britain has a state
religion. But they are all clearly and identifiably democracies. To
have "democracy" mean, subjectively, "a good government" makes it
analytically useless.

Constitutional liberalism, on the other hand, is not about the procedures for selecting government but, rather, government's goals. It
refers to the tradition, deep in Western history, that seeks to protect
an individual's autonomy and dignity against coercion, whatever the
source—state, church, or society. The term marries two closely connected ideas. It is liberal* because it draws on the philosophical strain,
beginning with the Greeks and Romans, that emphasizes individual
liberty. It is constitutional because it places the rule of law at the center of politics. Constitutional liberalism developed in Western Europe
and the United States as a defense of an individual's right to life and

---

*I use the term "liberal" in the nineteenth-century sense, meaning concerned
with individual economic, political, and religious liberty, which is sometimes called
"classical liberalism," not in the modern, American sense, which associates it with
the welfare state, affirmative action, and other policies.

property and the freedoms of religion and speech. To secure these rights, it emphasized checks on the power of government, equality under the law, impartial courts and tribunals, and the separation of church and state. In almost all of its variants, constitutional liberalism argues that human beings have certain natural (or "inalienable") rights and that governments must accept a basic law, limiting its own powers, to secure them. Thus in 1215 at Runnymede, England's barons forced the king to limit his own authority. In the American colonies these customs were made explicit, and in 1638 the town of Hartford adopted the first written constitution in modern history. In 1789 the American Constitution created a formal framework for the new nation. In 1975 Western nations set standards of behavior even for nondemocratic regimes. Magna Carta, the Fundamental Orders of Connecticut, the American Constitution, and the Helsinki Final Act are all expressions of constitutional liberalism.

Since 1945 Western governments have, for the most part, embodied both democracy and constitutional liberalism. Thus it is difficult to imagine the two apart, in the form of either illiberal democracy or liberal autocracy. In fact both have existed in the past and persist in the present. Until the twentieth century, most countries in western Europe were liberal autocracies or, at best, semidemocracies. The franchise was tightly restricted, and elected legislatures had limited power. In 1830 Great Britain, one of the most democratic European countries, allowed barely 2 percent of its population to vote for one house of Parliament. Only in the late 1940s did most Western countries become full-fledged democracies, with universal adult suffrage. But one hundred years earlier, by the late 1840s, most of them had adopted important aspects of constitutional liberalism—the rule of law, private property rights, and increasingly, separated powers and free speech and assembly. For much of modern history, what characterized governments in Europe and North America, and differentiated them from those around the world, was not democracy but constitutional liberalism. The "Western model of government" is best symbolized not by the mass plebiscite but the impartial judge.

For decades the tiny island of Hong Kong was a small but revealing illustration that liberty did not depend on democracy. It had one of the highest levels of constitutional liberalism in the world but was in no way a democracy. In fact in the 1990s, as the Chinese takeover of Hong Kong drew near, many Western newspapers and magazines fretted about the dangers of this shift to Hong Kong's democracy. But of course Hong Kong had no democracy to speak of. The threat was to its tradition of liberty and law. We continue to confuse these two concepts. American and Israeli politicians have often chided the Palestinian Authority for its lack of democracy. But in fact Yasser Arafat is the only leader in the entire Arab world who has been chosen through reasonably free elections. The Palestinian Authority's problem lies not in its democracy—which while deeply flawed is at least half-functioning—but in its constitutional liberalism, or lack thereof.

Americans in particular have trouble seeing any tension between democracy and liberty because it is not a dominant theme in our own history—with one huge exception. Slavery and segregation were entrenched in the American South through the democratic system. From the founding of the republic, those who abhorred slavery faced the problem that the majority of southern voters defended it passionately. In the end, slavery died not because it was lost in a vote but because the forces of the North crushed the South. Eventually the Jim Crow system that succeeded slavery in the South was destroyed during the 1950s and 1960s not by democracy but despite it. Although the final act of emancipation, the Civil Rights Act of 1964, was passed by Congress, all previous progress took place through the executive branch's fiat—as with the desegregation of the armed forces—or the Supreme Court's writ—as with school desegregation. In America's greatest tragedy, liberty and democracy were often at odds.

## The American Model

During the 1990s, an American scholar traveled to Kazakhstan on a U.S. government-sponsored mission to help the country's new parliament draft its electoral laws. His counterpart, a senior member of the Kazak parliament, brushed aside the many options the American expert was outlining, saying emphatically, "We want our parliament to be just like your Congress." The American was horrified, recalling, "I tried to say something other than the three words that had immediately come screaming into my mind: 'No you don't!' " This view is not unusual. Americans in the democracy business tend to see their own system as an unwieldy contraption that no other country should put up with. In fact, the philosophy behind the U.S. Constitution, a fear of accumulated power, is as relevant today as it was in 1789. Kazakhstan, as it happens, would be particularly well served by a strong parliament—like the American Congress—to check the insatiable appetite of its president.

It is odd that the United States is so often the advocate of unrestrained democracy abroad. What is distinctive about the American system is not how democratic it is but rather how undemocratic it is, placing as it does multiple constraints on electoral majorities. The Bill of Rights, after all, is a list of things that the government may not do, regardless of the wishes of the majority. Of America's three branches of government, the Supreme Court—arguably the paramount branch—is headed by nine unelected men and women with life tenure. The U.S. Senate is the most unrepresentative upper house in the world, with the lone exception of the House of Lords, which is powerless and in any event on the verge of transformation. Each American state sends two senators to Washington, D.C., regardless of its population. Thus California's 30 million people have as many votes in the Senate as Arizona's 3.7 million—hardly one man, one vote.* In state and local legislatures all over the United States, what is striking is not the power of the majority party but the protections accorded to the minority party, often to an individual legislator. Pri-

*This particular aspect of American democracy has had mostly terrible effects, giving small states with tiny populations huge political influence and massive subsidies. Still, American democracy benefits greatly from most of its "undemocratic" features.

vate businesses and other nongovernmental groups—what Alexis de Tocqueville called "intermediate associations"—make up yet another crucial stratum within society. This rich fabric of civil society has been instrumental in shaping the character of American democracy.

But it is wearing thin, producing America's own version of illiberal democracy. America's problems are different from—and much smaller than—those that face Third World countries. But they are related. In America, laws and rights are firmly established. The less-formal constraints, however, that are the inner stuffing of liberal democracy are disappearing. Many of these social and political institutions—political parties, professions, clubs, and associations—are undemocratic in their structure. They are all threatened by a democratic ideology that judges the value of every idea and institution by one simple test: Is power as widely dispersed as it can be? Are they, in other words, as democratic as they can be? Thus the U.S. Congress, although by definition democratic, used to function in a hierarchical and closed manner, at some distance from public pressures. Now it is a transparent body, utterly open to its constituents' views and pressures. Congress has become a more responsive, more democratic, and more dysfunctional body.

Or consider America's political parties, which are Potemkin organizations today. They no longer play their historic role as selectors and adjudicators in the American electoral process. With primaries and polls dominant, parties serve merely as vessels to be filled with the public's taste of the moment—neoliberal, conservative, whatever. Or look at America's professional elites—lawyers, most notably—who once formed a kind of local aristocracy with duties and responsibilities toward their towns and cities. They have lost their prestige and public purpose, becoming anxious hustlers. Medicine, accounting, and banking have all followed a similar path. The forces that guided democracy are quickly being eroded.

What has replaced them is the poll. When historians write about these times they will surely be struck by our constant, never-ending search for the pulse of the people. Politicians, corporations, and journalists spend vast amounts of time, money, and energy trying to divine the public's views on everything from Social Security to the afterlife to carbonated drinks. It is a race, actually, to be the first to genuflect before them. Pollsters have become our modern soothsayers, interpreting public opinion surveys with the gravity with which their predecessors read chicken entrails. Of course polls, like chicken entrails, can be ambiguous or people can change their minds—which happens from time to time—at which point there is a lemminglike rush to the newly popular view. Thus the very businessmen who were hailed as geniuses in 2000 became crooks in 2002. Newt Gingrich, the mastermind of the 1994 electoral landslide, became a bumbling extremist one year later. When president, Bill Clinton's image moved almost weekly from that of a scoundrel to a political legend. All through this roller-coaster ride the only constant is the ritual homage to the American public. "The American people are not stupid," politicians say endlessly, even when explaining the public's persistent desire for lower taxes and more government benefits. "The American people want to know," a politician will say, when in fact it is the politician—and perhaps the politician alone—who has a question. "We have heard from the American people," a third will declare, as if announcing a divine visitation. A commonplace assertion today has the force of a biblical revelation if ascribed to the American people.*

## Freedom and Restraint

The people, on the other hand, sense a problem. Americans have a lower regard for their political system than ever before. In this they

---

*As with all observations about America, Tocqueville said it first and best: "The French under the old monarchy held it for a maxim that the king could do no wrong," he wrote, "and if he did do wrong, the blame was imputed to his advisors. . . . The Americans entertain the same opinion with respect to the majority." In a similar vein, Michael Kinsley collected his *New Republic* columns together in a book with an admonishing title, calling the American people *Big Babies*.

are not alone. Most Western countries show the same historically low regard for their politics. In fact the recent rise of anti-establishment populism in every European country suggests that these feelings may already have become quite strong. This rising trend of dissatisfaction and anger with existing political systems comes at a bad time. Western democracies are under stress as they confront fundamental new challenges such as terrorism, demographic shifts, immigration, and cultural clashes. Governments have to protect societies from new dangers, revamp the welfare state, and encourage immigration without producing cultural war—a tall order at any time. But the political system has never been as dysfunctional. Perpetual campaigning and pandering, money-raising, special interests, and lobbying—most acute in America—have all discredited the system in people's eyes and voter turnouts are shockingly low. Western democracy remains the model for the rest of the world, but is it possible that like a supernova, at the moment of its blinding glory in distant universes, Western democracy is hollowing out at the core?

Many believe the contrary—that the increasing democratization of all spheres of society is an unqualified good. Out of the breakdown of the old systems, the opening up of access, and the empowerment of everyman will come ever-increasing individual freedom and happiness. During the last years of the heady 1990s the consulting firm Accenture published advertisements to tout its farseeing analysis. One of these was a mock newspaper headline that read, "THE INTERNET WILL BRING DEMOCRACY TO CHINA," followed by their tagline, "*Now* It Gets Interesting." While the fervor of the dot-com era has faded, technology enthusiasts point out that the Internet is in its infancy and eventually it will bring democracy to China, prosperity to India, and make us all our own bankers, lawyers, editors, and even legislators. The last trend is already visible in states like California, where government-by-referendum is well underway. Others are following the lead. How can you argue against more democracy?

But what if liberty comes not from chaos but from some measure of order as well—not from unfettered, direct democracy but from regulated, representative democracy? What if, as in much of life, we need guides and constraints? And what if liberty is truly secure only when these guardrails are strong? This alternate theory is, at any rate, what produced modern, liberal democracy. The democracy we have lived with in the West has always been what Aristotle called a "mixed regime." It had an elected government, to be sure, but also constitutional laws and rights, an independent judiciary, strong political parties, churches, businesses, private associations, and professional elites. Political democracy was an essential, indeed crucial, element of the whole—the people had ultimate power—but the system was a complex one with many parts, not all of them subject to elections. Indeed the purpose of many of these undemocratic institutions and groups was to temper public passions, educate citizens, guide democracy, and thereby secure liberty. When the Harvard Law School hands its graduates their diplomas, it reminds them to think of law as "the wise restraints that make men free." The national hymn, "America the Beautiful," declares, "America, America / God mend thine every flaw. / Confirm thy soul in self-control / Thy liberty in law."

This book is a call for self-control, for a restoration of balance between democracy and liberty. It is *not* an argument against democracy. But it is a claim that there can be such a thing as too much democracy—too much of an emphatically good thing. The essence of liberal democratic politics is the construction of a rich, complex social order, not one dominated by a single idea. America's founding fathers, for example, sought to create such a pluralistic society when many believed that a single religious ideology should dominate societies. Democracy is also a single ideology, and, like all such templates, it has its limits. What works in a legislature might not work in a corporation.

To undertake a restoration is not to seek the return of an old order. We like the democratic changes that we have lived through and cherish their achievements. The goal is liberal democracy not as it was practiced in the nineteenth century but as it should be practiced in the twenty-first century. Democratic societies need new buffers and guides, designed for modern problems and times. And yet any such undertaking must begin with a return to history, to the struggle for liberty and democracy that began in the West and spread elsewhere. If we want to renew the perennial quest for life, liberty, and the pursuit of happiness, we must recall the forces that produced them in the first place. Only by understanding freedom's past can we help secure its future.

## CHAPTER 1

# A Brief History of Human Liberty

I T ALL STARTED when Constantine decided to move. In A.D. 324 the leader of the greatest empire in the world went east, shifting his capital from Rome to Byzantium, the old Greek colony, at the mouth of the Black Sea, which he promptly renamed Constantinople. Why abandon Rome, the storied seat of the empire? Constantine explained that he did it "on command of God." You can't really argue with that kind of logic, though vanity and ambition surely played some part as well. Constantine desperately wanted to leave behind a grand legacy and, short of winning a war, what better way to do so than to build a new capital city? The move was also politically smart. Constantinople was closer to the great cultural and economic centers of the day, such as Athens, Thessalonika, and Antioch. (Rome in those days was considered a backwater.) And Constantinople was a more strategic point from which to defend the empire against its enemies, mainly Germanic tribes and Persian armies. In the fourth century, the pivots of history lay in the east.

Emperors don't travel light, and Constantine was no exception. He shifted not just the capital but tens of thousands of its inhabitants and commandeered immense quantities of food and wine from Egypt, Asia Minor, and Syria to feed his people. He sent his minions across the empire to bring art for the "new Rome." Such was the pillage that the historian Jacob Burckhardt described it as "the most disgraceful and extensive thefts of art in all history . . . committed for the purpose of decorating [Constantinople]."[1] Senators and other notables were given every inducement to move; exact replicas of their homes were waiting for them in the new city. But although he took most of his court, Constantine left one person behind: the bishop of Rome. This historic separation between church and state was to have fateful, and beneficial, consequences for humankind.

Although the bishop of Rome had nominal seniority—because the first holder of that office, Peter, was the senior apostle of Christ—Christianity had survived by becoming a decentralized religion, comprising a collection of self-governing churches. But Rome was now distant from the imperial capital. Other important priests, such as the bishop of Byzantium and those of nearby Antioch, Jerusalem, and Alexandria, now lived in the shadow of the emperor and quickly became appendages of state authority. But, far from palace power and intrigue, the Roman church flourished, asserting an independence that eventually allowed it to claim the mantle of spiritual leadership of the Christian peoples. As a result of this separation, the great English classical scholar Ernest Barker observed, the East (Byzantium) fell under the control of the state and the West (Rome) came under the sovereignty of religion. It would be more accurate to say that in the West sovereignty was contested; for 1,500 years after Constantine's move, European history was marked by continual strife between church and state. From the sparks of those struggles came the first fires of human liberty.

## Liberty, Old and New

Obviously it is an oversimplification to pick a single event to mark the beginnings of a complex historical phenomenon—in this case, the development of human liberty—but stories have to start some-where. And the rise of the Christian Church is, in my view, the first important source of liberty in the West—and hence the world. It highlights the central theme of this chapter, which is that liberty came to the West centuries before democracy. Liberty led to democracy and not the other way around. It also highlights a paradox that runs through this account: whatever the deeper structural causes, liberty in the West was born of a series of power struggles. The consequences of these struggles—between church and state, lord and king, Protestant and Catholic, business and the state—embedded themselves in the fabric of Western life, producing greater and greater pressures for individual liberty, particularly in England and, by extension, in the United States.

Some might contest this emphasis on the Christian Church, pointing fondly to ancient Greece as the seedbed of liberty. They will think of Pericles' famous funeral oration, delivered in 431 B.C., which conjured a stirring vision of the Athens of his day, dedicated to freedom, democracy, and equality. For much of the nineteenth century, British and German university curricula assumed that the greatest flowering of human achievement took place in the city-states of Greece around the fifth century B.C. (The study of ancient Greece and Rome at Oxford and Cambridge is still colloquially called "Greats.") But the Victorian obsession with Greece was part fantasy. Ancient Greece was an extraordinary culture, fertile in philosophy, science, and literature. It was the birthplace of democracy and some of its associated ideas, but these were practiced in only a few, small city-states for at most a hundred years and died with the Macedonian conquest of Athens in 338 B.C. Over a millennium later, Greece's experiment became an inspiration for democrats, but in the intervening centuries, it left no tangible or institutional influences on politics in Europe.

More to the point, Greece was not the birthplace of liberty as we understand it today. Liberty in the modern world is first and foremost the freedom of the individual from arbitrary authority, which has meant, for most of history, from the brute power of the state. It implies certain basic human rights: freedom of expression, of association, and of worship, and rights of due process. But ancient liberty, as the enlightenment philosopher Benjamin Constant explained, meant something different: that everyone (actually, every male citizen) had the right to participate in the governance of the community. Usually all citizens served in the legislature or, if this was impractical, legislators were chosen by lottery, as with American juries today. The people's assemblies of ancient Greece had unlimited powers. An individual's rights were neither sacred in theory nor protected in fact. Greek democracy often meant, in Constant's phrase, "the subjection of the individual to the authority of the community."[2] Recall that in the fourth century B.C. in Athens, where Greek democracy is said to have found its truest expression, the popular assembly—by democratic vote—put to death the greatest philosopher of the age because of his teachings. The execution of Socrates was democratic but not liberal.

If the Greek roots of Western liberty are often overstated, the Roman ones are neglected. When Herodotus wrote that the Greeks were "a free people" he meant that they were not slaves under foreign conquest or domination—an idea we would today call "national independence" or "self-determination." (By this definition, the North Koreans today are a free people.) The Romans emphasized a different aspect of freedom: that all citizens were to be treated equally under the law. This conception of freedom is much closer to the modern Western one, and the Latin word for it, *libertas*, is the root of ours. Whereas Greece gave the world philosophy, literature, poetry, and art, Rome gave us the beginnings of limited government and the rule of law. The Roman Republic, with its divided government (three branches), election of officials to limited terms, and emphasis on equality under law has been a model for governments ever since, most consciously in the founding of the American Republic. To this day Roman political concepts and terms endure throughout the Western world: senate, republic, constitution, prefecture. Western law is so filled with Roman legacies that until the early twentieth century, lawyers had to be well versed in Latin. Most of the world's laws of contract, property, liability, defamation, inheritance, and estate and rules of procedure and evidence are variations on Roman themes. For Herbert Asquith, the gifted amateur classicist who became prime minister of the United Kingdom, Rome's greatest gift to the ages was that "she founded, developed and systematized the jurisprudence of the world."[3]

The gaping hole in Roman law, however, was that as a practical matter, it didn't apply to the ruling class, particularly as the republic degenerated into a monarchy by the first century. Emperors such as Nero, Vitellius, and Galba routinely sentenced people to death without trial, pillaged private homes and temples, and raped and murdered their subjects. Caligula famously had his horse appointed senator, an act that probably violated the implicit, if not explicit, rules of that once-august body. Traditions of law that had been built carefully during Rome's republican years crumbled in the decadence of empire. The lesson of Rome's fall is that, for the rule of law to endure, you need more than the good intentions of the rulers, for they may change (both the intentions and the rulers). You need institutions within society whose strength is independent of the state. The West found such a countervailing force in the Catholic Church.

## The Paradox of Catholicism

Rome's most concrete legacy has been the Roman Catholic Church, which the English philosopher Thomas Hobbes called "the ghost of the deceased Roman Empire sitting crowned upon [its] grave."[4] The culture of Rome became the culture of Catholicism. Through the church were transmitted countless traditions and ideas—and, of course, Latin, which gave educated people all over Europe a common language and thus strengthened their sense of being a single community. To this day the ideas and structure of the Catholic Church—its universalism, its hierarchy, its codes and laws—bear a strong resemblance to those of the Roman Empire.

The Catholic Church might seem an odd place to begin the story of liberty. As an institution it has not stood for freedom of thought or even, until recently, diversity of belief. In fact, during the Middle Ages, as it grew powerful, it became increasingly intolerant and oppressive, emphasizing dogma and unquestioning obedience and using rather nasty means to squash dissent (recall the Spanish Inquisition). To this day, its structure remains hierarchical and autocratic. The church never saw itself as furthering individual liberty. But from the start it tenaciously opposed the power of the state and thus placed limits on monarchs' rule. It controlled crucial social institutions such as marriage and birth and death rites. Church properties and priests were not subject to taxation—hardly a small matter since at its height the church owned one-third of the land in Europe. The Catholic Church was the first major institution in history that was independent of temporal authority and willing to challenge it. By doing this it cracked the edifice of state power, and in nooks and crannies individual liberty began to grow.

The struggles between church and state began just over fifty years after Constantine's move. One of Constantine's successors, the emperor Theodosius, while in a nasty dispute with the Thessalonians, a Greek tribe, invited the whole tribe to Milan—and orchestrated a blood-curdling massacre of his guests: men, women, and children. The archbishop of Milan, a pious priest named Ambrose, was appalled and publicly refused to give the emperor Holy Communion. Theodosius protested, resorting to a biblical defense. He was guilty of homicide, he explained, but wasn't one of the Bible's heroic kings, David, guilty not just of homicide but of adultery as well? The archbishop was unyielding, thundering back, in the English historian Edward Gibbon's famous account, "You have imitated David in his crime, imitate then his repentance."[5] To the utter amazement of all, for the next eight months the emperor, the most powerful man in the world, periodically dressed like a beggar (as David had in the biblical tale) and stood outside the cathedral at Milan to ask forgiveness of the archbishop.

As the Roman Empire crumbled in the East, the bishop of Rome's authority and independence grew. He became first among the princes of the church, called "Il Papa," the holy father. In 800, Pope Leo III was forced to crown the Frankish ruler Charlemagne as Roman emperor. But in doing so, Leo began the tradition of "investiture," whereby the church had to bless a new king and thus give legitimacy to his reign. By the twelfth century, the pope's power had grown, and he had become a pivotal player in Europe's complex political games. The papacy had power, legitimacy, money, and even armies. It won another great symbolic battle against Holy Roman Emperor Henry IV, who in 1077 challenged—unsuccessfully—Pope Gregory VII's expansion of the power of investiture. Having lost the struggle, Henry, so the legend goes, was forced to stand barefoot in the snow at Canossa to seek forgiveness from the holy father. Whether or not that tale is true, by the twelfth century the pope had clearly become, in power and pomp, a match for any of Europe's kings, and the Vatican had come to rival the grandest courts on the continent.

## The Geography of Freedom

The church gained power in the West for a simple reason: after the decline of the Roman Empire, it never again faced a single emperor of Europe. Instead, the Catholic Church was able to play one European prince against another, becoming the vital "swing vote" in the power struggles of the day. Had one monarch emerged across the continent, he could have crushed the church's independence, turning it into a handmaiden of state power. That is what happened to the Greek Orthodox Church and later the Russian Orthodox Church (and, for that matter, to most religions around the world). But no ruler ever conquered all of Europe, or even the greater part of it. Over the millennia only a few tried—Charlemagne, Charles V,

Napoleon, Kaiser Wilhelm, and Hitler. All were thwarted, most fairly quickly.

What explains this? Probably mountains and rivers. Europe is riven with barriers that divide its highlands into river valleys bordered by mountain ranges. Its rivers flow into sheltered, navigable bays along the long, indented Mediterranean coastline—all of which means that small regions could subsist, indeed thrive, on their own. Hence Europe's long history of many independent countries. They are hard to conquer, easy to cultivate, and their rivers and seas provide ready trade routes. Asia, by contrast, is full of vast flatlands—the steppes in Russia, the plains in China—through which armies could march unhindered. Not surprisingly, these areas were ruled for millennia by centralized empires.*

Europe's topography made possible the rise of communities of varying sizes—city-states, duchies, republics, nations, and empires. In 1500 Europe had within it more than 500 states, many no larger than a city. This variety had two wondrous effects. First, it allowed for diversity. People, ideas, art, and even technologies that were unwelcome or unnoticed in one area would often thrive in another. Second, diversity fueled constant competition between states, producing innovation and efficiency in political organization, military technology, and economic policy. Successful practices were copied; losing ways were cast aside. Europe's spectacular economic and political success—what the economic historian Eric Jones has termed "the European miracle"—might well be the result of its odd geography.[6]

---

*Africa is particularly unlucky in its geography. Despite being the second-largest continent in the world it has the shortest coastline, much of which is too shallow to develop ports. So it has historically had little trade. Its rivers are not navigable, because they are either too shallow or, where deep, scarred by rapids and waterfalls (dramatic scenery makes for disastrous commerce in this case). Add to this tropical heat and accompanying disease and one has a sad structural explanation for Africa's underdevelopment.

## Lords and Kings

Geography and history combined to help shape Europe's political structure. The crumbling of the Roman Empire and the backwardness of the German tribes that destroyed it resulted in decentralized authority across the continent; no ruler had the administrative capacity to rule a far-flung kingdom comprising so many independent tribes. By contrast, in their heyday, Ming and Manchu China, Mughal India, and the Ottoman Empire controlled vast lands and diverse peoples. But in Europe local landlords and chieftains governed their territories and developed close ties with their tenants. This became the distinctive feature of European feudalism—that its great landowning classes were independent. From the Middle Ages until the seventeenth century, European sovereigns were distant creatures who ruled their kingdoms mostly in name. The king of France, for example, was considered only a duke in Brittany and had limited authority in that region for hundreds of years. In practice if monarchs wanted to do anything—start a war, build a fort—they had to borrow and bargain for money and troops from local chieftains, who became earls, viscounts, and dukes in the process.

Thus Europe's landed elite became an aristocracy with power, money, and legitimacy—a far cry from the groveling and dependent courtier-nobles in other parts of the world. This near-equal relationship between lords and kings deeply influenced the course of liberty. As Guido de Ruggiero, the great historian of liberalism, wrote, "Without the effective resistance of particular privileged classes, the monarchy would have created nothing but a people of slaves."[7] In fact monarchs did just that in much of the rest of the world. In Europe, on the other hand, as the Middle Ages progressed, the aristocracy demanded that kings guarantee them certain rights that even the crown could not violate. They also established representative bodies— parliaments, estates general, diets—to give permanent voice to their claims. In these medieval bargains lie the foundations of what we today call "the rule of law." Building on Roman traditions, these rights were secured and strengthened by the power of the nobility. Like the clash between church and state, the conflict between the aristocracy and the monarchy is the second great power struggle of European history that helped provide, again unintentionally, the raw materials of freedom.

The English aristocracy was the most independent in Europe. Lords lived on their estates, governing and protecting their tenants. In return, they extracted taxes, which kept them both powerful and rich. It was, in one scholar's phrase, "a working aristocracy": it maintained its position not through elaborate courtly rituals but by taking part in politics and government at all levels.[8] England's kings, who consolidated their power earlier than did most of their counterparts on the continent, recognized that their rule depended on co-opting the aristocracy—or at least some part of it. When monarchs pushed their luck they triggered a baronial backlash. Henry II, crowned king in 1154, extended his rule across the country, sending judges to distant places to enforce royal decrees. He sought to unify the country and create a common, imperial law. To do this he had to strip the medieval aristocracy of its powers and special privileges. His plan worked but only up to a point. Soon the nobility rose up in arms— literally—and after forty years of conflict, Henry's son, King John, was forced to sign a truce in 1215 in a field near Windsor Castle. That document, Magna Carta, was regarded at the time as a charter of baronial privilege, detailing the rights of feudal lords. It also had provisions guaranteeing the freedom of the church and local autonomy for towns. It came out (in vague terms) against the oppression of any of the king's subjects. Over time the document was interpreted more broadly by English judges, turning it into a quasi constitution that enshrined certain individual rights. But even in its day, Magna Carta was significant, being the first written limitation on royal authority in Europe. As such, the historian Paul Johnson noted, it is "justly classified as the first of the English Statutes of the Realm,*

---

*The collection of English laws that make up its "unwritten constitution."

from which English, and thus American, liberties can be said to flow."[9]

## Rome versus Reform

After church versus state and king versus lord, the next great power struggle, between Catholics and Protestants, was to prove the longest and bloodiest, and once again it had accidental but revolutionary implications for freedom. Its improbable instigator was a devout German monk who lived in a small backwater town called Wittenberg. It was the early sixteenth century, and across Europe there was already great dissatisfaction with the papacy, which had become extraordinarily powerful and corrupt. Rome's most scandalous practice was the widespread sale of indulgences: papal certificates absolving the buyer of sins, even those not yet committed. The money financed the church's never-ending extravagance, which even by the glittering standards of the Baroque era was stunning. Its newest project was the largest, grandest cathedral ever known to man—St. Peter's in Rome. Even today, when one walks through the acres of marble in the Vatican, gazing at gilt, jewels, tapestries, and frescos from wall to wall and floor to ceiling, it is easy to imagine the pious rage of Martin Luther.

There had been calls for reform before Luther—Erasmus, for one, had urged a simpler, stripped down form of worship—but none had frontally challenged the authority of the church. Luther did so in ninety-five tightly reasoned theses, which he famously nailed to the door of the Castle Church in Wittenberg on the morning of October 31, 1517. Luther may have had right on his side, but he also had luck. His heresy came at an opportune moment in the history of technology. By the time the Catholic Church reacted and responded to his action, strictly forbidding the dissemination of his ideas, the new printing presses had already circulated Luther's document all over Europe. The Reformation had begun. One hundred and fifty bloody years later, almost half of Europe was Protestant.

Were Martin Luther to see Protestantism today, with its easygoing doctrines that tolerate much and require little, he would probably be horrified. Luther was not a liberal. On the contrary, he had accused the Vatican of being too lax in its approach to religion. In many ways he was what we would today call a fundamentalist, demanding a more literal interpretation of the Bible. Luther's criticisms of the papacy were quite similar to those made today by Islamic fundamentalists about the corrupt, extravagant regimes of the Middle East that have veered from the true, devout path. Luther was attacking the pope from the conservative end of the theological spectrum. In fact some have said that the clash between Catholicism and Protestantism illustrates the old maxim that religious freedom is the product of two equally pernicious fanaticisms, each canceling the other out.

Most of the sects that sprang up as a consequence of the Reformation were even more puritanical than Lutheranism. The most influential of them was a particularly dour creed, Calvinism, which posited the wretched depravity of man and the poor chances of salvation for all but a few, already chosen by God. But the various Protestant sects converged in rejecting the authority of the papacy and, by implication, all religious hierarchy. They were part of a common struggle against authority and, although they didn't know it at the time, part of the broader story of liberty.*

For all their squabbles, these small Protestant sects in northern Europe opened up the possibility of a personal path to truth, unmediated by priests. To the extent that they imagined any clergy at all, it was to be elected by a self-governing congregation. Often minority sects within a larger community, they fought for the rights of all minorities to believe and worship as they chose. Together, they

*Visitors to the city of Geneva, which has long seen itself as the spiritual birthplace of Protestantism, find in its grandest public park a memorial to the Reformation. Built in 1909, it is a vast wall with sculptures and bas-reliefs celebrating the legacy of the Reformation. It honors all the once-feuding fathers of the movement, such as Luther, John Calvin, and even Oliver Cromwell and the American Puritans. That many of these sects opposed one another is forgotten—as perhaps it should be.

opened up the space for religious freedom in the Western world. They helped shape modern ideas about not only freedom of conscience and of speech but also critical scientific inquiry, first of religious texts such as the Bible, then of all received wisdom. Science, after all, is a constant process of challenging authority and contesting dogma. In that sense modern science owes an unusual debt to sixteenth-century religious zealots.

The more immediate, political effect of Protestantism was to give kings and princes an excuse to wrest power away from the increasingly arrogant Vatican, something they were looking to do anyway. The first major assault took place not in support of Protestant ideals but for the less-exalted reason that a restless monarch wanted an heir. Henry VIII of England asked Pope Clement VII to annul his marriage to Catherine of Aragon because she had not produced an heir to the throne. (Not for lack of effort: in eight years she had given birth to one daughter and five infants who had died, and had miscarried twice.) The pope refused and King Henry broke with the Vatican, proclaiming himself head of the Church of England. Henry had no doctrinal dispute with the Catholic Church. In fact he had defended the pope against Luther in an essay, for which the Vatican honored him as "Defender of the Faith," a title his successors, strangely, bear to this day. The newly independent Anglican Church was thus Catholic in doctrine—except for the small matter of the pope.

The English break was the first and most prominent of a series of religious revolts and wars against the Vatican involving virtually every state in Europe and lasting almost 150 years after Luther's act of defiance. The wars resulting from the Reformation came to an end in 1648. The Peace of Westphalia, as it was called, ended the Thirty Years' War among the Germans and rendered unto Caesar that which was Caesar's—plus a good bit of that which used to be God's (actually, the pope's). It revived a 1555 idea—*cuius regio eius religio* (whoever's domain, his religion prevails)—that princes could choose their state religions, and it explicitly permitted religious toleration and migration. The year 1648 is not a clean point of separation between church and state, but it does symbolize an important shift in Western history. Westphalia laid to rest the idea that Europe was one great Christian community—"Christendom"—governed spiritually by the Catholic Church and temporally by the holy Roman emperor.* The future belonged to the state.

## The Enlightened State

By the eighteenth century, the real challenge to princely power came not from religion but from local authorities: the princes, dukes, barons, and counts. But over the course of this century the prince would best his rivals. He strengthened his court and created a central government—a state—that dwarfed its local rivals. The state triumphed for several reasons: technological shifts, heightened military competition, the stirrings of nationalism, and the ability to centralize tax collection. One consequence, however, is worth noting. The strengthening of the state was not good for liberty. As the power of monarchs grew, they shut down most of the medieval parliaments, estates, assemblies, and diets. When France's Estates General were summoned in the spring of 1789—on the eve of the revolution—it was their first assembly in 175 years! The newly powerful royals also began abolishing the multilayered system of aristocratic privileges, regional traditions, and guild protections in favor of a uniform legal code, administered by the monarch. The important exception was the English Parliament, which actually gained the upper hand in its struggle with the monarchy after the Glorious Revolution of 1688.[10]

On the face of it the weakening of the aristocracy might seem a victory for equality under law, and it was presented as such at the time. As Enlightenment ideas swept through seventeenth century

---

*The idea of a worldwide community of believers still exists in Islam: the *umma*. There is, however, no Muslim equivalent of the Catholic Church or the pope (see Chapter 4).

Europe, philosophers such as Voltaire and Diderot fantasized about the "rationalization" and "modernization" of government. But in practice these trends meant more power for the central government and the evisceration of local and regional authority. "Enlightened absolutism," as it was later called, had some progressive elements about it. Rulers such as Frederick II of Prussia, Catherine II of Russia, and Joseph II of Austria tolerated religious dissent, enacted legal reforms, and lavished money and attention on artists, musicians, and writers (which might help explain the good press they received). But the shift in power weakened the only groups in society capable of checking royal authority and excess. Liberty now depended on the largesse of the ruler. When under pressure from abroad or at home, even the most benign monarch—and his not-so-benign successors— abandoned liberalization and squashed dissent. By the end of the eighteenth century, with war, revolution, and domestic rebellion disturbing the tranquility of Europe, enlightened absolutism became more absolutist than enlightened.

The monarchy reached its apogee in France under Louis XIV. Feudalism in France had always been different from that in England. Sandwiched between hostile neighbors, France was perpetually mobilizing for war, which kept its central government strong. (Louis XIV was at war for thirty of his fifty-four years of rule.) The monarchy exploited these geopolitical realities to keep the nobles distant from their power base, which was their land. Building on the foundation laid by the brilliant Cardinal Richelieu, Louis XIV edged nobles out of local administration and put in their place his own regional officials. He also downgraded regional councils and assemblies. Louis was called the "Sun King" not because of his gilded possessions, as is often thought, but because of his preeminent position in the country. All other forces paled in comparison. Louis XIV brought France's aristocrats to Paris permanently, luring them with the most glittering court in Europe. His purpose was to weaken them. The legendary excess of the French monarchy—the ceaseless games, balls, hunts, and court rituals, the wonder of Versailles—was at one level a clever political device to keep the lords in a gilded cage. Behind the sumptuous silks and powdered wigs, the French aristocracy was becoming powerless and dependent.[11]

The French Revolution (1789) changed much in the country, but not these centripetal tendencies. Indeed, the revolution only centralized the country further. In contrast to England's Glorious Revolution (1688), which had strengthened the landed aristocracy, the French Revolution destroyed it. It also crippled the church and weakened local lords, parishes, and banks. As the great nineteenth century scholar-politician Lord Acton observed, the revolution was not so much about the limitation of central power as about the abrogation of all other powers that got in the way. The French, he noted, borrowed from Americans "their theory of revolution not their theory of government—their cutting but not their sewing." Popular sovereignty took on all the glory and unchecked power of royal sovereignty. "The people" were supreme, and they proclaimed their goals to be *liberté, égalité, fraternité*. Once dependent on royal largesse, liberty now depended on the whims of "the citizens," represented of course by the leaders of the revolution.

But there was another model of liberty and it took a Frenchman to see it. Montesquieu—actually Charles-Louis de Secondat, baron de La Brède et de Montesquieu—like many Enlightenment liberals in the eighteenth century admired England for its government. But Montesquieu went further, identifying the genius of the English system: that it guaranteed liberty in fact rather than proclaiming it in theory. Because government was divided between the king, aristocrats (House of Lords), and commoners (House of Commons), no one branch could grow too strong. This "separation of powers" ensured that civil liberties would be secure and religious dissent tolerated. Montesquieu did not put blind faith in the mechanics of government and constitutions; his major work was titled, after all, *The Spirit of the Laws*.

In fact, over the centuries, the British monarch's powers had been so whittled away that by the late eighteenth century, Britain, although formally a monarchy, was really an aristocratic republic, ruled by its landed elite. Montesquieu's flattering interpretation strongly influenced the British themselves. The preeminent English jurist of the era, William Blackstone, used Montesquieu's ideas when writing his commentaries on English law. The American political philosopher Judith Shklar pointed out that during the founding of the American Republic "Montesquieu was an oracle." James Madison, Thomas Jefferson, John Adams, and others consciously tried to apply his principles in creating a new political system. He was quoted by them more than any modern author (only the Bible trumped him). His appeal was so widespread, noted Shklar, that "both those who supported the new constitution and those who opposed it relied heavily on Montesquieu for their arguments."[12]

## The Consequences of Capitalism

By the eighteenth century, Britain's unusual political culture gained a final, crucial source of strength: capitalism.* If the struggles between church and state, lords and kings, and Catholics and Protestants cracked open the door for individual liberty, capitalism blew the walls down. Nothing has shaped the modern world more powerfully than capitalism, destroying as it has millennia-old patterns of economic, social, and political life. Over the centuries it has destroyed feudalism and monarchism with their emphasis on bloodlines and birth. It has created an independent class of businesspeople who owe little to the state and who are now the dominant force in every advanced society in the world. It has made change and dynamism—rather than order and tradition—the governing philosophy of the modern age. Capi-

---

*Books have been written on the varying definitions of "capitalism." I am using it in a very basic sense, which accords with most dictionary definitions, including that of the *Oxford Paperback Encyclopedia* (1998): "A system of economic organization, based on market competition, under which the means of production, distribution, and exchange are privately owned and directed by individuals or corporations. . . ."

talism created a new world, utterly different from the one that had existed for millennia. And it took root most firmly in England.

It started elsewhere. By the fourteenth century, trade and commerce, frozen during much of the Middle Ages, was once again thriving in parts of Europe. A revolution in agricultural technology was producing surpluses of grain, which had to be sold or bartered. Market towns and port cities—Antwerp, Brussels, Venice, Genoa—became centers of economic activity. Double-entry bookkeeping, the introduction of Arabic numerals, and the rise of banking turned money-making from an amateur affair into a systematic business. Soon the commercial impulse spread inland from the port cities, mostly in the Low Countries and later in England, where it was applied to all kinds of agriculture, crafts, manufacturing, and services. Why capitalism spread to these areas first is still debated, but most economic historians agree that a competent state that protected private property was an important factor. Where capitalism succeeded it was "in the main due to the type of property rights created," write the leading historians on the subject, Douglass North and Robert Thomas.[13] By the sixteenth century a consensus was developing across Europe that "Property belongs to the family, sovereignty to the prince and his magistrates." A fifteenth-century jurist in Spain had explained, "To the king is confided solely the administration of the kingdom and not dominion over things."[14] Only in England, however, was a king (Charles I) actually executed, in large part for levying arbitrary taxes.

The systematic protection of property rights transformed societies. It meant that the complex web of feudal customs and privileges—all of which were obstacles to using property efficiently—could be eliminated. The English landed elite took a leading role in modernizing agriculture. Through the enclosures system, a brutal process of asserting their rights over the pastures and commons of their estates, they forced the peasants and farmers who had lived off these lands into more specialized and efficient labors. The pastures were then used for grazing sheep, to service the highly profitable wool trade. By adapting to the ongoing capitalist revolution, the English landed classes secured their power but also helped modernize their society. The French aristocrats, in contrast, were absentee landlords who did little to make their properties more productive and yet continued to extract hefty feudal dues from their tenants. Like many continental aristocracies, they disdained commerce.

Beyond enterprising nobles, capitalism also created a new group of wealthy and powerful men who owed their riches not to land grants from the crown but to independent economic activity. Ranging from minor aristocrats to enterprising peasants, these English "yeomen" were, in the words of one historian, "a group of ambitious, aggressive small capitalists."[15] They were the first members of the bourgeoisie, the industrious property-owning class that Karl Marx defined as "the owners of the means of production of a society and employer of its laborers." Marx accurately recognized that this class was the vanguard of political liberalization in Europe. Since its members benefited greatly from capitalism, the rule of law, free markets, and the rise of professionalism and meritocracy, they supported gradual reforms that furthered these trends. In a now-legendary work of social science, the Harvard scholar Barrington Moore, Jr., studied the pathways to democracy and dictatorship around the world and presented his central conclusion in four words: "No bourgeoisie, no democracy."[16]

British politics was revolutionized as entrepreneurial activity became the principal means of social advancement. The House of Commons, which had wrested power from the king in the seventeenth century and ran the country, now swelled with newly rich merchants and traders. The number of titled nobles in Britain was always tiny: fewer than 200 by the end of the eighteenth century.[17] But beneath them lay a broad class, often called the "English gentry." The gentry usually had some connection to the aristocracy and often took on responsibilities in local government, but it ultimately drew its prestige and power from business, professional work, or efficient farming. Many of these men entered public life, and with a healthy distance from the old order, pushed for progressive reforms such as free trade, free markets, individual rights, and freedom of religion.

The three most powerful British prime ministers of the nineteenth century—Robert Peel, William Gladstone, and Benjamin Disraeli—all came from the ranks of the gentry. This newly powerful class adopted many of the traits of the aristocracy—manor houses, morning coats, hunting parties—but it was more fluid. "Gentlemen" were widely respected and, even more than lords, became the trendsetters of their society. Indeed, by the eighteenth century, the English gentleman became an almost mythic figure toward which society aspired. A nurse is said to have asked King James I to make her son a gentleman. The monarch replied, "A gentleman I could never make him, though I could make him a lord." A visiting Frenchman ridiculed the tendency of the English aristocracy to ape the gentry: "At London, masters dress like their valets and duchesses copy after their chambermaids."[18] Today the English gentleman is remembered mostly as a dandy, whose aesthetic sensibility is marketed worldwide by Ralph Lauren. But his origins are intimately connected with the birth of English liberty.

## Anglo-America

Despite the rise of capitalism, limited government, property rights, and constitutionalism across much of Europe by the eigtheenth century, England was seen as unique. It was wealthier, more innovative, freer, and more stable than any society on the continent. As Guido de Ruggiero noted, "The liberties of the individual, especially security of person and property, were solidly assured. Administration was decentralized and autonomous. The judiciary bodies were wholly independent of the central government. The prerogatives of the crown were closely restricted. . . . [P]olitical power was concentrated in the hands of Parliament. What similar spectacle could the continent offer?" Many observers at the time drew similar conclusions, praising England's constitution and national character. Some focused more specifically on economics. For Voltaire, "commerce which has enriched the citizens of England has helped make them free . . . that liberty has in turn expanded commerce." Rather than cultivating the decadent pleasures of its nobility, the observant French clergyman Abbe Coyer remarked, the English government had helped "the honest middle class, that precious portion of nations."[19] Free markets helped enrich the middle class, which then furthered the cause of liberty. It seemed a virtuous circle.

The lands most like England were its colonies in America. The colonists had established governments that closely resembled those they had left behind in Tudor England. In 1776, when they rebelled against George III, the colonists couched their revolution as a call for the return of their rights as Englishmen. As they saw it, their long-established liberties had been usurped by a tyrannical monarch, forcing them to declare independence. In some ways it was a replay of England's own Glorious Revolution, in which Parliament rebelled against an arbitrary monarch whose chief sin was also to have raised taxes without the consent of the governed—or rather, the taxed. The winners in both 1688 and 1776 were the progressive, modernizing, and commercially minded elites. (The losers, in addition to the king, were the old Tories, who remained loyal to the crown both in seventeenth-century England and eighteenth-century America.

But if England was exceptional, America was a special case of a special case. It was England without feudalism. Of course America had rich, landed families, but they were not titled, had no birthrights, and were not endowed with political power comparable to that of the members of the House of Lords. To understand eighteenth-century America, the historian Richard Hofstadter wrote, one had to imagine that unique possibility, "a middle class world."[20] Aristocratic elements in the economy and society, though present, rarely dominated. In the North, they began to wane by the close of the eighteenth century. The historian Gordon Wood noted, "In the 1780s we can actually sense the shift from a premodern society to a modern one where business interests and consumer tastes of ordinary people were coming to dominate." The American Revolution, which produced, in Wood's words, "an explosion of entrepreneurial power," widened the gulf between America and Europe.[21] America was now openly bourgeois and proud of it. Days after arriving in the United States in 1831, Tocqueville noted in his diary that in America "the whole society seems to have melted into a middle class."

The American path to liberal democracy was exceptional. Most countries don't begin their national experience as a new society without a feudal past. Free of hundreds of years of monarchy and aristocracy, Americans needed neither a powerful central government nor a violent social revolution to overthrow the old order. In Europe liberals feared state power but also fantasized about it. They sought to limit it yet needed it to modernize their societies. "The great advantage of the Americans," Tocqueville observed famously, "is that they have arrived at a state of democracy without having to endure a democratic revolution. . . . [T]hey are born equal without having to become equal."

By the early nineteenth century in the United Kingdom and the United States, for the most part, individual liberty flourished and equality under law ruled. But neither country was a democracy. Before the Reform Act of 1832, 1.8 percent of the adult population of the United Kingdom was eligible to vote. After the law that figure rose to 2.7 percent. After further widening of the franchise in 1867, 6.4 percent could vote, and after 1884, 12.1 percent.[22] Only in 1930, once women were fully enfranchised, did the United Kingdom meet today's standard for being democratic: universal adult suffrage. Yet it was widely considered the model of a constitutional liberal state—one that protected liberty and was governed by law.

The United States was more democratic than the United Kingdom, but not by as much as people think. For its first few decades, only white male property owners were eligible to vote—a system quite similar to that in the country whose rule it had just thrown off. In 1824—48 years after independence—only 5 percent of adult Americans cast a ballot in the presidential election. That number rose dramatically as the Jacksonian revolution spread and property qualifications were mostly eliminated. But not until the eve of the Civil War could it even be said that every white man in the United States had the right to vote. Blacks were enfranchised in theory in 1870, but in fact not until a century later in the South. Women got the vote in 1920. Despite this lack of democracy, for most of the nineteenth century, the United States and its system of laws and rights were the envy of the world. And with time, constitutional liberalism led to democracy, which led to further liberty, and so it went.

The rest of Europe followed a more complex path to liberal democracy than did the United Kingdom and the United States, but it eventually got there. What happened in Britain and America slowly and (mostly) peacefully happened on the continent in a jerky and bloody fashion (as will be discussed in the next chapter). Still, most became liberal democracies by the late 1940s and almost all the rest have done so since 1989, with consolidation taking place fast and firmly. The reason is clear: all Western countries shared a history that, for all its variations, featured the building of a constitutional liberal tradition. The English case is what scholars call the "ideal type," which makes it useful to highlight. But by the eighteenth century, even the most retrograde European power was a liberal regime when compared with its counterparts in Asia or Africa. Citizens had explicit rights and powers that no non-Western subject could imagine. Monarchs were restrained by law and tradition. A civil society of private enterprise, churches, universities, guilds, and associations flourished without much interference from the state. Private property was protected and free enterprise flowered. Often these freedoms were stronger in theory than in practice, and frequently they were subject to abuse by autocratic monarchs. But compared with the rest of the world the West was truly the land of liberty.

## Culture as Destiny

This brief history of liberty might seem a discouraging guide. It suggests that any country hoping to become a liberal democracy should probably relocate to the West. And without a doubt, being part of the Western world—even if on the periphery—is a political advantage. Of all the countries that gained independence after the Soviet empire collapsed, those that have shared what one might call "the Western experience"—the old lands of the Austrian and German empires—have done best at liberal democracy. The line that separated Western and Eastern Christendom in 1500 today divides successful liberal regimes from unsuccessful, illiberal ones. Poland, Hungary, and the Czech Republic, which were most securely a part of Europe, are furthest along in consolidating their democracies; the Baltic states are next in line. Even in the Balkans, Slovenia and Croatia, which fall on the western side of that East-West line, are doing well while Serbia and Albania (on the east) are having a far more troubled transition.

Does this mean that culture is destiny? This powerful argument has been made by distinguished scholars from Max Weber to Samuel Huntington. It is currently a trendy idea. From business consultants to military strategists, people today talk about culture as the easy explanation to most puzzles. Why did the U.S. economy boom over the last two decades? It's obvious: our unique entrepreneurial culture. Why is Russia unable to adapt to capitalism? Also obvious: it has a feudal, antimarket culture. Why is Africa mired in poverty? And why is the Arab world breeding terrorists? Again, culture.

But these answers are too simple. After all, American culture also produced stagflation and the Great Depression. And the once-feudal cultures of Japan and Germany seem to have adapted to capitalism well, having become the second- and third-richest countries in the world, respectively. A single country can succeed and fail at different times, sometimes just a few decades apart, which would suggest that something other than its culture—which is relatively unchanging—is at work.

Singapore's brilliant patriarch Lee Kuan Yew once explained to me that if you want to see how culture works, compare the performance of German workers and Zambian workers anywhere in the world. You will quickly come to the conclusion that there is something very different in the two cultures that explains the results. Scholars make similar arguments: in his interesting work *Tribes*, Joel Kotkin argues that if you want to succeed economically in the modern world, the key is simple—be Jewish, be Indian, but above all, be Chinese.

Lee and Kotkin are obviously correct in their observation that certain groups—Chinese, Indians, Jews—do superbly in all sorts of settings. (In fact I find this variant of the culture theory particularly appealing, since I am of Indian origin.) But if being Indian is a key to economic success, what explains the dismal performance of the Indian economy over the first four decades after its independence in 1947—or, for that matter, for hundreds of years before that? Growing up in India I certainly did not think of Indians as economically successful. In fact I recall the day a legendary member of the Indian parliament, Piloo Mody, posed the following question to Indira Gandhi during the prime minister's "question hour" in New Delhi: "Can the prime minister explain why Indians seem to thrive economically under every government in the world except hers?"

Similar questions might be asked of China, another country that did miserably in economic terms for hundreds of years until three decades ago. If all you need are the Chinese, China has billions of them. As for Jews, although they have thrived in many places, the one country where they are a majority, Israel, was also an economic mess until recently. Interestingly, the economic fortunes of all three countries (India, China, Israel) improved markedly around the 1980s. But this was not because they got themselves new cultures, but because their governments changed specific policies and created a more market-friendly system. China is today growing faster than India, but that has more to do with the fact that China is reforming its economy more extensively than India is, than with any supposed superiority of the Confucian ethic over the Hindu mind-set.

It is odd that Lee Kuan Yew is such a fierce proponent of cultural arguments. Singapore is culturally not very different from its neighbor Malaysia. It is more Chinese and less Malay, but compared to the rest of the world, the two countries share much in common. But much more than its neighbors, Singapore has had an effective government that has pursued wise economic policies. That surely, more than innate cultural differences, explains its success. The key to Singapore's success, in other words, is Lee Kuan Yew, not Confucius. The point is not that culture is unimportant; on the contrary it matters greatly. It represents the historical experience of a people, is embedded in their institutions, and shapes their attitudes and expectations about the world. But culture can change. German culture in 1939 was very different from what it became in 1959, just twenty years later. Europe, once the heartland of hypernationalism, is now postnationalist, its states willing to cede power to supranational bodies in ways that Americans can hardly imagine. The United States was once an isolationist republic with a deep suspicion of standing armies. Today it is a hegemon with garrisons around the world. The Chinese were once backward peasants; now they are smart merchants. Economic crises, war, political leadership—all these things change culture.

A hundred years ago, when East Asia seemed immutably poor, many scholars—most famously Max Weber—argued that Confucian-based cultures discouraged all the attributes necessary for success in capitalism.[23] A decade ago, when East Asia was booming, scholars had turned this explanation on its head, arguing that Confucianism actually emphasized the traits essential for economic dynamism. Today the wheel has turned again and many see in "Asian values" all the ingredients of crony capitalism. In his study Weber linked northern Europe's economic success to its "Protestant ethic" and predicted that the Catholic south would stay poor. In fact, Italy and France have grown faster than Protestant Europe over the last half-century. One may use the stereotype of shifty Latins and a *mañana* work ethic to explain the poor performance of some countries, but then how does one explain Chile? Its economy is doing as well as that of the strongest of the Asian "tigers." Its success is often attributed to another set of Latin values: strong families, religious values, and determination.

In truth we cannot find a simple answer to why certain societies succeed at certain times. When a society does succeed it often seems inevitable in retrospect. So we examine successful societies and search within their cultures for the seeds of success. But cultures are complex; one finds in them what one wants. If one wants to find cultural traits of hard work and thrift within East Asia, they are there. If you want instead to find a tendency toward blind obedience and nepotism, these too exist. Look hard enough and you will find all these traits in most cultures.

Culture is important. It can be a spur or a drag, delaying or speeding up change. It can get codified in institutions and practices, which are often the real barriers to success. Indian culture may or may not hurt its chances for economic growth, but Indian bureaucracy certainly does. The West's real advantage is that its history led to the creation of institutions and practices that, although in no sense bound up with Western genes, are hard to replicate from scratch in other societies. But it can be done.

## The East Asian Model

Looking at the many non-Western transitions to liberal democracy over the last three decades one can see that the countries that have moved furthest toward liberal democracy followed a version of the European pattern: capitalism and the rule of law first, and then democracy. South Korea, Taiwan, Thailand, and Malaysia were all governed for decades by military juntas or single-party systems. These regimes liberalized the economy, the legal system, and rights of worship and travel, and then, decades later, held free elections. They achieved, perhaps accidentally, the two essential attributes of good government that James Madison outlined in the Federalist Papers. First, a government must be able to control the governed, then it must be able to control itself. Order plus liberty. These two forces will, in the long run, produce legitimate government, prosperity, and liberal democracy. Of course, it's easier said than done.

In the 1950s and 1960s, most Western intellectuals scorned East Asia's regimes as reactionary, embracing instead popular leaders in Asia and Africa who were holding elections and declaring their faith in the people—for example in Ghana, Tanzania, and Kenya. Most of these countries degenerated into dictatorships while East Asia moved in precisely the opposite direction. It should surely puzzle these scholars and intellectuals that the best-consolidated democracies in Latin America and East Asia—Chile, South Korea, and Taiwan—were for a long while ruled by military juntas. In East Asia, as in western Europe, liberalizing autocracies laid the groundwork for stable liberal democracies.

In almost every case the dictatorships opened the economy slowly and partially, but this process made the government more and more liberal. "An unmistakable feature in East Asia since World War II," wrote a leading scholar of East Asia, Minxin Pei,

> is the gradual process of authoritarian institutionalization. . . . At the center of this process was the slow emergence of modern political institutions exercising formal and informal constraining power through dominant parties, bureaucracies, semi-open electoral procedures, and a legal system that steadily acquired a measure of autonomy. The process had two beneficial outcomes—a higher level of stability and security of property rights (due to increasing constraints placed on rulers by the power of market forces and new political norms).[24]

East Asia is still rife with corruption, nepotism, and voter fraud—but so were most Western democracies, even fifty years ago. Elections in Taiwan today are not perfect but they are probably more free and fair than those in the American South in the 1950s (or Chicago in the 1960s). Large conglomerates (*chaebols*) have improper influence in South Korean politics today, but so did their equivalents in Europe and the United States a century ago. The railroads, steel companies, shipbuilders, and great financiers of the past were probably more powerful than any East Asian tycoon today. They dominated America during its late-nineteenth-century Gilded Age. (Can you even name the political contemporaries of J. P. Morgan, E. H. Harriman, and John D. Rockefeller?) One cannot judge new democracies by standards that most Western countries would have flunked even thirty years ago. East Asia today is a mixture of liberalism, oligarchy, democracy, capitalism, and corruption—much like the West in, say, 1900. But most of East Asia's countries are considerably more liberal and democratic than the vast majority of other non-Western countries.

An even more striking proof that a constitutional liberal past can produce a liberal democratic present was identified by the late political scientist Myron Weiner in 1983. He pointed out that, as of then, "every single country in the Third World that emerged from colonial rule since the Second World War with a population of at least one million (and almost all the smaller colonies as well) with a continuous democratic experience is a former British colony."[25] British rule meant not democracy—colonialism is almost by definition undemocratic—but limited constitutional liberalism and capitalism. There are now other Third World democracies but Weiner's general point still holds. To say this is not to defend colonialism. Having grown up in a postcolonial country I do not need to be reminded of the institutionalized racism and the abuse of power that was part of the imperial legacy. But it is an undeniable fact that the British Empire left behind a legacy of law and capitalism that has helped strengthen the forces of liberal democracy in many of its former colonies—though not all.* France, by contrast, encouraged little constitutionalism or free markets in its occupied lands, but it did enfranchise some of its colonial populations in northern Africa. Early democratization in all those cases led to tyranny.

The Western path has led to liberal democracy far from the Western world. But the sequence and timing of democratization matter.

---

*In many of the colonies the British acquired late in their imperial age and decolonized within a few decades—in Africa and the Middle East, for instance—they did little by way of building institutions and creating a rule of law. Worse, they drew bad borders, saddling the states with ethnic and religious problems from the start of their independent lives. But in South Asia, the Caribbean, and of course the settler colonies (Canada, Australia, and New Zealand), the connection between British rule and democracy is undeniable.

Most Third World countries that proclaimed themselves democracies immediately after their independence, while they were poor and unstable, became dictatorships within a decade. As Giovanni Sartori, Columbia University's great scholar of democracy, noted about the path from constitutional liberalism to democracy, "the itinerary is not reversible." Even European deviations from the Anglo-American pattern—constitutionalism and capitalism first, only then democracy—were far less successful in producing liberal democracy. To see the complications produced by premature democratization, we could return to the heart of Europe—back in time to the early twentieth century.

## CHAPTER 2

# The Twisted Path

VIENNA AT THE turn of the last century was a glittering metropolis, cosmopolitan in flavor, avant-garde in art, and adventurous in politics. In that one city Richard Strauss and Gustav Mahler composed, Gustav Klimt and Egon Schiele painted, Robert Musil and Arthur Schnitzler wrote fiction, Theodor Herzl penned newspaper articles, Sigmund Freud practiced psychoanalysis, and Leon Trotsky held forth at cafés. Vienna was famous for its coffeehouses, at which central Europe's intelligentsia gathered for a heady mix of alcohol, tobacco, and conversation. At one such café—probably the Landtman—in the spring of 1895, Sigmund Freud lit a cigar. As might have been expected with Freud, the cigar was more than just a cigar. It was a celebration of liberty—against democracy.[1]

That March Vienna had elected an ultranationalist, Karl Lueger, as mayor. Lueger's politics were ugly. He regularly likened Jews to locusts, demanding that they be crushed into the ground like fertilizer or packed onto ships and drowned at sea. The Habsburg emperor, Franz Joseph I, decided that Lueger's election was a threat to the city's civic liberties and, in an unprecedented move, refused to honor it. He was supported in this decision by Austria's other ancient and authoritarian institution, the Catholic Church. Vienna's intellectuals, traditionally opposed to the monarchy and the church, found themselves in the awkward position of siding with the king, against the people. Freud wanted to publicly applaud the emperor's decision, which is why he lit that cigar, a traditional act of celebration.

No one would think of Lueger as a model democrat, but he rose to power as a direct result of the expansion of democracy in Austria. In the 1860s and 1870s only the rich and the educated middle class voted in Austria, and their great causes were free speech, constitutionalism, and economic liberalism. Vienna's famed cosmopolitan and progressive character was a product of its limited franchise. In the 1880s and 1890s the electorate was broadened—ironically, at the urging of liberals—to allow most adult males to vote, and the country's atmosphere soon changed. The newly empowered workers and peasants were uninterested in the civic reforms of the bourgeoisie and easily swayed by the fiery rhetoric of socialists (who appealed to the workers) or ultra-nationalists (who appealed to the peasants). Lueger brilliantly constructed a program that combined both nationalist and communist impulses—calling it Christian socialism. Adolf Hitler, who lived in Vienna during Lueger's reign, would later single him out for praise in *Mein Kampf,* and Hitler's National Socialism bore a distinct resemblance to Lueger's Christian socialism.

Hitler's own rise to power was fueled by many of the same democratic dynamics that helped Lueger. It is sometimes assumed that the Nazis came to power in Germany by an electoral fluke or covert coup. In fact, in 1930—just eleven years after its founding —the Nazi Party came in second in a crowded political field with 18 percent of the vote. In 1932 Germany held two national elections, and the Nazis came in first in both, getting 37 and 33 percent of the vote (the runner-up, the Social Democrats, received 21 and 20 percent). And in the famous election of 1933 the Nazis received 44 percent of the vote, as much as the next three parties put together, and was asked to form the government.[2] The Weimar Republic, established in Germany after World War I, was a well-designed democracy with a free press and fair elections. The Nazi Party made full use of the democratic process to organize and spread into small towns and cities. As Germany was wracked by one crisis after another in the 1920s and 1930s, the traditional institutions of government lost credibility. Liberalism and constitutionalism seemed hollow phrases in the face of an increasingly desperate reality. Reeling from the effects of the Depression and hyperinflation, Germany's masses and middle classes grasped at Hitler's promise of bold leadership that would make the nation strong again. The more extreme Hitler's rhetoric, the more popular he got. In his careful study of democratization, the political scientist Jack Snyder concluded, "Racist authoritarian nationalism triumphed at the end of the Weimar Republic not despite the democratization of political life but because of it."[3]

Vienna and Weimar were hardly unusual in experiencing this clash between liberty and democracy. Across Europe in the late nineteenth and early twentieth centuries, liberalism was under siege from mass politics. Usually the latter won. In the case of Lueger, Emperor Franz Joseph held out for two years but, after the fourth election, in 1897, reluctantly swore him in as mayor of Vienna. In France the tradition of antimonarchical liberalism (republicanism) grew strong, particularly after 1871. But it came under relentless attack from both the left (by socialists) and the right (by monarchists, aristocrats, and the church). A few decades later, even the United Kingdom, the birthplace and stronghold of modern liberal politics, saw its once-great Liberal Party fade into irrelevance, squeezed out by the more radical Labor Party and the more traditional Conservatives.[4] As democracy expanded, the moderate, liberal agenda of individual rights, free-market economics, and constitutionalism withered before the gut appeal of communism, religion, and nationalism.

It wasn't just socialists and ultra-nationalists who whipped up populist fury. The legendary German chancellor Otto von Bismarck introduced universal male suffrage in the newly united Germany in 1871 because he believed that a limited franchise helped elect urban liberals who tended to be critics of the monarchy. The masses, Bismarck believed, would always vote for the pro-monarchical conservatives. He was right. His conservative confederate Benjamin Disraeli made a similar calculation in the United Kingdom, throwing the support of the Tories behind the Second Reform Act of 1882, which widened suffrage, allowing most adult British males to vote. But in order to secure the vote of the newly empowered working classes and peasantry, conservative elites had to court them.

Bismarck and his successors fought every election from then on using raw appeals to nationalism and employing all the symbols of patriotism at their disposal. It worked: they always won. In fact even the middle class split, some allying with the conservatives' calls for pride in the fatherland while others stayed true to their liberal roots. In wooing these new voters, Germany's political elite became increasingly willing to use scare tactics and promote divisive politics. Catholics, socialists, and other "enemies of the Reich" were demonized and persecuted. The strategy required the identification of enemies within and without. Politicians, eager to propitiate influential lobbying groups such as the Navy League, grew more and more militarist, building offensive weaponry and defining the country's national interests in expansive, aggressive ways. The result was a series of irresponsible policies, wildly popular at home, that were partly responsible for plunging Europe into a general war in 1914.

## Why Wasn't Germany England?

Democracy did not lead directly to liberty in Germany. Only after major shocks to the country—that is to say, losing the Second World War, being dismembered and occupied, and having a new political order imposed from outside—did West Germany become a full-fledged liberal-democratic society. But Germany, particularly under Bismarck and Kaiser Wilhelm I, had strong liberal, progressive elements within it, as did most European countries.[5] Two traditions battled within much of continental Europe: liberalism and populist authoritarianism of the kind exemplified by Lueger and Hitler. Liberalism lost out in the first half of the twentieth century, and populist authoritarianism was crushed and discredited in the second half. Because of this struggle, for much of Europe the path to liberal democracy was twisted and bloody, often detouring into nasty episodes of social revolution, fascism, and war. Of course some places in Europe had a pattern much closer to the British one—Denmark, Belgium, the Netherlands, the countries of Scandinavia—and for similar reasons (the early development of capitalism, for example). But the history of continental Europe's great nations—Germany, Austria-Hungary, France—is more troubled. As such it might provide clues into the troubles of democratization today, for few places in the world today have the peculiar combination of circumstances that produced liberal democracy in England and the United States. Countries in Asia, Latin America, and Africa are likely to have many of the mixed and complicated features that existed, in some measure, in continental Europe. Already one can see in the world's new democracies some of the turbulence that characterized twentieth-century Vienna and Berlin.

In comparing the British case to those of other European countries, scholars have asked a simple question. British political scientist Ralf Dahrendorf put it bluntly in 1968: "Why wasn't Germany England?"[6] It's a useful question, since it might help us understand how to get to liberal democracy in the modern, imperfect world.

The answer is complex, but a good part of it is that Germany lacked one crucial feature of the English model—the economic and political independence of its bourgeoisie. The English bourgeoisie, born of the Industrial Revolution and bred on free trade and property rights, battled the old feudal order and, as it triumphed, remade the country in its own image—commercial, acquisitive, socially mobile, and dynamic. A new elite of merchants had emerged and England became, in Napoleon's derisive phrase, "a nation of shopkeepers." In Germany, by contrast, industrialization was jump-started and prodded by government subsidies, regulations, and tariffs. As a result its bourgeoisie was weak, divided, and subservient to the state and its ruling feudal elite. Marx contemptuously described Germany's business class as "a bourgeoisie without a world historical purpose."[7]

Germany had a strong bureaucratic tradition of which it was understandably proud. Its state had been far more progressive and efficient at handling many of the problems of industrialization and urbanization—such as public health, transportation, and pensions—than any other European country. But as a result, instead of maintaining independence from state authority, German entrepreneurs eagerly sought favors and honors from the state. Being a businessman with the title of *Kommerziellrat* (commercial officer) was considered a great honor. "Men did not aspire to the nobility of a landed estate," explained one historian, "they aspired to the title of sanitary councillor." Or consider the contrast in the role of the press. In England the free press served as an important voice of political dissent, and journalists were independent—often fiercely—of the state. The first newspapers in Prussia, by contrast, were set up by Frederick the Great as organs of state propaganda. For much of the nineteenth century instead of pressing for liberal reforms the German business classes compromised with the feudal ruling elite. Thus even as it industrialized, Germany remained a mixed regime, with elements of the new bourgeois society combined with the old pre-industrial order. Friedrich Nauman, a liberal intellectual, wrote in 1909 about Germany's "industrial society in the political apparel of an agrarian state. Our political situation is a little bit like the modern factory built in what were old farm buildings. The most modern machinery stands under the old roof beams, and iron girders are drawn through mud walls."

The old order retained a vise-like grip on the reins of government. In 1891, 62 percent of the Prussian domestic administration was of noble birth. The concentration was even greater in the foreign service. In 1914, the German foreign service included eight princes, 29 counts, 20 barons, 54 minor nobles, and 11 commoners.[8] France, with its traditions of a strong state and a weak civil society, also took a long, meandering path to liberal democracy. The social forces that sped the United Kingdom along were weak in France, which had a dependent aristocracy and merchant class. Looking at the eighteenth century, the *Cambridge Economic History of Europe* lists the "distinguishing features of bourgeois representative government"—rule of law, equality before the law, private property, free enterprise, civil liberties, etc.—and then adds, "all of them were absent in France before the revolution."[9] So postrevolutionary France embraced democracy without a developed tradition of constitutional liberalism. Liberty was proclaimed in theory rather than being secured in practice (by a separation of powers and by the strength of nonstate institutions such as private business, civil society, and an independent church). The revolutionaries believed that Montesquieu was utterly misguided in asking for limited and divided government. Instead the absolute power of the king was transferred intact to the new National Assembly, which proceeded to arrest and murder thousands, confiscate their property, and punish them for their religious beliefs, all in the name of the people. Some scholars have aptly called the Jacobin regime "totalitarian democracy." It is the first example in modern history of illiberal democracy.[10]

France placed the state above society, democracy above constitutionalism, and equality above liberty. As a result, for much of the nineteenth century it was democratic, with broad suffrage and elections, but hardly liberal. It was certainly a less secure home for individual freedom than was England or America. The emperor Louis Napoleon, who ruled France from 1848 to 1870, personified France's mixed regime. He governed with popular consent, elections, and referenda—all the while using the methods of a police state to suppress liberty of thought, word, and action. France's Third Republic, like many of Europe's liberal experiments, eventually perished. The country finally got both liberalism and democracy after World War II, more than 150 years after its revolution, having gone through two monarchies, two empires, five republics, and one proto-fascist dictatorship. Even today it has a regime that its founder, Charles de

Gaulle, called an "elective and democratic monarchy." He meant this as a compliment.

## Almost Democratic

There was another, better side to continental Europe, one that contained within it the seeds of liberal democracy. The liberal tradition, although often defeated, was always present, even in Germany, the country that went most badly awry in the 1930s. In fact especially in Germany. Around 1900 Germany was seen by many serious observers as the most progressive state in the world. It had a modern, written constitution, highly developed administrative governance at all levels, and the first welfare state. It had a liberal political culture and, in cities such as Berlin, an avant-garde, aesthetic sensibility. In 1887 one of the leading American scholars of comparative government, Woodrow Wilson, then a professor at Princeton University, praised Prussia for an "admirable system . . . the most studied and most nearly perfected . . . [It] transformed arrogant and perfunctory [bureaucracies] into public-spirited instruments of just government."[11] (It is an irony of history that Wilson, a great admirer of Germany, would lead his country to war against it.) Political scientists of the time often compared Germany favorably to England, which they thought had an overly centralized political system that vested too much power in the House of Commons, an anachronistic upper house full of eccentric lords, no written constitution, and mystical traditions that made innovation frustratingly difficult.

Germany at the turn of the century seemed to be moving in the right direction toward democracy. Then came World War I, which killed 2 million Germans and left the country devastated and was closed with the punitive and humiliating peace of Versailles. The years after Versailles saw the mass flight of ethnic Germans from Poland, Russia, and other eastern lands into Germany (a migration that produced immense social turmoil); hyperinflation; and finally the Great Depression. The liberalizing strains in German society were overwhelmed by much darker ones, and political order collapsed. In particular, hyperinflation—which Niall Ferguson has aptly called an "anti-bourgeois revolution"—wiped out the savings of the middle class and utterly alienated them from the Weimar Republic. The country became easy prey for extreme ideologies and leaders. It is common to read history backward and assume that Germany was destined to become what it became under Hitler. But even the United Kingdom and the United States had their ugly sides and desperate demagogues who grew in strength during the Great Depression. Had those countries gone through twenty years of defeat, humiliation, chaos, economic depression, and the evisceration of their middle classes, perhaps they, too, would have ended up being governed by demagogues such as Huey Long and Oswald Mosley rather than the statesmen Franklin Roosevelt and Winston Churchill.

In much of Europe World War I tossed out the monarchs but it also wrought such devastation that the nations of Europe became breeding grounds for fascism and dictatorship. Liberalism in the 1930s came under attack from the right by fascists and from the left by communists, some of whom used democracy to destroy liberalism. It took another war to finally crush the demagogues. After 1945, with generous help from the United States, Europe set about building a new political order. Within fifty years it had succeeded beyond anyone's hopes.

The threat to liberal democracy from the right—first feudal, then fascist—had died almost completely by 1945 (except on the Iberian Peninsula, but neither Spain's Francisco Franco nor Portugal's Antonio Salazar had any interest in exporting his regime). The threat to democracy then came from the communist parties of the left, often backed by Moscow. But the Western alliance effectively contained that specter. What followed was a remarkable, little-noted transformation. Western Europe, where for two centuries liberalism had tussled with extremist ideologies of the right and the left, quietly and without any grand declarations embraced moderate, constitutional politics. The University of Chicago scholar Mark Lilla describes this process as "the other velvet revolution." He writes,

> In retrospect one can now see that the peace guaranteed by American oversight, the affluence brought by three decades of unprecedented economic growth, and the expansion of the welfare state worked together to erode the traditional working class bases of left-wing parties. . . . Today every single Western European nation has a limited constitutional government, an independent judiciary, multiparty elections, universal suffrage, civilian control of the military and police, rights to free assembly and worship, a large middle class, and a developed consumer economy. Despite the presence of new nationalist and regionalist parties, despite outbursts of ethnic violence and contentious debates over immigration, no government in Western Europe faces the kind of challenge to its legitimacy that all liberal governments faced in the 1920s.[12]

Greece, Spain, and Portugal were the last three western European countries to become fully democratic, which they did in the 1970s. The revolutions of 1989 made for the final act in the drama of European liberalism. Many of the countries of eastern Europe shared much of the historical background of the western European states but, having had the bad luck to have been "liberated" by the Red Army in 1945, were imprisoned within the communist empire. In retrospect we can see that the forces—familiar from our own story—that helped them battle the Soviet Union also helped liberalize their societies: the church and labor unions in Poland, civil-society groups in Czechoslovakia, a reformist elite in Hungary, and a small middle class in all three countries. Free of the Soviet embrace, they moved rapidly to establish liberal democracy, which has taken remarkably firm root. Formerly communist countries such as Romania and Bulgaria are still going through tough transitions toward liberal democracy, some more succesfully than others. But little more than a decade after the collapse of communism, Europe is coming tantalizingly close to becoming, in the elder George Bush's phrase, "whole and free."

## The Wealth of Nations

No country can give itself a new past. But it can alter the future and help its chances of developing into a liberal democracy. For a developing country today, even a middle-income country in Latin America, consolidating into a genuine democracy is proving to be the most important and difficult challenge. To better understand these countries' chances of success we must draw lessons from history and ask what factors produce liberal democracy.

The simplest explanation for a new democracy's political success is its economic success—or, to be more specific, high per capita national income. In 1959, the social scientist Seymour Martin Lipset made a simple, powerful point: "the more well-to-do a nation, the greater its chances to sustain democracy."[13] Lipset argued that as countries develop economically, their societies also developed the strengths and skills to sustain liberal democratic governance. Lipset's thesis has spawned schools and counter-schools, gathering data, running regressions, and checking assumptions. After forty years of research, with some caveats and qualifications, his fundamental point still holds.

Of course some poor countries have become democracies. But when countries become democratic at low levels of development, their democracy usually dies. (There are exceptions, such as India, about which more later.) The most comprehensive statistical study of this problem, conducted by political scientists Adam Przeworski and Fernando Limongi, looked at every country in the world between the years 1950 and 1990. It calculated that in a democratic country that has a per capita income of under $1,500 (in today's dollars), the regime on average had a life expectancy of just eight years. With between $1,500 and $3,000 it survived on average for about eighteen years. Above $6,000 it became highly resilient. The chance that a democratic regime would die in a country with an income above $6,000 was 1 in 500. Once rich, democracies become immortal. Thirty-two democratic regimes have existed at incomes above roughly $9,000 for a combined total of 736 years. Not one has died. By contrast, of the 69 democratic regimes that were poorer, 39 failed—a death rate of 56 percent.[14]

Thus one might conclude that a country that attempts a transition to democracy when it has a per capita GDP of between $3,000 and $6,000 will be successful. This zone of transition to democracy holds true even going back in history. The per capita GDPs of European countries in 1820, when most of them had taken the first steps toward widening the franchise, hovered around $1,700 dollars (in 2000 U.S. dollars), growing to about $2,700 in 1870 and $4,800 in 1913, before the devastation of World War I.[15] Historical GDP figures are based on heroic assumption and guesswork but clearly these figures would fall somewhere within the zone of transition, albeit at the low end. Also, many of these countries became securely liberal democratic only after 1945, at which point most had achieved an approximately $6,000 per capita GDP. If one looks at the success stories of the last thirty years, from Spain, Greece and Portugal onward, almost every one became democratic at the high end of this transitional GNP range. Among eastern European countries after 1989, those that had income levels at the high end of this range—Poland, the Czech Republic, Hungary—consolidated their democracy rapidly. Those at the bottom end or below—Romania, Albania—are taking much longer. So even in Europe, even historically, the correlation holds. No one factor tells the whole story, but given the number of countries being examined, on different continents, with vastly different cultures, and at different historical phases, it is remarkable that one simple explanation—per capita GDP—can explain so much.

All this talk of GDP might suggest that I am minimizing the importance of leadership in the struggle for democracy. Far from it. No successful political transition can take place without leaders and movements that demand and press for freedom. People such as

Vaclav Havel, Nelson Mandela, Lech Walesa, and Kim Dae Jung have an honored place in the history of liberty. But as a matter of scholarship one must ask why they succeeded when they did. One writer has angrily reacted to such concerns, writing that it was not per capita income that brought democracy to South Korea but "moral will."[16] Of course. But surely there are determined, moral men and women in Uganda and Belarus and Egypt who have nonetheless failed time and again in their efforts to bring democracy to these lands. South Korean activists themselves failed during the 1960s, 1970s, and 1980s. In fact Seoul's dissident-turned-president, Kim Dae Jung, was in jail for many of those years. What made him fail in the 1970s but succeed in the 1990s? Did he suddenly gain "moral will" in the 1990s? The fiery Taiwanese political leader Lei Chen, editor of *Free China*, tried to bring democracy to Taiwan in 1960 when he organized the Chinese Democratic Party. He was no less brave than Chen Shui-bian, the human rights lawyer who was elected president of Taiwan in 2000. Why did one human rights activist fail and the other succeed?

Even with the best historical insights, one can't predict when a country will embrace democracy. It often depends on a complex mix of historical facts particular to each country. Why did Spain move to democracy only in 1977 and not earlier? Because its dictator-for-life, Franco, died two years earlier. Why Hungary in 1989? Because that year the Soviet Union stopped threatening it with a military invasion if it liberalized its politics. Why India in 1947? Because that's when Britain liquidated its empire on the subcontinent. And so on. The more interesting question, however, is *what makes democracy endure*. Political regimes change for varied reasons—war, economic crises, death. But when an autocratic regime does collapse and people try to establish a democracy, what makes it last? Historically, the best single answer to that question has been wealth.

Why is wealth good for liberty? Remember the European examples: the process of economic development usually produces the two elements that are crucial to the success of liberal democracy.

First, it allows key segments of society—most important, private businesses and the broader bourgeoisie—to gain power independent of the state. Second, in bargaining with these elements the state tends to become less rapacious and capricious and more rule-oriented and responsive to society's needs, or at least to the needs of the elite of that society. This process results in liberalization, often unintentionally. Minxin Pei describes Taiwan's road to liberal democracy in the 1980s and 1990s in terms that parallel the European experience:

> Rapid growth had liberalizing consequences that the ruling regime had not fully anticipated. With the economy taking off, Taiwan displayed the features common to all growing capitalist societies: The literacy rate increased; mass communication intensified; per capita income rose; and a differentiated urban sector—including labor, a professional middle class, and a business entrepreneurial class—came into being. The business class was remarkable for its independence. Although individual enterprises were small and unorganized they were beyond the capture of the party-state.[17]

This story was repeated in most of East Asia, with local variations. As in Europe, economic liberalization produced a bourgeoisie and civil society and then, after decades, reasonably liberal democracy. As in Europe, the autocrats didn't think they were democratizing. But by spurring growth and modernity, they unleashed forces that they couldn't contain. The historian Phillip Nord describes the process:

> Dictatorships believe they want growth but actually they make a serious mistake in fostering it. Development favors the expansion of an educated middle class; it engenders a "pluralistic infrastructure," a ramifying civil society ever more difficult to manage from above. . . . [T]he authoritarian state may opt at this juncture to relax its grip on public life. The decision is a fatal one, for into the openings created by liberalization pour accumulated discon-

tents that, now articulated, take on the character of outright opposition.[18]

Nord is describing how France democratized in the late nineteenth century, but his work explains East Asia in the late twentieth century just as well.

## Blessed Are the Poor

Money in and of itself does not produce liberty. It must be earned wealth. Over the last half-century some regimes grew rich and yet remained autocracies: for example, the Persian Gulf sheikdoms, Nigeria, and Venezuela. It turns out that the wealth of the oil-rich states does not produce positive political change because their economic development is fundamentally different from the European and Asian models. These economies did not develop along capitalist lines, moving systematically from agriculture to industry to high-level services, but rather exploited their vast oil or mineral reserves in order to buy modernity, in the form of new buildings, hospitals, mansions, cars, and televisions. The people who lived in these countries remained substantially as they had been before—uneducated and unskilled. The societies remained primitive. In fact, the state had to import knowledge and even people from overseas to run the hospitals, schools, and television stations. The result was a business class that, instead of being independent of the state, was deeply dependent on it.

Some numbers make the point. In Saudi Arabia, for example, despite high per capita income, adult literacy stands at only 62 percent, and only 50 percent of adult women are able to read. Kuwait, Qatar, and the United Arab Emirates do a little better, with adult literacy rates that hover in the high 70s. For comparison, the Philippines and Thailand, two countries from which the Gulf states obtain a significant proportion of their unskilled labor, have adult literacy rates in the mid 90s, still among the lowest rates in East Asia. If an educated populace—or at least a literate one—is a prerequisite for democratic and participatory government, it is one that the oil-producing Arab states are still lacking after decades of fabulous wealth.

For liberal democracy the best economic growth is capitalist growth. Marx was among the first to recognize this when he observed that capitalism produced as its favored form of government, bourgeois democracy (of course he didn't mean this as a compliment). Marx argued that capitalism threw up an entrepreneurial bourgeoisie that inevitably destroyed the old aristocratic order and established one that protected property, contracts, rules, and other liberties. Where the bourgeosie does not have such a character, as in nineteenth-century Germany, the society remains unreformed. Consider Latin America. Through much of the twentieth century, business in Latin America grew through a kind of state-sponsored capitalism. Local oligarchs allied with the military and bureaucracy and protected their industries, creating a Byzantine structure of tariffs and regulations that kept the powerful fat and happy. This system impeded genuine economic development and was bad for politics as well. The broader business class remained weak and subservient to the state. Until recently Latin American political development was a variation of the nineteenth-century German model. It is no accident that the one Latin American country that moved first and most strongly away from that tradition and toward free markets and free trade is now its most successful economy and stable country: Chile.

Wealth in natural resources hinders both political modernization and economic growth. Two Harvard economists, Jeffrey D. Sachs and Andrew M. Warner, looked at ninety-seven developing countries over two decades (1971–89) and found that natural endowments were strongly correlated with economic failure. On average the richer a country was in mineral, agricultural, and fuel deposits, the slower its economy grew—think of Saudi Arabia or Nigeria. Countries with almost no resources—such as those in East Asia—grew the fastest. Those with some resources—as in western Europe—grew at rates between these two extremes. There are a few exceptions: Chile, Malaysia, and the United States are all resource rich yet have developed economically and politically. But the basic rule holds up strikingly well.[19]

Why are unearned riches such a curse? Because they impede the development of modern political institutions, laws, and bureaucracies. Let us cynically assume that any government's chief goal is to give itself greater wealth and power. In a country with no resources, for the state to get rich, society has to get rich so that the government can then tax this wealth. In this sense East Asia was blessed in that it was dirt poor. Its regimes had to work hard to create effective government because that was the only way to enrich the country and thus the state. Governments with treasure in their soil have it too easy; they are "trust-fund" states. They get fat on revenues from mineral or oil sales and don't have to tackle the far more difficult task of creating a framework of laws and institutions that generate national wealth (think of Nigeria, Venezuela, Saudi Arabia). A thirteenth-century Central Asian Turkish poet, Yusuf, put this theory simply and in one verse:

> To keep the realm needs many soldiers, horse and foot;
> To keep these soldiers needs much money.
> To get this money, the people must be rich;
> For the people to be rich, the laws must be just.
> If one of these is left undone, all four are undone;
> If these four are undone, kingship unravels.[20]

A version of this theory holds that any state that has access to easy money—say, by taxing shipping through a key canal (as with Egypt) or even because of foreign aid (as with several African countries)—will remain underdeveloped politically. Easy money means a government does not need to tax its citizens. When a government taxes people it has to provide benefits in return, beginning with services, accountability, and good governance but ending up with liberty and representation. This reciprocal bargain—between taxation and representation—is what gives governments legitimacy in the modern world. If a government can get its revenues without forging any roots in society, it is a court, not a state, and its businessmen courtiers, not entrepreneurs.* The Saudi royal family offers its subjects a different kind of bargain: "We don't ask much of you economically and we don't give much to you politically." It is the inverse of the slogan of the American Revolution—no taxation, but no representation either.

This is not to say that countries should hope to be poor in natural resources. Many poor countries become neither democratic nor capitalist. Political institutions, leadership, and luck all matter. Similarly, some countries develop even though they are rich—just as some trust-fund kids turn out well. Most European countries began democratizing when they were better off than the rest of the world. But, as Chapter 1 detailed, Europe had unique advantages. Its long history of battles between church and state, Catholics and Protestants, and kings and lords created liberal institutions and limited state power. Some non-European countries have had variations of these struggles. For example, the political diversity of India, with its dozens of regions, religions, and languages, might actually secure its democratic future rather than threaten it. Polish democracy has been strengthened by a strong and independent church. In general it is fair to conclude that although certain historical and institutional traits help, capitalist growth is the single best way to overturn the old feudal order and create an effective and limited state.

## In Praise of the State

Supporters of free markets often make the mistake of thinking of capitalism as something that exists in opposition to the state. When it is time to pay taxes, this view can seem self-evident. But the reality is more complex. Although in the twentieth century many states grew so strong as to choke their economies, in a broader historical perspec-

---

*This notion can shed some light even in developed democracies: oil and patronage politics went hand in hand in states like Texas until quite recently.

tive, only a legitimate, well-functioning state can create the rules and laws that make capitalism work. At the very least, without a government capable of protecting property rights and human rights, press freedoms and business contracts, antitrust laws and consumer demands, a society gets not the rule of law but the rule of the strong. If one wanted to see what the absence of government produces, one need only look at Africa—it is not a free-market paradise.

In the developing world, the state has often had to jump-start capitalism. Again this mirrors the European example, where modern capitalism began with the state taking large tracts of agricultural land from the hands of feudal lords and using it in ways that were more market-friendly. This move broke the back of the large landowners, the most politically reactionary group in society. As important, millions of acres of land were moved out of stagnant feudal estates, where they lay underutilized, and into a market system. The new owners, often the farmers who tilled the land, used the land more efficiently, since they now had an incentive to do so, or they rented or sold the land to someone who would. In other words, it took a massive redistribution of wealth to make capitalism work.

The modernization of agriculture took centuries in Europe. In the Third World over the last half-century, when it has been implemented, land reform has had similar effects. It has moved property away from feudal landlords who had theoretical title to it, giving it to tenants who have lived and worked on it for generations. Aside from the equity of the matter, this process frees up land—often the most valuable resource in any pre-industrial country—and brings it into the market economy. Land reform was one of the keys to economic and political success in East Asia (particularly in Japan, Taiwan, and South Korea) and, where it was applied, in Latin America (most clearly in Costa Rica, Mexico, and Chile).

Western conservatives often opposed land reform during the Cold War because it sounded vaguely Marxist and its advocates were often left-wingers. But actually it promotes capitalism and thus democracy. Land reform is a crucial step in the process of turning a backward peasant society into a modern capitalist and democratic one. Third World countries where land reform has failed—in parts of Central and Latin America, Pakistan, Zimbabwe, and many other African countries—never managed to commercialize agriculture, retained a strong quasi-feudal elite, and thus have had a tortured experience with democracy. Even in India, the parts of the country where democracy is most dysfunctional (in the northern states of Uttar Pradesh and Bihar) are those where land reform failed. Americans understand implicitly the connection between privately held land and freedom, which is why their government granted land freely to its citizens under the Homestead Act after the Civil War. As the Peruvian intellectual-turned-activist Hernando de Soto has argued, the unwillingness of most Third World countries to give full-fledged property rights to the poor remains one of the chief obstacles to their economic (and, I would add, political) development.[21]

## The Next Wave

Where will we next see democracy flourish and deepen? We cannot accurately predict where democracy will next be tried; that depends on chance. But we can suggest where it might take root. The most promising major country that has moved toward democracy recently is Mexico, which is promising precisely because it followed, in a fashion, the East Asian path (itself a version of the European path). Economic reform first, followed by political reform.

Mexico was tightly run as a one-party state ever since its modern founding in 1926. Mexico's Institutional Revolutionary Party (PRI) dominated all levels of government. Despite the facade of elections and parliaments, however, democracy in Mexico was a sham. But after the debt crisis of the early 1980s, the PRI decided to embark on an ambitious path of economic reform, opening itself up to the world economy and loosening its system of domestic economic controls. As always, economic reform required legal reform and other relaxations of power. The reforms got their greatest boost with the

North American Free Trade Agreement, which locked in Mexico's outward, capitalist orientation. By the late 1990s the PRI began instituting political reforms as well, and in 2001 President Ernesto Zedillo made an extraordinarily courageous and farsighted decision to allow genuinely free elections for the first time in Mexican history. The opposition candidate won and in December 2000, Vicente Fox became the first democratically elected president of Mexico.

If Mexico followed a trajectory similar to that of East Asia, it also received similar treatment in much of the Western press. Despite major legal and economic liberalization, the PRI was usually described as a hard-line authoritarian government in newspapers and magazines. During the 1990s Mexico was routinely spoken of as an authoritarian state, despite twenty years of liberalization. Mexico's transition to democracy took place when its per capita income was just over $9,000, which alone suggests that it will be secure in its new political orientation. Let us return to that simple measure (per capita income) and search for countries that are in the upper reaches of the band of transition to democracy—i.e., between $5,000 and $6,000. Eliminating all countries whose wealth derives almost exclusively from natural resources, we are left with the following major countries: Romania, Belarus, Bulgaria, Croatia, Malaysia, Turkey, Morocco, Tunisia, and Iran.* These are the most likely prospects where democracy, if tried, could over time become genuine and liberal.

Romania ($6,800), Belarus ($7,550), Bulgaria ($5,530), and Croatia ($7,780) have per capita incomes around $6,000, which places the odds of consolidation strongly in their favor. As in the past, these European countries may be able to make the transition at even lower income levels because of their history of independent institutions. Belarus is an unusual case because its economy depends so heavily on Russia's, but if it could rid itself of its elected autocrat, Alexander Lukashenko, it might make progress surprisingly quickly.

*Even though Iran is an oil state, it is worth adding to this list because it has always had a strong non-resource-based economy as well. For more on Iran see Chapter 4.

Among countries with partially authoritarian and partially democratic systems, Malaysia ($8,360) and Turkey ($7,030) have incomes well above $6,000, so they also have good chances of success. Malaysia has mostly followed the East Asian path, first liberalizing its economy while keeping politics locked up (alas, literally in the case of the jailed political leader Anwar Ibrahim) and slowly allowing genuine democratization. Turkey is also a very promising complex case. It is not a full-fledged democracy; its military has three and a half times overthrown an elected head of state (the half came in 1998, when it nudged aside an elected government headed by an Islamic party, in what a Turkish journalist, Jengiz Candar, called a "postmodern coup"). The Turkish military sees itself as the guardian of the secular character of the state and, along with some like-minded judges, enforces this secularism heavy-handedly. On the whole these elites have played a modernizing and stabilizing role in Turkish society, but their zeal has outlived its usefulness. Turkey has one main force working for liberal change: the prospect of European Union (EU) membership, which has forced the country to put its house in order. The Turkish parliament passed thirty-four constitutional amendments in October 2001 to bring itself in line with EU standards. It has since implemented more major reforms. If the EU had a broader strategic vision, its members would see that bringing Turkey within its fold sooner rather than later would have enormous benefits for both sides—and demonstrate to the world that a Muslim society that is modern and democratic would be embraced by the West.

Two other intriguing possibilities are Tunisia ($6,090) and Morocco ($3,410). Tunisia is a dictatorship, Morocco a monarchy. But both have taken some steps toward loosening up the system, particularly economically. Tunisia's president, Zine el-Abidine Ben Ali, is now in his second decade of rule. He runs the country tightly, allowing little political openness nor even much movement toward legal reform. But Tunisia's economic growth has been impressive and widespread. By some estimates the middle class in Tunisia has grown almost tenfold, to include more than half the population. These economic reforms are bound to begin spilling over into the areas of law, travel, and information, but progress is slow so far. Morocco is even worse off, with more talk than action. The king, Mohammed VI, inherited an almost medieval structure of political authority from his father, Hassan II. The young king has made impressive speeches calling for economic reform, the rule of law, equal rights for women, and greater freedoms for all his subjects. Three years into his reign, however, little has happened. Still, Tunisia and Morocco are reasonably open societies when compared with the rest of the Arab world. Were they to succeed in liberalizing their economies and then their polities, they would send a powerful signal around the world that no culture, no religion, no region, is inherently resistant to democracy.

## You Can't Stop the Machine

The single most important test of the connection between capitalism and democracy will take place in China over the next few decades. The images of China's rulers that are sometimes presented in the media are grim. Some politicians and commentators use phrases like "the butchers of Beijing" to describe them. There is obviously some reality behind them; Tiananmen Square was a brutal massacre. But a more accurate way to think of China's ruling elite is as nervous apparatchiks, gingerly watching as they try to reform the world's most populous country while holding on to power. If things go well, they will be respected as builders of an industrialized world power. If their experiment goes awry, they will be dead or exiled to Outer Mongolia.

"The experiment" is the Chinese leaders' attempt to modernize China by opening its economy but holding political change in check. It is too easy to caricature them as trying to graft capitalism onto a fascist state. They know that to introduce capitalism into China requires much more than economic changes, so they have allowed significant reforms of the administrative and legal systems as well. The debate on how best to liberalize the system is actually a fairly

open and freewheeling one in China. The regime has even introduced open elections in some villages and allowed businessmen to
join the Communist Party. But the political system is still tightly
controlled and brutal in its suppression of dissent. China's rulers
believe that premature democratization in a country as vast, poor, and
diverse as China will produce chaos. They have more selfish reasons
as well: the Communist Party would lose its total monopoly on
power.

The economic results of China's reforms have been staggering.
Between 1980 and 2000 the average person's income in China almost
tripled, from $1,394 to $3,976. Some 170 million people have moved
above the poverty line. Exports from the dynamic coastal provinces
have skyrocketed. Shenzen sold $17 million worth of goods in 1981;
ten years later that figure was $5.9 billion; today it is over $30 billion.
Foreign investment into these areas has surged. Other changes have
been more halting. State-owned enterprises—large government fac-
tories—still account for almost half of China's industrial output,
although that figure is down from 80 percent in 1980, and dropping
fast. Land reform has slowed considerably. But if trends continue to
move in the direction they have been going, the next two decades
will produce a prosperous country with a market economy that is
integrated into the world economy. This would be a staggering
change for China. For China to implement its agreements with the
World Trade Organization (WTO) the regime will have to force
transparency, accountability, and market discipline across large swaths
of the domestic economy. China's entry into the WTO is likely to be
a slow but seismic change.

Some people see China's transformation as impressive but proof
that economic liberalization does not lead to political change. After
all, the Communists are still in charge. But China is still a relatively
poor Third World country with a relatively small bourgeoisie.
Besides, because it is still ruled utterly undemocratically, it is easy to be
blind to the enormous political and social changes that have already
taken place there. The first decade of economic reform, roughly from

1979 to 1989, saw the rapid growth of political dissent. The "democracy wall" movement, which began in Beijing, spread to more than twenty cities and at its peak produced more than forty dissident publications. In November 1987, the premier of the Communist Party, Zhao Zhiyang, even sought to legitimize political opposition, arguing in a famous report to the Thirteenth Party Congress that the central task of the congress was to accelerate and deepen economic and political reform. He described the goal of the Party as "turn[ing] China into a prosperous, strong, *democratic*, culturally advanced and modern socialist country" (italics are mine). Different groups of people may have different interests and views, he said, and they too need opportunities and channels for the exchange of ideas.

By the late 1980s, the economy and political dissent were growing at heady rates. Partly because of mismanagement, partly because of corruption, the economy spiraled out of control, with inflation jumping in 1988 from 8 percent to 18 percent. Political criticism of the regime became much more intense and more broad-based—even private business leaders started supporting the protesters. When the de facto leader of the opposition movement, liberal party leader Hu Yaobang, died in April 1989, his funeral began a series of demonstrations and sit-ins. Two months later they ended in a blaze of fire when Chinese troops moved into Tiananmen Square and, using tanks, bullets, and tear gas, disbanded the demonstrators. The political openings that Hu and Zhao had championed were shut down, and Zhao was purged from the leadership.

The economic reforms continued after a decent interval. Stock markets were set up in Shanghai and Shenzen in 1990 and 1991. The exchange rate became more sensitive to international market pressures. Foreign investment laws were further loosened, causing a new flood of funds from abroad. In 1992 China's supreme leader, Deng Xiaoping, visited the entrepreneurial coastal regions of Guangzhou and Shenzen and blessed their free-market policies. Since then opposition to economic reforms has been marginalized. China continues to reduce the power and role of the state in its economy and to integrate itself into world markets, accepting their rules and regulations. But less has happened in the political sphere, although the government has openly celebrated the new business class and admitted it into its fold. It has also signed international covenants on social, economic, cultural, civil, and political rights. These are only parchment promises. But just as the Soviet Union's acceptance of the Helsinki Final Act placed some pressure on it, so these treaties will surely put some limits on the Chinese regime's behavior.

Although political dissent in China might seem to have quieted in recent years, many scholars believe it is finding new paths in legal and administrative attacks on the ruling establishment. Here, as in East Asia, the regime's desire to modernize the economy has unintended political effects. For example, to implement its agreements with the WTO, the government has made wide-ranging reforms of Chinese law, creating stronger economic and civil rights. As a result, litigation has exploded, including administrative litigation. Chinese citizens are suing the government—and winning—in record numbers (90,557 suits in 1997 versus 0 in 1984). Harvard's scholar of Chinese law, William Alford, often a skeptic about Chinese political reform, explained the unintended consequences of China's legal reform:

> The regime has not only through its law provided a legal, moral, and political vocabulary with which those who wish to take it to task might articulate their concerns, but also has proffered these individuals a singular platform from which their concerns might be broadcast. In seeking to deploy formal legality for highly instrumental purposes, the regime has unwittingly handed its opponents a keenly honed instrument through which to seek to accomplish their own, very different ends.

The veteran dissident Xu Wenli agreed with this analysis, explaining that from now on China's opposition movement should be "open and in conformity with the Chinese constitution."

When speaking about dissent in China, it is easy to believe that more democracy would mean more liberty. In fact, in the short term, the opposite is true. The Chinese government on many important issues is more liberal than its people. When Beijing forced down an American reconaissance plane in March 2001, Americans were outraged that the Chinese government was being so demanding in its negotiations with Washington. But in China, to the extent that it could be measured, the public felt that the government was being too soft on the Americans. On a wide range of issues, from law and order to attitudes regarding Taiwan, Japan, and the United States, the Beijing regime is less populist, nationalist, aggressive, and intolerant than its people.

Of course it is difficult to measure public opinion in China. One ends up relying on the few surveys that the government allows, the bursts of public opinion in Internet chat rooms, good reporting by foreign newspapers, and other such indications. But surely it is indicative that all these sources point in the same direction. In this respect, China might be following a historical pattern. Germany, Austria-Hungary, and other late modernizing countries at the turn of the nineteenth century were, like China today, trapped between regimes that wouldn't liberalize enough and powerful mass movements that were hyper-nationalist, fascist, communist—and ultimately, illiberal. This suggests that the current regime in Beijing should not suppress dissent or slow down political reform. On the contrary, only legal, social, and political reform will allow China's leaders to manage the volatile domestic circumstances they face. But they would do well to liberalize with care and incrementally.

China's Communist Party elites—like all modernizing autocrats before them—believe that they can manage this balancing act, mixing economic liberalization with political control. Their role model is former prime minister Lee Kuan Yew of Singapore. Lee achieved the dream of every strongman: to modernize the economy, even the society, of his country, but not the politics. All liberalizing autocrats have believed that they can, like Lee, achieve modernity but delay democracy. But they can't.

Other than the oil-rich Gulf states, Singapore is the only country with a per capita GDP over $10,000 that is not a democracy (its GDP is $26,500). It is a small city-state that lives in the shadow of large neighbors and has had remarkably clever political leadership. It is an obvious exception to the rule and one that will not last. Singapore already has very strong strands of constitutional liberalism. It has a vigorous free economy, and rights of property, belief, travel, etc., are staunchly protected. The country is open to the world. (Even its absurd bans on certain foreign newspapers are becoming a thing of the past because of unrestricted internet access.) Its people are educated, cosmopolitan, and well informed about the rest of the world. In fact the World Economic Forum and other independent bodies have regularly rated Singapore one of the most economically free countries in the world, with the cleanest administrative system. But it has a limited free press, an even more limited political opposition, and no free elections. Anyone who has visited Singapore can see that it is changing. The younger generation of Singaporeans is less willing to accept a closed political system and the elders recognize that the system will open up. If Lee's successors democratize the country in the next fifteen years on their own terms, they will have a chance to maintain their power and political base. If not, change will happen suddenly and they will likely lose power. But one way or the other, Singapore will be a fully functioning liberal democracy within a generation.

In Europe, most liberalizing autocrats met a bad end. They were ousted or executed after losing a war or presiding over a depression—sometimes both. Wars and economic crises often fulfilled a useful function: getting rid of the old regime. World War I discredited many of the ruling monarchies of Europe; World War II dispensed with the fascists. In East Asia, this process has been more benign, with economic downturns playing the role that war did in Europe. A sharp economic dislocation in the mid-1980s rattled South Korea's military junta, which never recovered. President Suharto of Indonesia and Thailand's old ruling elites were eased out as they floundered during the 1998 Asian financial crisis. Were China to go through large-scale economic turmoil, the legitimacy of the Communist Party would probably be called into question. The role of the modernizing autocrat is biblical; like Moses, he can lead his country forward, but he rarely makes it to the promised land himself.

China's Communists should re-read their Marx. Karl Marx understood that when a country modernizes its economy, embraces capitalism, and creates a bourgeoisie, the political system will change to reflect that transformation. Changes in the "base," in Marxist lingo, always produce changes in the "superstructure." Whatever the intentions of its rulers, the Middle Kingdom has embarked on a journey that will end in democracy or chaos. Which one it will be depends on the government in Beijing. Will it accept new realities and allow economic liberalization to lead to political liberalization, like the other autocrats in East Asia? Or will it fight to the end and hold on to all reins of power? It is not an exaggeration to say that the prospects for peace and freedom in Asia—indeed the world—rest on that decision.

| CHAPTER 3 |

# Illiberal Democracy

I F ONE IMAGE symbolizes the final death of Soviet communism
it is Boris Yeltsin standing on a tank. It was August 19, 1991.
That morning a faction of the Politburo had declared a state of
emergency in the Soviet Union. The self-appointed Committee for
the State of Emergency had placed the Communist Party general
secretary, Mikhail Gorbachev, under house arrest, sent the army into
the streets to maintain order, and announced the reversal of Gorbachev's liberal reforms. The commissars might well have succeeded
in reimposing a dictatorship on the Soviet Union. But Yeltsin, recently
and overwhelmingly elected president of the Russian Republic,
fought back. He denounced the coup, urged Russians to resist, and
called on the military troops to disobey their orders. Showing both
extraordinary courage and a gift for political theater, he walked up to
the troops who had surrounded the marble-clad Russian parliament
building—their "White House"—climbed atop a tank, shook hands
with the astonished crew, and held a press conference. The rest, quite
literally, is history.

That was a great moment for Russia. Yet even at the pinnacle of
its democratic triumph one could forsee Russia's democratic

tragedy. What Yeltsin actually did on top of that tank was read decrees, unilateral presidential edicts that would become a hallmark of his eight-year reign. In August 1991 (and then again in 1993 when he disbanded the legislature and introduced a new constitution) Yelstin was fighting for the survival of a fragile democracy against communist thugs. But rule by decree became standard operating procedure. Whenever confronted with a difficult problem, he would not marshal his supporters and fight it politically, nor would he compromise. Instead he invariably issued a presidential fiat, sometimes of dubious legality, using his power and popularity to override the normal give and take of politics. When local authorities fought back, he disbanded the entire system of local government. When governors defied him, he fired them. When Russia's constitutional court challenged one of his decrees, Yeltsin refused to implement its ruling, and then deprived the chief justice of his pay, forcing him to resign in despair. Yeltsin had little regard for the country's institutions, other than his own office. He weakened the legislature and courts at every turn. He prosecuted a brutal war in Chechnya, ignoring the routine processes of consultation, let alone checks and balances. In his final months in office, Yeltsin implemented what historian Richard Pipes (who had strongly supported Yeltsin) called "a coup d'état": he resigned six months before the scheduled presidential elections and appointed his prime minister, Vladimir Putin, as acting president. This made the upcoming election irrelevant, a ratification of power rather than a genuine contest. Putin ran as the incumbent, with the aura and authority of the head of state (and one who was conducting a war), against a bunch of hacks.

By the end of his reign Yelstin was regarded in his own country and much of the world as a figure from the past. Mercurial, aging, unhealthy, and often drunk, he seemed a political fossil. But in fact, Yeltsin may prove to have been a herald of the future, a political leader of a type that is becoming increasingly common: the popular autocrat. Since the fall of communism, countries around the world are being governed by regimes like Russia's that mix elections and authoritarianism—illiberal democracies.

## Russia Redux

Russia and China are the two most important countries in the world that are not liberal democracies. Their search for political and economic systems that work for them is of enormous global significance. Were both to become Western-style liberal democracies, all the major powers in the world would be stable regimes governed by popular consent and the rule of law. This would not mean permanent peace, nor would it abolish international rivalries. But it would likely mean a different and probably more benign world. As of now, however, the two countries are on somewhat different paths. China has moved to reform its economy and, very slowly, other aspects of its legal and administrative system, but it has taken few steps to introduce democracy. Russia, by contrast, moved first and most quickly on political reform. Even under Gorbachev, there was more glasnost (political openness) than perestroika (economic restructuring). After communism, Russia moved rapidly to free and fair elections in the hope that they would produce Western-style liberal democracy. It also initiated a burst of economic reforms, in the early 1990s, in the hope that this would produce Western-style capitalism, but most didn't work. To oversimplify, China is reforming its economics before its politics, whereas Russia did the reverse.

Today, Russia is a freer country than China. It has greater respect for individual rights and press freedoms, and even its economy is in theory more open to competition and foreign investment. China remains a closed society run by the Communist Party, but it is being steadily liberalized along several fronts, chiefly economic and legal. Which will ultimately prove to have taken a more stable route to liberal democracy? If economic development and a middle class are keys to sustaining democracy, China is moving in the right direction. Its economy has grown dramatically over the last twenty-five years.

Russia's gross national product, by contrast, has shrunk almost 40 percent since 1991 and has begun to recover only in the last few years, largely because oil prices moved higher. If China continues on its current path and continues to grow, further develops its rule of law, builds a bourgeoisie, and then liberalizes its politics—and these are huge ifs—it will have achieved an extraordinary transformation toward genuine democracy.

If Russia continues down *its* path—and this, too, is a big if—of slipping toward an elected autocracy with more and more of its freedoms secure in theory but violated in practice, with corruption embedded into the very system of politics and economics, it could well remain democratic and illiberal. It might settle into a version of the regimes that dominated Latin America in the 1960s and 1970s: quasi-capitalist, with a permanent governing alliance among the elites. In Latin America this alliance was between big business and the military; in Russia it is between the oligarchs and the former Communist elite. This type of regime appears to have taken hold in much of the former Soviet Union—Central Asia, Belarus, Ukraine— the notable exceptions being the three Baltic states.

The Russian path has, wittingly or not, violated the two key lessons that one can glean from the historical experience of democratization: emphasize genuine economic development and build effective political institutions. Moscow is failing on both counts.

Russia's fundamental problem is not that it is a poor country struggling to modernize, but rather that it is a rich country struggling to modernize. Schoolchildren in the Soviet era were taught that they lived in the richest country in the world. In this case communist propaganda was true. If natural resources were the measure of national wealth, Russia would probably rank on top globally, with its vast endowments of oil, natural gas, diamonds, nickel, and other minerals. These resources probably prolonged the life of Soviet communism for a generation. They also helped produce a dysfunctional state.

In the never-never land of Soviet communism, the state needed no tax revenues, since it owned the entire economy. Much of the manufacturing sector was, by the 1970s, worthless. In fact products were often "value-subtracted," which is to say that the raw materials were more valuable than the finished goods they were turned into. The Soviet state relied almost entirely on revenues from natural resources to fund itself. Thus, unlike dictatorships in South Korea and Taiwan, it never created rules and policies to facilitate economic growth. Rich regimes with faltering legitimacy often bribe their citizens with benefits so that they don't revolt (e.g., Saudi Arabia). The Soviet Union terrorized them instead. Moscow was not inclined to give away resources to its citizens, having much grander purposes for these funds, such as maintaining a huge defense establishment and propping up Third World proxies. When Soviet communism collapsed, Gorbachev's successors inherited a state strong enough to terrorize its people but too weak to administer a modern economy.

Unfortunately Yeltsin added to the problems of Russia's political development. His supporters have justified his autocratic actions by pointing out, correctly, that the president was fighting well-entrenched and nasty antidemocratic forces. But a political founder must follow his acts of destruction with greater acts of construction. Jawaharlal Nehru spent almost thirteen years in jail fighting the British colonial authorities, but as prime minister of independent India he spent many more years preserving British institutions. Nelson Mandela approved of radical and violent resistence to apartheid, but once in power he reached out to South Africa's whites to create a multiracial South Africa.

But unlike Nehru and Mandela, Yeltsin did little to build political institutions in Russia. In fact he actively weakened almost all competing centers of power—the legislature, the courts, regional governors. The 1993 constitution he has bequeathed to Russia is a disaster, creating a weak parliament, a dependent judiciary, and an out-of-control presidency. Perhaps most lamentably, Yeltsin did not found a political party. He could have done so easily, uniting all the reformist elements within Russia. More than any other action this could have ensured that Russian democracy would deepen and become genuine.

But he didn't. This may seem like a small point, but parties are the mechanism through which people in modern societies express, reconcile, and institutionalize their moral and political values. The historian of American democracy Clinton Rossiter once wrote, "No America without democracy, no democracy without politics, no politics without parties." His statement is true everywhere. Without parties, politics becomes a game for individuals, interest groups, and strongmen. That is a fair description of Russian democracy today.

Putin has strengthened Yeltsin's chief legacy, which is not liberal reform but rather a superpresidency. In his first year in office, Putin shrank the rest of Russia's government. His main targets have been regional governors, whom he effectively disempowered by appointing seven "supergovernors" to oversee the eighty-nine regions and threw the governors out of parliament where they had seats in the upper house. They were replaced by legislators appointed by the Kremlin. Additionally, any governor can now be fired if the president believes that he has broken the law. Putin also persuaded the Duma to enact legislation reducing the tax revenues sent to the provinces. Putin's other targets have been the media and Russia's infamous oligarchs, whom he has threatened with raids, arrests, and imprisonment. As a strategy of intimidation, it has worked. Freedom of the press in Russia barely exists anymore. In April 2000, a Kremlin-allied consortium took over NTV, the country's last independent nationwide broadcaster, firing most of its senior staff. And when journalists who resigned over the takeover sought refuge at another TV station owned by NTV founder Vladimir Gusinsky, they found their new employer under immediate assault by the tax authorities. The print media is still nominally independent but now toes the government line on all matters.[1]

In doing all this Putin is following the wishes of his electorate. In a 2000 poll conducted by the Public Opinion Fund, 57 percent of Russians approved of his censorship of the media. Even more approved of his attacks on the oligarchs, many of whom are questionable figures. Russia's oligarchs acquired their wealth using shady means and maintain it in even more dubious ways. The regional governors are often local bosses with enormous appetites for corruption. But when Putin unleashes the secret police on businessmen or politicians whom he dislikes, he is undermining the rule of law. A minor oligarch (with a fairly clean reputation) once told me in Moscow, "We have all broken some law or other. You cannot do business in Russia without breaking the law. Putin knows that. So to say that he is simply enforcing the law is nonsense. He is selectively using it for political ends." The use of law as a political weapon perverts the idea of equality under law.

More important is the long-term effect of Putin's whittling down of his opponents. Pluralism rests on competing centers of power. Vladimir Ryzkhov, one of Russia's few liberals in parliament, made an explicit comparison with Europe's past: "The earls and barons who battled royal power were hardly virtuous themselves. But they kept a check on the crown. Our problem in Russia if Putin succeeds is that there will be absolutely no one left to check the Kremlin. We are left trusting once again in a good czar."[2] Putin is a good czar. He wants to build a modern Russia. He believes that Russia needs order and a functioning state in order to liberalize its economy. Perhaps he even believes that eventually, Russia will be able to democratize its political system. If he succeeds, Putin could help Russia become a normal industrialized country with some of the liberal features that this moniker implies. "The model for Russia in the early 1990s was Poland after communism. Now it's Chile under [Augusto] Pinochet," says Ryzkhov. The Pinochet model is certainly possible; Pinochet did eventually lead his country to liberal democracy.

But it is an odd argument in favor of Russia's democratic path to say that it has made possible a leader who crushes the opposition, stifles the media, bans political parties, and then liberalizes the economy by fiat, which will eventually bring true democracy. Illiberal democracy is good, in this thesis, because it has—by chance—produced a liberal autocrat who may eventually lead his country to genuine liberal democracy. This is an argument in favor of liberal autocrats, not democracy. There is always the possibility, of course, that Putin, or more likely one of his successors, will turn out to be a bad czar and use his enormous powers for less noble goals. It has happened in the past.

## The Wrong Way

The Russian path is familiar. In contrast to the Western and East Asian models, during the last two decades in Africa and in parts of Asia and Latin America, dictatorships with little background in constitutional liberalism or capitalism have moved toward democracy. The results are not encouraging. In the Western Hemisphere, with elections having been held in every country except Cuba, a 1993 study by one of the leading scholars of democratization, Stanford's Larry Diamond, determined that ten of the twenty-two principal Latin American countries had "levels of human rights abuse that are incompatible with the consolidation of [liberal] democracy." Since then, with a few important exceptions such as Brazil, things have only gotten worse.

Consider Venezuela's Hugo Chavez. A colonel in the army, he was cashiered and jailed for his part in an unsuccessful coup d'état in 1992. Six years later, running on an angry, populist platform, he was elected president with a solid 56 percent of the vote. He proposed a referendum that would replace Venezuela's constitution, eviscerate the powers of the legislature and the judiciary, and place governing authority under a "Constituent Assembly." The referendum passed with 92 percent of the vote. Three months later his party won 92 percent of the seats in the new assembly. The proposed new constitution increased the president's term by one year, allowed him to succeed himself, eliminated one chamber of the legislature, reduced civilian control of the military, expanded the government's role in the economy, and allowed the assembly to fire judges. "We are heading toward catastrophe," warned Jorge Olavarria, a longtime legislator and former Chavez supporter. "This constitution will set us back 100 years, and the military will become an armed wing of the political movement."[3] The new constitution passed in December 1999 with 71 percent of the vote. Despite the fact that Venezuela went through grim economic times during his first few years, Chavez never dropped below 65 percent in public approval ratings.

By early 2002 it seemed as if his luck was finally running out. Public discontent with his thuggish rule and a failing economy combined to spark massive demonstrations. The army and business elites plotted a coup and, in March 2002, Chavez was ousted—for two days. Chavez, who is skilled at organizing "people power"—and who was helped by the blatantly undemocratic nature of the coup—was comfortably back in power within a week.

Venezuela has the telltale sign of democratic dysfunction: abundant natural resources, including the largest oil reserves outside the Middle East. This has meant economic mismanagement, political corruption, and institutional decay. Four out of five Venezuelans live below the poverty line in a country that, twenty years ago, had among the highest living standards in Latin America. In some ways the country was ripe for a revolution. But what it got was a new caudillo, a strongman who claims to stand up for his country against the world (which usually means the United States). This is why Chavez has shown his admiration for Fidel Castro, Saddam Hussein, and even the loony Mu'ammar Gadhafi. More dangerously, Chavez represents a persistent hope in Latin America that constructive change will come not through a pluralist political system, in which an array of political parties and interests grind away at the tedious work of incremental reform, but in the form of some new, messianic leader who can sweep away the debris of the past and start anew. This tendency has been gaining ground throughout the Andean region in the last few years. If Latin America's economic woes persist, it could become more widespread.

In Africa the past decade has been a crushing disappointment. Since 1990, forty-two of the forty-eight countries of sub-Saharan Africa have held multiparty elections, ushering in the hope that

Africa might finally move beyond its reputation for rapacious despots and rampant corruption. The *New York Times* recently compared this wave of elections to the transitions in eastern Europe after the fall of communism.[4] This is a highly misleading analogy, however. Although democracy has in many ways opened up African politics and brought people liberty, it has also produced a degree of chaos and instability that has actually made corruption and lawlessness worse in many countries. One of Africa's most careful observers, Michael Chege, surveyed the wave of democratization in the 1990s and concluded that the continent had "overemphasized multiparty elections . . . and correspondingly neglected the basic tenets of liberal governance."[5] These tenets will prove hard to come by, since most of Africa has not developed economically or constitutionally. It is surely not an accident that the two countries in Africa that are furthest along on the path toward liberal democracy, South Africa and Botswana, have per capita incomes above the zone of transition to democracy, which was from $3,000 to $6,000. South Africa's is $8,500 and Botswana's $6,600; both are artificially high because of natural-resource wealth. None of this is to say that Africa was better off under its plundering dictators, but it does suggest that what Africa needs more urgently than democracy is good governance. There are some extraordinary success stories, such as Mozambique, which ended a sixteen-year civil war and is now a functioning democracy with a market economy. But it has had enormous help in establishing good government from the international community and the United Nations, a pattern unlikely to recur in every African country.

In Central Asia, elections, even when reasonably free, as in Kyrgyzstan, have resulted in strong executives, weak legislatures and judiciaries, and few civil and economic liberties. Some countries have held no elections; there, popular autocrats hold sway. Azerbaijan's president, Gaidar Aliyev, for example, is a former head of the Soviet-era intelligence bureau, the KGB, and a former member of the Soviet Politburo. He ousted his predecessor in a coup in 1993, but most serious observers of the region suspect that if a free and fair election were held today, Aliyev would win.[6] Even when heroes become leaders, it doesn't seem to change much. Georgia is run by the venerated Eduard Shevardnadze, Gorbachev's reformist foreign minister who helped end the Cold War. Still, Shevardnadze rigs elections in his favor (even though he would probably win a free one) and runs a country in which corruption is pervasive and individual liberties insecure.

Naturally, illiberal democracy runs along a spectrum, from modest offenders such as Argentina to near-tyrannies such as Kazakhstan, with countries such as Ukraine and Venezuela in between. Along much of the spectrum, elections are rarely as free and fair as in the West today, but they do reflect popular participation in politics and support for those elected. The mixture of democracy and authoritarianism varies from country to country—Russia actually holds freer elections than most—but all contain these seemingly disparate elements. The only data base that scores countries separately on their democratic and constitutional records shows a clear rise in illiberal democracy over the last decade. In 1990 only 22 percent of democratizing countries could have been so categorized; in 1992 that figure had risen to 35 percent; in 1997 it was 50 percent, from which peak it has since declined somewhat. Still, as of this writing close to half of the "democratizing" countries in the world are illiberal democracies.

Yet some call it simply a passing phase, the growing pains that young democracies must endure. The *Economist* has argued that constitutional liberalism "is more likely to occur in a democracy."[7] But is this commonly asserted view true? Do elections in places such as Central Asia and Africa open up political space in a country, forcing broader political, economic, and legal reforms? Or do these elections provide a cover for authoritarianism and populism? It is too soon to tell—most of these transitions are still underway—but the signs are not encouraging. Many illiberal democracies—almost all in Central Asia, for example—have quickly and firmly turned into dictatorships. Elections in these countries merely legitimized power grabs. In others, such as many in Africa, rapid moves toward democracy have undermined state authority, producing regional and ethnic challenges to central rule. Still others, such as Venezuela and Peru, retain some level of genuine democracy with lots of illiberal practices. Finally, there are cases such as Croatia and Slovakia, where an illiberal democratic system is evolving in a more constitutional and reformist direction. In these cases, the democratic element was a crucial spur to reform because it did what democracy does better than any other form of government: it threw the bums out, providing for a peaceful transfer of power from the old guard to a new regime. Note, however, that Croatia and Slovakia are both European countries with relatively high per capita incomes: $6,698 and $9,624, respectively. In general, outside Europe, illiberal democracy has not proved to be an effective path to liberal democracy.

Consider Pakistan. In October 1999, the Western world was surprised when Pakistan's army chief, General Pervez Musharraf, overthrew the freely elected prime minister, Nawaz Sharif. The surprising fact was not the coup—it was Pakistan's fourth in as many decades—but its popularity. Most Pakistanis were happy to be rid of eleven years of sham democracy. During that period, Sharif and his predecessor, Benazir Bhutto, abused their office for personal gain, packed the courts with political cronies, fired local governments, allowed Islamic fundamentalists to enact draconian laws, and plundered the state coffers. The headline of an essay in one of Pakistan's leading newspapers in January 1998 described the state of the country: "Fascist Democracy: Grab Power, Gag Opposition."[8] Western, particularly American, newspapers had a very different reaction. Almost all righteously condemned the coup. During the 2000 presidential campaign, George W. Bush confessed to not remembering the name of the new Pakistani leader, but said that he would "bring stability to the region." The *Washington Post* immediately denounced him for uttering such heresies about a dictator.

Two years later and with the transforming events of September 11 on his side, Musharraf had pursued a path of radical political, social, educational, and economic reform that even his supporters would not have predicted. Few elected politicians in Pakistan supported his moves. Musharraf has been able to promote these policies precisely because he did not have to run for office and cater to the interests of feudal bosses, Islamic militants, and regional chieftains. There was no guarantee that a dictator would do what Musharraf did. But in Pakistan no elected politician would have acted as boldly, decisively, and effectively as he did. As of this writing, Musharraf seems somewhat more autocratic and somewhat less liberal than he seemed at first flush. Yet he remains determined to modernize and secularize his country, although he is facing opposition from many feudal and religious factions in Pakistani society. Reforming Pakistan—economically and politically—is a near-impossible task. But as with Russia, if genuine liberalization and even democracy come to Pakistan it will come not because of its history of illiberal democracy but because it stumbled on a liberal autocrat.

## Problems of Democracy

Current concerns about elected autocrats in Russia, Central Asia, and Latin America would not have surprised nineteenth-century liberals such as John Stuart Mill. Mill opened his classic *On Liberty* by noting that as countries became democratic, people tended to believe that "too much importance had been attached to the limitation of [governmental] power itself. That . . . was a response against rulers whose interests were opposed to those of the people." Once the people were themselves in charge, caution was unnecessary; "The nation did not need to be protected against its own will." As if confirming Mill's fears, Aleksandr Lukashenko, after being elected president of Belarus overwhelmingly in a free 1994 election, when asked about limiting his powers, said, "There will be no dictatorship. I am of the people, and I am going to be for the people."

The tension between constitutional liberalism and democracy centers on the scope of governmental authority. Constitutional liberalism is about the limitation of power; democracy is about its accumulation and use. For this reason, many eighteenth- and nineteenth-century liberals saw democracy as a force that could undermine liberty. The tendency for a democratic government to believe it has absolute sovereignty (that is, power) can result in the centralization of authority, often by extraconstitutional means and with grim results. What you end up with is little different from a dictatorship, albeit one that has greater legitimacy.

Over the past decade, elected governments claiming to represent the people have steadily encroached on the powers and rights of other elements in society, a usurpation that is both horizontal (from other branches of the national government) and vertical (from regional and local authorities as well as private businesses and other nongovernmental groups such as the press). Putin, Lukashenko, and Chavez are only a few exemplars. Even a bona fide reformer such as former Argentine president Carlos Menem passed close to 300 presidential decrees in his eight years in office, about three times as many as were passed by all previous Argentine presidents put together, going back to 1853. Kyrgyzstan's Askar Akayev, elected with 60 percent of the vote, proposed enhancing his powers in a referendum that passed easily in 1996. His powers now include appointing all top officials except the prime minister, although he can dissolve parliament if it turns down three of his nominees for that post.

Horizontal usurpation is more obvious, but vertical usurpation is more common. Over the past three decades, elected governments in India and Pakistan routinely disbanded state legislatures on flimsy grounds, placing regions under direct rule of the central government. In a less dramatic but typical move, the elected government of the Central African Republic ended the long-standing independence of its university system, making it part of the central state apparatus. The widespread use of security forces to intimidate journalists—from Peru to Ukraine to the Philippines—systematically weakens a crucial check on governmental power. In Latin America even a supposedly reformist democrat, like Peru's Alberto

Toledo, has routinely used his presidential powers to intimidate political opponents.

Usurpation is particularly widespread in Latin America and the former Soviet Union, perhaps because the states in these regions feature, for the most part, presidential systems. These systems tend to produce leaders who believe that they speak for the people—even when they have been elected by no more than a plurality. As the political scientist Juan Linz has pointed out, Salvador Allende was elected to the Chilean presidency in 1970 with only 36 percent of the vote. In similar circumstances in a parliamentary system, a prime minister would have had to share power in a coalition government. Presidents appoint cabinets of cronies, rather than senior party figures, maintaining few internal checks on their power. And when their views conflict with those of the legislature, or even the courts, presidents tend to "go to the nation," bypassing the dreary tasks of bargaining and coalition-building. Scholars debate the merits of presidential versus parliamentary forms of government, and certainly usurpation can occur under either, absent well-developed alternate centers of power such as strong legislatures, courts, political parties, and regional governments, as well as independent universities and news media. Many countries in Latin America actually combine presidential systems with proportional representation, producing populist leaders and multiple parties—an unstable combination.

Governments that usurp powers do not end up producing well-run, stable countries. A strong government is different from an effective government; in fact, the two may be contradictory. Africa has power-hungry and ineffective states. The United States has a government with limited powers and yet is a highly effective state. Confusing these two concepts has led many Western governments and scholars to encourage the creation of strong and centralized states in the Third World. Leaders in these countries have argued that they need the authority to break down feudalism, split entrenched coalitions, override vested interests, and bring order to chaotic societies. There is some truth to this concern, but it confuses legitimate government with one that is all-powerful. Governments that are limited, and thus seen as legitimate, can usually maintain order and pursue tough policies, albeit slowly, by building coalitions. The key test of a government's legitimacy is tax collection, because it requires not vast police forces but rather voluntary compliance with laws. No government has a large enough police force to coerce people to pay their taxes. Yet Third World governments have abysmally low tax-collection rates. This is because they—and their policies—lack legitimacy.

The case of Russia is again instructive. Since the fall of the Soviet Union, Western academics and journalists have fretted loudly about the weakness of the Russian state. Their analysis was based mostly on its inability to collect taxes—a dubious measure, since the Russian state had never done so before and thus was taking on a new task in the post-Soviet era. In fact, the Russian state after Soviet communism was still very powerful. It was, however, corrupt and widely viewed as illegitimate. Today, after years of stability and some important reforms (under Putin), the Russian government collects taxes at about the level of most European countries. Still, the earlier academic worrying had real effects on public policy. Western statesmen were far too understanding of Yeltsin's various decrees and power grabs. They believed him when he said that the central government was under siege and needed help.

As only a politician can, Putin ended this academic debate. Within months of his inauguration, he successfully reasserted the Kremlin's power against every competing authority and demonstrated that the old Soviet institutions have life in them yet. When formal measures were not enough he used his powers of "persuasion." Legislators and judges who refuse to vote with the Kremlin are denied their salaries and perks (the Russian parliament does not have control over its own salaries, let alone over other governmental funds). This explains why the upper house of parliament was willing to vote for the reduction of its own power and size, not an everyday occurrence in politics. As for taxes, the government collected 100 percent of its target tax revenues in 2000. It turns out that the problem in Russia was not that the state was sick but that Yeltsin was. With a living, breathing president, big government is back. This might prove to be an unfortunate development; the weakening of the central state was a needed corrective to the Soviet superstate.

Historically, unchecked centralization has been the enemy of liberal democracy. As political participation increased in Europe over the nineteenth century, it was accommodated smoothly in countries such as the United Kingdom and Sweden, where medieval assemblies, local governments, and regional councils had remained strong. Countries such as France and Prussia, on the other hand, where the monarchy had effectively centralized power (both horizontally and vertically), often ended up illiberal and undemocratic. It is no coincidence that in twentieth-century Spain, the beachhead of liberalism lay in Catalonia, for centuries a doggedly independent and autonomous region. In the United States, the presence of a rich variety of institutions—state, local, and private—made it much easier to accommodate the rapid and large extensions in suffrage that took place in the early nineteenth century. In 1922, the distinguished Harvard historian Arthur Schlesinger, Sr., documented how, during America's first fifty years, virtually every state, interest group, and faction tried to weaken and even break up the federal government.[9] In a more recent example, India's semiliberal democracy has survived because of, not despite, its strong regions and varied languages, cultures, and even castes. The point is logical, even tautological: decentralized government helps produce limited government.

## Tyranny of the Majority

If the first source of abuse in a democratic system comes from elected autocrats, the second comes from the people themselves. James Madison explained in the Federalist Papers that "the danger of oppression" in a democracy came from "the majority of the community." Tocqueville warned of the "tyranny of the majority," writing, "The very essence of democratic government consists in the absolute sovereignty of the majority." This problem, alive and urgent to Madison and Tocqueville, may seem less important in the West today because elaborate protections for individual and minority rights exist here. But in many developing countries, the experience of democracy over the past few decades has been one in which majorities have—often quietly, sometimes noisily—eroded separations of power, undermined human rights, and corrupted long-standing traditions of tolerance and fairness.

Let me illustrate this point with some reflections on India, the country in which I grew up. India has a hallowed place in discussions of democracy. Despite being desperately poor it has had a functioning democracy since 1947. Whenever someone wants to prove that you do not need to develop economically to become democratic they use as their one example—India. Much of this praise is warranted. India is a genuinely free and freewheeling society. But looking under the covers of Indian democracy one sees a more complex and troubling reality. In recent decades, India has become something quite different from the picture in the hearts of its admirers. Not that it is less democratic: in important ways it has become more democratic. But it has become less tolerant, less secular, less law-abiding, less liberal. And these two trends—democratization and illiberalism—are directly related.

India got its democracy from the United Kingdom and the Congress Party. The British built and operated most of the crucial institutions of liberal democracy in India: courts, legislatures, administrative rules, and a (quasi-) free press. It just didn't allow Indians to exercise much power within them. Once independent, in 1947, Indians inherited these institutions and traditions and built their democracy on them, led by the Indian National Congress, which had dominated the struggle for independence. Even the Congress Party, however, was modeled after a British political party, from its liberal nationalist ideology down to its committee structure. Indian courts followed British practice and precedents, often using British law as precedent. The New Delhi parliament followed Westminster rules and rituals, down to the prime minister's "Question Hour." Absent the British and the Congress Party it is difficult to imagine Indian democracy as it exists today.

India's first prime minister, Nehru, once described himself as "the last Englishman to rule India." He was right. He was the son of a highly Anglicized, pro-British barrister and was taught English history and literature by a tutor. His formative years were spent training to be an English gentleman. He attended Harrow, one of England's most prestigious private boarding schools, and went on to university at Cambridge. He then spent a few years training to be a barrister in London. Even after his subsequent turn toward Indian nationalism, his worldview was that of a left-wing British intellectual circa 1940.

Nehru's India—he was Prime Minister from 1947 to 1964—can best be described as a one-party democracy. Elections were free and fair, but as the party that liberated India and the only truly national party, the Congress Party dominated at every level, often winning two-thirds majorities in parliament and in state legislatures. This enviable position gave it all kinds of formal and informal advantages, making it impossible to mount a serious challenge to the Congress in many areas. Like America's Democratic Party in the old South, the Congress Party controlled every stage of the political process. India was a democracy, but one in which one political party was more equal than the others. It was also, however, quite liberal. The Congress Party was committed to building genuine traditions of constitutional governance. Nehru in particular was deeply respectful of liberal institutions and traditions, such as the prerogatives of parliament and the press. He supported an independent judiciary, even when this meant accepting political defeats in court. He was obsessive about secularism and religious tolerance. Despite his immense popularity, he allowed dissenting views to flourish and often win the day within both his party and his government.

When I was growing up in India in the late 1960s and 1970s, this tradition was still strong but fraying. The Congress Party had morphed from a vibrant grass roots organization into a fawning, imperial court, appointed by and adoring of its popular leader, Indira Gandhi. Mrs. Gandhi pursued populist policies that were often unconstitutional and certainly illiberal, such as nationalizing banks and abolishing the rights of India's princes. Still, the courts were largely independent, the press free, and religious tolerance sacred. But over time, the Congress Party's commitment to these institutions and values weakened. More importantly, the party declined as the dominant national institution. New challengers rose to fill the space, the most prominent of them being the Hindu fundamentalist Bharatiya Janata Party (BJP). The BJP, however, is only one among a host of energetic new parties that draw their appeal from regional, religious, or caste differences. As a result, new voters—almost all from poor, rural, and lower-caste backgrounds—have entered the political system. In the 1950s about 45 percent of the population voted; today that number is over 60 percent. Yogendra Yadav, an Indian political scientist studying this trend, argues that India is going through a "fundamental though quiet transformation" that is opening up its politics to a much broader group of people who were previously marginalized. These parties have made India more democratic, but they have also made it less liberal.

The BJP came to power by denouncing Nehruvian secularism, advocating a quasi-militant Hindu nationalism, and encouraging anti-Muslim and anti-Christian rhetoric and action. It organized a massive national campaign to destroy a mosque in northern India (in the city of Ayodhya) that had been built, some Hindus believed, on the site of the birthplace of Rama. That Rama is a mythological figure, that Hinduism advocates nonviolence and tolerance, and that India has had terrible experiences with religious violence (and did again in the wake of the Ayodhya affair) mattered little to the BJP. The rhetoric of hatred appealed to its core voters. Recently the BJP formed a governing coalition, and inevitably has had to tone down its anti-Muslim, anti-Christian, and anti-lower-caste rhetoric, lest it alienate the other members of its coalition. But it has still pursued a policy aimed at "Hinduizing" India, which has meant rewriting history texts to downplay or remove references to Muslims and other minorities, establishing departments of astrology at major universities, and encouraging the use of Hindu religious symbols in public settings. And whenever it has found itself in political trouble, it has stoked the fires of religious conflict, as it did in Gujarat in 2002. In Gujarat the local BJP government—in an unprecedented manner—allowed and even assisted in the massacre of thousands of innocent Muslim men, women, and children and the ethnic cleansing of tens of thousands from their neighborhoods and towns. It was in some ways India's first state-assisted pogrom. Most troubling, all evidence suggests that it has helped the BJP with its Hindu base. In fact the leader of the BJP in Gujarat hoped to cash in on the violence and scheduled elections a few months afterward. But the nonpartisan administrative body that runs elections in India—the Election Commission—courageously concluded that elections could not be held in such circumstances.

Religious intolerance is only the first glimpse of the new face of Indian democracy. Massive corruption and a disregard for the rule of law have transformed Indian politics. Consider Uttar Pradesh (UP), India's largest state, the political base of Nehru and the other titans of the Congress Party. UP is now dominated by the BJP and two lower-caste parties. The political system there can only be described as "bandit democracy." Every year elections are rigged, ballot boxes are stuffed. The winning party packs the bureaucracy—sometimes even the courts—with its cronies and bribes opposition legislators to defect to its ranks. The tragedy for the millions of new lower-caste voters is that their representatives, for whom they dutifully vote en masse, have looted the public coffers and become immensely rich and powerful while mouthing slogans about the oppression of their people.

The process reached its lowest point in November 1997, when the chief minister of UP secured his parliamentary majority by creating a cabinet of ninety-three ministers, so that all legislators who switched party affiliation and supported him could be appointed government officials. The new ministers had checkered pasts; nineteen of them had documented criminal backgrounds (and I don't mean speeding tickets). The science and technology minister, Hari Shankar Tiwari, for example, has a police file that names him as a suspect in nine murders, ten attempted murders, three robberies, and three kidnappings. The program implementation minister (whatever that means), Raghuraj Pratap Singh, was being investigated for two murders, three attempted murders, and several kidnappings (twenty-five crimes in all). Another one, Pratap Singh, used his newfound powers to turn himself into a feudal baron. *Outlook*, a leading Indian newsmagazine, describes the scene at his country home:

> He holds court in his courtyard and delivers instant justice—slaps fines on "erring subjects" or orders a sound thrashing. His subjects, poor men, women, and children, touch his feet with their foreheads, pleading for mercy. Outside his fortified Bainti Estate, people queue up every morning to offer salutations, their bodies bent at 90 degrees. . . . The 28-year-old [chieftain] rides majestic horses, keeps elephants, zips around in his [four-wheel drive vehicle] with his armed supporters in tow. Police records say that he kills his opponents, organizes kidnappings for ransom, commits robberies. But this has never prevented his career graph from soaring. He was barely 24 years old when he fought and won his first election in 1993. Three years later, he once again jumped into the fray and barring the BJP no one dared oppose him.[10]

This is the reality of democracy in India. And yet no one in the West wishes to look at it too closely. We prefer to speak romantically about the beauty of Indians voting and the joys of the world's largest democracy. Thoughtful Indians do not quite see it this way. The veteran journalist Kuldip Nayar has described what has happened in UP as "the daylight murder of democracy." Another well-known writer, Prem Shanker Jha, believes democracy there has regressed "by two hundred years." And UP is hardly an isolated case. Political corruption in neighboring Bihar and Haryana is much worse. And parliament and the government in New Delhi reflect many of these trends, though in less extreme form.

India's court system has gone from being the pride of its democracy to a corrupt handmaiden of political power. In 1975 a local judge unseated Prime Minister Indira Gandhi because he determined that she had violated a minor election law. In 1981 another local judge ruled against the most powerful regional politician in India, the chief minister of Maharashtra (India's wealthiest state, home to Bombay, India's economic capital). Today, when a party comes to power in any region of India, it often finds ways to pack the local courts. Judges, anticipating this process, now offer their services to political leaders so that they may remain secure in office and be rewarded in retirement. Other than the Supreme Court in New Delhi, no court in India has shown the independence that almost all of them showed routinely a generation ago.

Corruption has always existed in India, but until the 1970s, it was mostly petty corruption produced by the country's insane web of economic regulations. The typical act of corruption in the 1960s was a bureaucrat's taking a bribe to permit some private-sector undertaking. This was bad for economic growth, but it did not distort the entire political process. Political corruption existed, too, but it was limited. Nobody accused Nehru of corruption, nor his successor as prime minister, Lal Bahadur Shastri, nor any of the senior members of the government in the 1950s and 1960s. Perhaps most important, the judiciary was clean and had high standards. In 1958, Nehru appointed one of India's most eminent jurists, M. C. Chagla, as ambassador to the United States. The Bombay Bar Council immediately issued a formal denunciation, worried that appointing a judge to high office might compromise the image of the independence of the judiciary. Today, rewarding compliant judges with patronage posts is so common as to be unremarkable. As a result, although corruption and abuses of power have reached unheard-of proportions, no judge in any part of India has ruled against a powerful politician.

The only attempt to clean up the election process, spearheaded by a bureaucrat who headed the election commission, has sputtered out.

In retrospect it is clear that Nehru's Congress Party imposed a quasi-liberal order on India in the 1950s and 1960s that began withering as new, entrepreneurial parties competed for votes using raw appeals to caste, linguistic, and religious solidarity. Nowhere is this more evident than in the change in atmosphere and substance of my hometown. Bombay is a city built by its great minority communities: Parsi industrialists, Gujarati merchants, Muslim restaurateurs, and of course, the British. Unlike Calcutta and New Delhi, it was never capital of the British Raj. It was India's New York and Los Angeles rolled into one—nouveau riche, crass, but also vibrant, meritocratic, and tolerant. Like many great port cities, cosmopolitanism was in the city's salty air.

That Bombay is now a memory. In the last twenty years, the rise of Hindu nationalism and a local variant, Maratha chauvinism, has systematically destroyed the old city. The regional party that has spearheaded this movement, the Shiv Sena, is named after a seventeenth century chieftain, Shivaji, who opposed New Delhi's (Muslim) Mughal emperors. The party is determined to rid the state of Maharashtra, of which Bombay is the capital, of all "alien" influences. (The Muslims came to India beginning in the twelfth century; 800 years is apparently not long enough to be considered a native.) This is most evident in its campaign to rename cities, towns, roads, and buildings that have anything other than pure Hindu names. It culminated in the renaming of Bombay as Mumbai in 1996, an act that illustrates the invented quality of much of Hindu nationalism. Unlike Beijing (a long-standing city whose name was Anglicized into Peking by Westerners), Mumbai did not really exist as a city before the Portuguese and the British called it Bombay. Like Singapore and Hong Kong, it was a tiny fishermen's village. The city was a colonial creation. "Mumbai" is not a return to the past but the validation of a myth.

New names for cities and quotas might seem merely symbolic, but they represent a seismic shift in attitude. In crises, this shift can turn bloody. Over the last decade, Muslims, the largest minority in Bombay, have been the victims of some of the worst rioting since the bloodbaths of the Indian subcontinent's partition in 1947. Tens of thousands of people have been killed and hundreds of thousands more have fled Bombay into the countryside—a macabre reversal of the normal pattern of minorities flocking to cities for equality and opportunity. An independent commission charged the government and the police with abandoning the victims of the riots and even, occasionally, aiding the rioters. This led to attempts at revenge by the Muslims, leaving the atmosphere of the entire state more charged with religious antagonism than at any other time in many observers' lifetimes. This pattern recurs all over India—most recently in Gujarat—and not just against Muslims. During 1998 and 1999 four times as many Christians were killed in India in religiously motivated attacks than in the preceding thirty-five years. Since 1999 the data is less complete, but the numbers are still astonishingly high. In addition to murders, there have been waves of incidents of Bibles burnt, churches looted, and nuns raped. Again, the government has blocked and delayed most investigations into these crimes.

Ethnic conflict is as old as recorded history, and dictatorships are hardly innocent in fomenting it. But newly democratizing societies display a disturbingly common tendency toward it. The reason is simple: as society opens up and politicians scramble for power, they appeal to the public for votes using what ends up being the most direct, effective language, that of group solidarity in opposition to some other group. Often this stokes the fires of ethnic or religious conflict. Sometimes the conflict turns into a full-scale war.

## War

On December 8, 1996, Jack Lang made a dramatic dash to Belgrade. The French celebrity politician, formerly the minister of culture, had been inspired by the student demonstrations involving tens of thousands against Yugoslav president Slobodan Milosevic, a man Lang and many Western intellectuals held responsible for the war in the Balkans. Lang wanted to lend his moral support to the Yugoslav opposition. The leaders of the movement received him in their offices—the philosophy department of a university—only to boot him out, declare him "an enemy of the Serbs," and order him out of the country. It turned out that the students opposed Milosevic not for starting the war, but for failing to win it.

Lang's embarrassment highlights a common, and often mistaken, assumption: that the forces of democracy are the forces of ethnic harmony and peace. Not necessarily true. Mature liberal democracies can usually accommodate ethnic divisions without violence or terror and live in peace with other liberal democracies. But without a background in constitutional liberalism, the introduction of democracy in divided societies has actually fomented nationalism, ethnic conflict, and even war. The numerous elections held immediately after the collapse of communism were won in the Soviet Union and Yugoslavia by nationalist separatists and resulted in the breakup of those countries. This was not inherently bad, since those countries had been bound together by force. But the rapid secessions, without guarantees, institutions, or political power for the many minorities living within the emergent new countries, have caused spirals of rebellion, repression, and, in places such as Bosnia, Azerbaijan, and Georgia, war.

Elections require that politicians compete for people's votes. In societies without strong traditions of multiethnic groups or assimilation, it is easiest to organize support along racial, ethnic, or religious lines. Once an ethnic group is in power, it tends to exclude other ethnic groups. Compromise seems impossible; one can bargain on material issues such as housing, hospitals, and handouts, but how does one split the difference on a national religion? Political competition that is so divisive can rapidly degenerate into violence. Opposition movements, armed rebellions, and coups in Africa have often been directed against ethnically based regimes, many of which came to power through elections. Surveying the breakdown of African and

Asian democracies in the 1960s, two scholars concluded that democracy "is simply not viable in an environment of intense ethnic preferences."[11] Recent studies, particularly of Africa and Central Asia, have confirmed this pessimism. A distinguished expert on ethnic conflict, Donald Horowitz, concluded, "In the face of this rather dismal account . . . of the concrete failures of democracy in divided societies . . . one is tempted to throw up one's hands. What is the point of holding elections if all they do in the end is to substitute a Bemba-dominated regime for a Nyanja regime in Zambia, the two equally narrow, or a southern regime for a northern one in Benin, neither incorporating the other half of the state?"[12]

Over the past decade, one of the most spirited debates among scholars of international relations concerns the "democratic peace"—the assertion that no two modern democracies have gone to war against each other. The debate raises interesting substantive questions (Does the American Civil War count? Do nuclear weapons better explain the peace?), and even the statistical findings have raised interesting dissents. (As the scholar David Spiro has pointed out, given the small number of both democracies and wars over the last two hundred years, sheer chance might explain the absence of war between democracies. No member of his family has ever won the lottery, yet few offer explanations for this impressive correlation.) But even if the statistics are correct, what explains them?

Immanuel Kant, the original proponent of the democratic peace, contended that in democracies, those who pay for wars—that is, the public—make the decisions, so they are understandably cautious. But that claim suggests that democracies are more pacific than other states, when in fact, they are more warlike, going to war more often and with greater intensity than most other states. It is only with other democracies that the peace holds. When divining the cause behind this correlation, one thing becomes clear: the democratic peace is actually the liberal peace. Writing in the eighteenth century, Kant believed that democracies were tyrannical, and he specifically excluded them from his conception of "republican" governments, which lived in a zone of peace. Republicanism, for Kant, meant a separation of powers, checks and balances, the rule of law, protection of individual rights, and some level of representation in government (though nothing close to universal suffrage). Kant's other explanations for the "perpetual peace" are all closely linked to republics' constitutional and liberal character: a mutual respect for the rights of each other's citizens, a system of checks and balances assuring that no single leader can drag a country into war, and classical liberal economic policies—most important of which is free trade—that create an interdependence that makes war costly and cooperation useful. Michael Doyle, the leading scholar on the subject, confirms in his 1997 book *Ways of War and Peace* that without constitutional liberalism, democracy itself has no peace-inducing qualities:

> Kant distrusted unfettered, democratic majoritarianism, and his argument offers no support for a claim that all participatory polities—democracies—should be peaceful, either in general or between fellow democracies. Many participatory polities have been non-liberal. For two thousand years before the modern age, popular rule was widely associated with aggressiveness (by Thucydides) or imperial success (by Machiavelli). . . . The decisive preference of [the] median voter might well include "ethnic cleansing" against other democratic polities.

The distinction between liberal and illiberal democracies sheds light on another striking statistical correlation. Political scientists Jack Snyder and Edward Mansfield contend, using an impressive data set, that over the past 200 years democratizing states went to war significantly more often than either stable autocracies or liberal democracies.[13] In countries not grounded in constitutional liberalism, the rise of democracy often brings with it hypernationalism and war-mongering. When the political system is opened up, diverse groups with incompatible interests gain access to power and press their demands. Political and military leaders, who are often embattled remnants of the old authoritarian order, realize that to succeed they must rally the masses behind a national cause. The result is invariably aggressive rhetoric and policies, which often drag countries into confrontation and war. Noteworthy examples range from Napoleon III's France, Wilhelmine Germany, and Taisho Japan to the more recent Armenia and Azerbaijan and the former Yugoslavia. The democratic peace is real, but it turns out to have little to do with democracy.

## What Is to Be Done?

The problems with new democracies might seem an abstract topic, worth discussing at think tanks and universities. But theory often bangs into reality. Countries are often deciding how best to move along the path to democracy. And the United States is constantly formulating policies to deal with countries as they move—or slip— along that path. Getting the theory wrong means getting the practice wrong as well. Consider the case of Indonesia, whose democratization should have been handled much more carefully than it was in 1998, when the International Monetary Fund (IMF) and the United States helped force its long-standing dictator, Suharto, out of power and ushered in a new democracy. Or at least that was the hope.

Indonesia in 1998 was not an ideal candidate for democracy. Of all the East Asian countries it is most reliant on natural resources. Strike one. It was also bereft of legitimate political institutions, since Suharto ran the country through a small group of courtiers, paying little attention to the task of institution-building. Strike two. Finally, it attempted democratization at a low level of per capita income, approximately $2,650 in 1998. Strike three. The results have been abysmal. Since it embraced democracy, Indonesia's gross domestic product has contracted by almost 50 percent, wiping out a generation of economic progress and pushing more than 20 million people below the poverty line. The newly open political system has also thrown up Islamic fundamentalists who, in a country without much of a political language, speak a very familiar discourse—that of religion. Already almost 20 percent of the country's parliamentarians describe themselves as Islamic politicians. If successful, the rise of political Islam in Indonesia will threaten the secular character of the country and breed secessionist movements that will threaten its unity. In the midst of this chaos, corruption and cronyism have gotten even worse and economic reforms have been unwound.

Although they were not entirely to blame, the IMF and the U.S. government demanded immediate and radical reforms in Indonesia during its 1998 crisis, thereby helping delegitimize and topple the government. Had they recognized the political instability these reforms would produce, they might have moderated their demands and made do with a more incremental approach. Suharto was running a flawed regime but one that had achieved order, secularism, and economic liberalization—an impressive combination in the Third World. Most important, nothing better was available to replace it. Gradual political reform rather than wholesale revolution would have been preferable, certainly for the average Indonesian, who one assumes was the intended beneficiary of Western policies.

Nowhere are these tough choices between order and instability, liberalism and democracy, and secularism and religious radicalism more stark than in the Middle East today. And nowhere will it be more important that the United States get it right, in theory and in practice.

## CHAPTER 4

# The Islamic Exception

I T IS ALWAYS the same splendid setting, and the same sad story. A senior U.S. diplomat enters one of the grand presidential palaces in Heliopolis, the neighborhood of Cairo from which President Hosni Mubarak rules over Egypt. He walks through halls of marble, through rooms filled with gilded furniture—all a bad imitation of imperial French style that has been jokingly called "Louis Farouk" (after the last king of Egypt). Passing layers of security guards, he arrives at a formal drawing room where he is received with great courtesy by the Egyptian president. The two talk amiably about U.S.-Egyptian relations, regional affairs, and the state of the peace process between Israel and the Palestinians. Then the American gently raises the issue of human rights and suggests that Egypt's government might ease up on political dissent, allow more press freedoms, and stop jailing intellectuals. Mubarak tenses up and snaps, "If I were to do what you ask, Islamic fundamentalists will take over Egypt. Is that what you want?" The conversation moves back to the latest twist in the peace process.

Over the years Americans and Arabs have had many such exchanges. When President Bush urged Palestinian leader Yasser

Arafat to agree to the Camp David peace plan that had been negotiated in July 2001, Arafat reportedly responded with words to this
effect: "If I do what you want, Hamas will be in power tomorrow."
The Saudi monarchy's most articulate spokesman, Prince Bandar bin
Sultan, often reminds American officials that if they press his government too hard, the likely alternative to the regime is not Jeffersonian
democracy but a Taliban-style theocracy.

The worst part of it is, they may be right. The Arab rulers of the
Middle East are autocratic, corrupt, and heavy-handed. But they
are still more liberal, tolerant, and pluralistic than what would
likely replace them. Elections in many Arab countries would produce politicians who espouse views that are closer to Osama bin
Laden's than those of Jordan's liberal monarch, King Abdullah. Last
year the emir of Kuwait, with American encouragement, proposed
giving women the vote. But the democratically elected Kuwaiti
parliament—filled with Islamic fundamentalists—roundly rejected
the initiative. Saudi crown prince Abdullah tried something much
less dramatic when he proposed that women in Saudi Arabia be
allowed to drive. (They are currently forbidden to do so, which
means that Saudi Arabia has had to import half a million chauf-
feurs from places like India and the Philippines.) But the religious
conservatives mobilized popular opposition and forced him to
back down.

A similar dynamic is evident elsewhere in the Arab world. In
Oman, Qatar, Bahrain, Jordan, and Morocco, on virtually every political issue, the monarchs are more liberal than the societies over which
they reign. Even in the Palestinian territories, where secular national-
ists like Arafat and his Palestine Liberation Organization have long
been the most popular political force, militant and religious groups
such as Hamas and Islamic Jihad are gaining strength, especially
among the young. And although they speak the language of elections, many of the Islamic parties have been withering in their con-
tempt for democracy, which they see as a Western form of
government. They would happily come to power through an elec-

tion, but then would set up their own theocratic rule. It would be, as the saw has it, one man, one vote, one time.

Compare, for example, the wildly opposite reactions of state and society to the November 2001 videotape of a gloating bin Laden found by the U.S. armed forces in an Al Qaeda hideout in Kabul. On tape, bin Laden shows an intimate knowledge of the September 11 attacks and delights in the loss of life they caused. Most of the region's governments quickly noted that the tape seemed genuine and proved bin Laden's guilt. Prince Bandar issued a statement: "The tape displays the cruel and inhumane face of a murderous criminal who has no respect for the sanctity of human life or the principles of his faith." In contrast, Sheik Mohammad Saleh, a prominent Saudi cleric and opponent of the regime, declared, "I think this recording is forged." Abdul Latif Arabiat, head of Jordan's Islamist party, the Islamic Action Front, asked, "Do the Americans really think the world is that stupid that they would believe that this tape is evidence?"

In most societies, dissidents force their country to take a hard look at its own failings. In the Middle East, those who advocate democracy are the first to seek refuge in fantasy, denial, and delusion. The region is awash in conspiracy theories, such as those claiming that the Israeli intelligence service, Mossad, was actually behind the World Trade Center attacks. In a CNN poll conducted across nine Muslim countries in February 2002, 61 percent of those polled said that they did not believe that Arabs were responsible for the September 11 attacks. Al-Jazeera, the first independent satellite television station in the region, which has an enormous pan-Arab audience, is populist and modern. Many of its anchors are women. It broadcasts news that the official media routinely censor. And yet it fills its airwaves with crude appeals to Arab nationalism, anti-Americanism, anti-Semitism, and religious fundamentalism.

The Arab world today is trapped between autocratic states and illiberal societies, neither of them fertile ground for liberal democracy. The dangerous dynamic between these two forces has produced a political climate filled with religious extremism and violence. As the state becomes more repressive, opposition within society grows more pernicious, goading the state into further repression. It is the reverse of the historical process in the Western world, where liberalism produced democracy and democracy fueled liberalism. The Arab path has instead produced dictatorship, which has bred terrorism. But terrorism is only the most noted manifestation of this dysfunctional relationship between state and society. There is also economic paralysis, social stagnation, and intellectual bankruptcy.

The Middle East today stands in stark contrast to the rest of the world, where freedom and democracy have been gaining ground over the past two decades. In its 2002 survey, Freedom House finds that 75 percent of the world's countries are currently "free" or "partly free." Only 28 percent of Middle Eastern countries could be so described, a percentage that has fallen during the last twenty years. By comparison, more than 60 percent of African countries today are classified as free or partly free.

Since September 11 the political dysfunctions of the Arab world have suddenly presented themselves on the West's doorstep. In the back of everyone's mind—and in the front of many—is the question why. Why is this region the political basket case of the world? Why is it the great holdout, the straggler in the march of modern societies?

## Islam's Wide World

Bin Laden has an answer. For him the problem with Arab regimes is that they are insufficiently Islamic. Only by returning to Islam, he tells his followers, will Muslims achieve justice. Democracy for bin Laden is a Western invention. Its emphasis on freedom and tolerance produces social decay and licentiousness. Bin Laden and those like him seek the overthrow of the regimes of the Arab world—perhaps of the whole Muslim world—and their replacement by polities founded on strict Islamic principles, ruled by Islamic law (*sharia*) and based on the early Caliphate (the seventh-century Islamic kingdom of Arabia). Their more recent role model was the Taliban regime in Afghanistan.

There are those in the West who agree with bin Laden that Islam is the reason for the Middle East's turmoil. Preachers such as Pat Robertson and Jerry Falwell and writers such as Paul Johnson and William Lind have made the case that Islam is a religion of repression and backwardness. More serious scholars have argued—far more insightfully—that the problem is more complex: for the fundamentalists, Islam is considered a template for all life, including politics. But classical Islam, developed in the seventh and eighth centuries, contains few of the ideas that we associate with democracy today. Elie Kedourie, an eminent student of Arab politics, wrote "The idea of representation, of elections, of popular suffrage, of political institutions being regulated by laws laid down by a parliamentary assembly, of these laws being guarded and upheld by an independent judiciary, the ideas of the secularity of the state . . . all these are profoundly alien to the Muslim political tradition."[1]

Certainly the Quranic model of leadership is authoritarian. The Muslim holy book is bursting with examples of the just king, the pious ruler, the wise arbiter. But the Bible has its authoritarian tendencies as well. The kings of the Old Testament were hardly democrats. The biblical Solomon, held up as the wisest man of all, was after all an absolute monarch. The Bible also contains passages that seem to justify slavery and the subjugation of women. The truth is that little is to be gained by searching in the Quran for clues to Islam's true nature. The Quran is a vast book, filled with poetry and contradictions—much like the Bible and the Torah. All three books praise kings, as do most religious texts. As for mixing spiritual and temporal authority, Catholic popes combined religious authority and political power for centuries in a way that no Muslim ruler has ever been able to achieve. Judaism has had much less involvement with political power because, until Israel's founding, Jews were a minority everywhere in the modern world. Yet the word "theocracy" was coined by Josephus to describe the political views of the ancient

Jews.[2] The founding religious texts of all faiths were, for the most part, written in another age, one filled with monarchs, feudalism, war, and insecurity. They bear the stamp of their times.

Still, Western scholars of the nineteenth and early twentieth centuries often argued that Islam encourages authoritarianism. This assertion was probably influenced by their view of the Ottoman Empire, a community of several hundred million Muslims laboring docilely under the sultan in distant Constantinople, singing hosannas to him before Friday prayers. But most of the world at the time was quite similar in its deference to political authority. In Russia the czar was considered almost a god. In Japan the emperor was a god. On the whole Asian empires were more despotic than Western ones, but Islamic rule was no more autocratic than Chinese, Japanese, or Russian versions.

Indeed if any intrinsic aspect of Islam is worth noting, it is not its devotion to authority, but the opposite: Islam has an anti-authoritarian streak that is evident in every Muslim land today. It originates, probably, in several hadith—sayings of the Prophet Mohammed—in which obedience toward the ruler is incumbent on the Muslim only so far as the ruler's commands are in keeping with God's law.* If the ruler asks you to violate the faith, all bets are off. ("If he is ordered to do a sinful act, a Muslim should neither listen to [his leader] nor should he obey his orders."[3]) Religions are vague, of course. This means that they are easy to follow—you can interpret their prescriptions as you like. But it also means that it is easy to slip up—there is always some injunction you are violating. But Islam has no religious establishment—no popes or bishops—that can declare by fiat which is the correct interpretation. As a result, the decision to oppose the

---

*The hadith are often more important than the Quran because they tell Muslims how to implement the sometimes general Quranic injunctions. For example, the Quran commands Muslims to pray, but it does not tell them how to pray; this is found in the hadith. (There are, of course, many hadith, many of dubious authenticity, and sometimes they contradict each other.)

state on the grounds that it is insufficiently Islamic belongs to anyone who wishes to exercise it. This much Islam shares with Protestantism. Just as any Protestant with just a little training—Jerry Falwell, Pat Robertson—can declare himself a religious leader, so also any Muslim can opine on issues of faith. In a religion without an official clergy, bin Laden has as much—or as little—authority to issue fatwas as does a Pakistani taxi driver in New York City. The problem, in other words, is the absence of religious authority in Islam, not its dominance.

Consider the source of the current chaos in Arab lands. In Egypt, Saudi Arabia, Algeria, and elsewhere, Islamist* groups wage bloody campaigns against states that they accuse of betraying Islam. Bin Laden and his deputy, the Egyptian Ayman Zawahiri, both laymen, began their careers by fighting their own governments because of policies they deemed un-Islamic (for Zawahiri it was Egyptian president Anwar Sadat's 1978 peace treaty with Israel; for Bin Laden it was King Fahd's decision to allow American troops on Saudi soil in 1991). In his 1996 declaration of jihad, bin Laden declared that the Saudi government had left the fold of Islam, and so it was permissible to take up arms against it: "The regime betrayed the *ummah* [community of believers] and joined the *kufr* [unbelievers], assisting and helping them against the Muslims." Bin Laden called for rebellion against rulers, and many responded to his call. The rulers of the Middle East probably wish that Muslims were more submissive toward authority.

There is also the question of timing: If Islam is the problem, then why is this conflict taking place now? Why did Islamic fundamentalism take off only after the 1979 Iranian revolution? Islam and the West have coexisted for fourteen centuries. There have been periods

*"Islamist" refers to people, like bin Laden, who want to use Islam as a political ideology, setting up an Islamic state that follows Islamic law strictly. I use this term interchangeably with the more commonly used "Islamic fundamentalist," although many scholars prefer the former.

of war but many more periods of peace. Many scholars have pointed out that, until the 1940s, minorities and particularly Jews were persecuted less under Muslim rule than under any other majority religion. That is why the Middle East was for centuries home to many minorities. It is commonly noted that a million Jews left or were expelled from Arab countries after the creation of Israel in 1948. No one asks why so many were living in Arab countries in the first place.

The trouble with thundering declarations about "Islam's nature" is that Islam, like any religion, is not what books make it but what people make it. Forget the rantings of the fundamentalists, who are a minority. Most Muslims' daily lives do not confirm the idea of a faith that is intrinsically anti-Western or antimodern. The most populous Muslim country in the world, Indonesia, has had secular government since its independence in 1949, with a religious opposition that is tiny (though now growing). As for Islam's compatibility with capitalism, Indonesia was until recently the World Bank's model Third World country, having liberalized its economy and grown at 7 percent a year for almost three decades. It has now embraced democracy (still a fragile experiment) and has elected a woman as its president. After Indonesia, the three largest Muslim populations in the world are in Pakistan, Bangladesh, and India (India's Muslims number more than 120 million.) Not only have these countries had much experience with democracy, all three have elected women as prime minister, and they did so well before most Western countries. So although some aspects of Islam are incompatible with women's rights, the reality on the ground is sometimes quite different. And South Asia is not an anomaly with regard to Islamic women. In Afghanistan, before its twenty-year descent into chaos and tyranny, 40 percent of all doctors were women and Kabul was one of the most liberated cities for women in all of Asia. Although bin Laden may have embraced the Taliban's version of Islam, most Afghans did not—as was confirmed by the sight of men in post-Taliban Kabul and Mazar-e-Sharif lining up to watch movies, listen to music, dance, shave, and fly kites.

Then there is Turkey, with the fifth largest Muslim population in the world, a flawed but functioning liberal democracy, a member of the North Atlantic Treaty Organization and perhaps soon to be a member of the European Union. Add fledgling democracies such as Nigeria and Mali and you have a more rounded view of the world of Islam. It is not the prettiest picture. Most Muslim countries are in the Third World and share the Third World's problems of poverty, corruption, and misgovernment. But there is no simple link between Islam and repression. As Freedom House noted, "the majority of the world's Muslims live in electoral democracies today." If there is a fundamental incompatibility between Islam and democracy, 800 million Muslims seem unaware of it.

The real problem lies not in the Muslim world but in the Middle East. When you get to this region you see in lurid color all the dysfunctions that people conjure up when they think of Islam today. In Iran,* Egypt, Syria, Iraq, the West Bank, the Gaza Strip, and the Persian Gulf states, dictatorships pose in various stripes and liberal democracy appears far from reach. The allure of Islamic fundamentalism seems strong, whether spoken of urgently behind closed doors or declared in fiery sermons in mosques. This is the land of flag-burners, fiery mullahs, and suicide bombers. America went to war in Afghanistan but not a single Afghan was linked to any terrorist attack against Americans. Afghanistan was the campground from which an Arab army was battling America.

The Arab world is an important part of the world of Islam—its heartland. But it is only one part and in numerical terms a small one. Of the 1.2 billion Muslims in the world, only 260 million live in Arabia. People in the West often use the term "Islamic," "Middle Eastern," and "Arab" interchangeably. But they do not mean the same thing.

*In this chapter I often lump Iran together with Arab countries. It is technically not one of them; Iranians speak Farsi not Arabic. But Iran's Islamic Revolution of 1979 gave an enormous fillip to the broader fundamentalist movement and, for now, has dulled the age-old divide between the two largest sects of Islam: Sunni (most Arabs) and Shia (most Iranians).

## The Arab Mind

Have I just passed the buck? Having shown Islam in practice to be less hostile to democracy and liberalism than many have argued, have I simply moved to another cultural theory, this time about the Arabs? This, too, is an argument that has long been made by Westerners, beginning with the British colonial officers who ruled Arabia in the nineteenth and early twentieth centuries. A typical verdict was that rendered by John Bagot Glubb, the British commander of Jordan's Arab Legion from 1939 to 1956:

> We have given them self-government for which they are totally unsuited. They veer naturally towards dictatorship. Democratic institutions are promptly twisted into engines of intrigue—thus the same bunch crop up after each coup in a different guise, until disposed of by assassination.[4]

Even T. E. Lawrence—the British officer-adventurer, a friend of the Arabs, immortalized in David Lean's film *Lawrence of Arabia*—paints a picture of a romantic race, easily swayed by any demagogue who happens to come along:

> Arabs could be swung on an idea as on a cord; for the unpledged allegiance of their minds made them obedient servants. . . . Their mind was strange and dark, full of depressions and exaltations, lacking in rule, but with more of ardour and more fertile in belief than any other in the world.[5]

Less sentimental, though equally damning of the Arabs' ability to run their own affairs, is the analysis of Evelyn Baring, later Lord Cromer, who single-handedly ran Egypt for the British crown from 1883 to 1907. In his massive history of modern Egypt, he contrasts the "Oriental" and "Occidental" minds:

Want of accuracy, which easily degenerates into untruthfulness, is in fact the main characteristic of the Oriental mind. . . . The mind of the Oriental . . . like his picturesque streets, is eminently wanting in symmetry. His reasoning is of the most slipshod description.[6]

Today, such characterizations of "the Oriental" have about them the whiff of illegitimacy, reminders of the days when ideas such as phrenology passed for science. (And if "Orientals" are to include the Chinese and the Indians—as they did then—then what to make of the stunning success of these groups at science, math, and other such manifestations of rationality?) But things have moved from one extreme to the other. Those who have resorted to such cultural stereotypes, the "Orientalists," have been succeeded by a new generation of politically correct scholars who will not dare to ask why it is that Arab countries seem stuck in a very different social and political milieu than the rest of the world. Nor is there any self-criticism in this world. Most Arab writers are more concerned with defending their national honor against the pronouncements of dead Orientalists than with trying to understand the predicament of the Arab world.

The reality is impossible to deny. Of the twenty-two members of the Arab League, not one is an electoral democracy, whereas 63 percent of all the countries in the world are. And although some—Jordan, Morocco—have in some senses liberal authoritarian regimes, most do not. The region's recent history is bleak. Its last five decades are littered with examples of Arab crowds hailing one dictator after another as a savior. Gamal Abdel Nasser in Egypt, Mu'ammar Gadhafi in Libya, and Saddam Hussein in Iraq all have been the recipients of the heartfelt adulation of the Arab masses.

The few Arab scholars who venture into the cultural field point out that Arab social structure is deeply authoritarian. The Eygptian-born scholar Bahgat Korany writes that "Arab political discourse [is] littered with descriptions of the enlightened dictator, the heroic leader, the exceptional Za'im, the revered head of family."[7] The

Lebanese scholar Halim Barakat suggests that the same patriarchal relations and values that prevail in the Arab family seem also to prevail at work, at school, and in religious, political, and social organizations. In all of these, a father figure rules over others, monopolizing authority, expecting strict obedience, and showing little tolerance of dissent. Projecting a paternal image, those in positions of responsibility (as rulers, leaders, teachers, employers, or supervisors) securely occupy the top of the pyramid of authority. Once in this position, the patriarch cannot be dethroned except by someone who is equally patriarchal.[8]

We can see the prototypical Arab patriarch in the novels of the Egyptian Nobel laureate Naguib Mahfouz. His famous trilogy— *Bain Al-Qasrain* (Palace walk), *Qasr al-Shawq* (Palace of desire), and *Sukariyya* (Sugar Street)—follows the life of an Egyptian merchant, Al-Sayyid Ahmad Al-Jawad. Sil Sayyid (Mister Lord), as he is called by his wife, is the undisputed sultan of his household. His family cows before him, standing at attention as he sits alone to enjoy his dinner; only when he has finished are his wife and children allowed to eat. When his wife ventures out of the house without his permission, he banishes her to her parents' household. Today, Egyptians use the name Sil Sayyid to refer to everything from a domineering husband to their national leader.

We can see the shades of Sil Sayyid in most Arab leaders: in Nasser, a charismatic but dictatorial leader who inspired both fear and devotion in his people; in Sadat, his successor, who called his people "my children" even as he demonstrated a capacity for unusual cruelty. We see Sil Sayyid in the Gulf monarchs with their monthly *majlis*, in which citizen-supplicants are given the opportunity to present their (carefully prescreened) grievances to the sheikh. This one's daughter is sick, that one has a land dispute with his neighbor. The sheikh refers one to the Ministry of Health, the other to the Ministry of the Interior. The petitioners kiss his hands and praise Allah for blessing them with such a kind ruler. He waves them off, as if to say that he is only doing his job. "I would like to stay in close contact with my people always, as in this way their wishes can be carried out. For that reason, my *majlis* will be open to all who wish to attend," King Abdul Aziz ibn Saud, the founder of Saudi Arabia, is supposed to have said.

But as foreign as all this will sound to modern Western ears, none of it—patriarchy, strongmen, romanticism—is peculiarly Arab. Those withering critiques of Arab culture penned by British soldiers quoted above were similar to those they wrote about the Chinese, the Japanese, the Indians, indeed all "Orientals" and "Asiatics." And until quite recently most Asian and African countries were also run by strongmen who were regarded by their people with fear and awe; think of Indonesia's Sukarno, Tanzania's Julius Nyerere, Argentina's Juan Peron, and Yugoslavia's Tito. Even recent Western history is littered with examples of powerful dictators and often adoring crowds. Francisco Franco, Antonio Salazar, Benito Mussolini, and Adolf Hitler were all at one time admired by large sections of their countries. More broadly, although the West has been more progressive and liberal for centuries, it also had a firmly patriarchal structure for millennia. After all, women were considered the property of men until a few centuries ago. But while the West progressed and parts of the non-Western world also began modernizing—particularly in the last fifty years or so—the Arab world stayed stuck in primitive political and social arrangements. Arab politics is not culturally unique; it is just stuck in a time warp.

If one looked at the Arab world in the middle of the twentieth century, newly independent of the colonial empires of Europe, one would not have thought it was destined to become a swamp. Other Asian countries, such as South Korea or Malaysia, in far worse shape back then, have done much better. Few would have predicted these outcomes in 1945. In fact many observers at the time noted that, compared with other decolonizing countries, the Arabs were doing well. Beirut, Damascus, Cairo, and Baghdad were more cultured, more commercial, more progressive than most Asian and African capitals. It made sense. The Arabs, after all, belonged to a great civilization, with a long history of science, philosophy, and military success. They invented algebra, preserved Aristotle when he had been forgotten in the West, and won wars against the greatest powers of the day. Islamic art and culture were sophisticated when Europe was in the Dark Ages.

In the 1940s and 1950s there was much hope in the Arab world that it would recapture its past glory. During that period, even though these countries had the usual postcolonial suspicion of the West, they looked up to the United States. Egypt's most famous journalist, Mohammed Heikal, explained, "The whole picture of the United States . . . was a glamorous one. Britain and France were fading, hated empires. The Soviet Union was 5,000 miles away and the ideology of communism was anathema to the Muslim religion. But America had emerged from World War II richer, more powerful and more appealing than ever."[9] These new elites had a modern, secular attitude toward religion. In 1956 the Arab intellectual Ishaq Husseni could write in a survey for the *Atlantic Monthly,* "Today Islam is moving toward a position more like that of Western religion, with separation of church and state." However strange it seems now, it was an accurate representation of the conventional wisdom of the time.

Something happened between then and now. In order to understand the contemporary crisis in the Arab world, we need to understand this downward spiral. We need to plumb not the last 400 years of history but the last 40.

## The Failure of Politics

It is difficult to conjure up the excitement in the Arab world in the late 1950s as Nasser consolidated power in Egypt. For decades Arabs had been ruled by colonial governors and decadent kings. Now they were achieving their dreams of independence, and Nasser was their new savior, a modern man for the postwar era. He had been born under British rule, in Alexandria, a cosmopolitan city that was more Mediterranean than Arab. His formative years had been spent in the army, the most Westernized segment of Egyptian society. With his tailored suits and fashionable dark glasses, he cut a daring figure on the world stage. "The Lion of Egypt" spoke for all the Arab world.

Nasser believed that Arab politics needed to be fired by ideas such as self-determination, socialism, and Arab unity. These were modern notions; they were also Western ones. Like many Third World leaders of the time, Nasser was a devoted reader of the British *New Statesman*. His "national charter" of 1962 reads as if it were written by left-wing intellectuals in Paris or London. Even his most passionately pursued goal, pan-Arabism, was European inspired. It was a version of the nationalism that had united first Italy and then Germany in the 1870s—the idea that those who spoke one language should be one nation.

Before wealth fattened the Gulf states into golden geese, Egypt was the leader of the Middle East. Thus Nasser's vision became the region's. Every regime, from the Baathists and generals in Syria and Iraq to the conservative monarchies of the Gulf, spoke in similar terms and tones. They were not simply aping Nasser. The Arab world desperately wanted to become modern, and it saw modernity in an embrace of Western ideas, even if it went hand in hand with a defiance of Western power.

In this respect, Arabia was like many non-Western lands. Having seen the rise of the West, the civilizations that were left behind— China, India, the Ottoman Empire—wondered how they could catch up. For much of modern history, Islamic elites seemed more eager to do so than most. Ever since their defeat of the Ottomans in 1683 outside Vienna, Arabs realized that they had much to learn from the West. When the West set ashore in Arab lands, in the form of Napoleon's conquest of Egypt in 1798, the locals were fascinated by this powerful civilization. As the historian Albert Hourani has documented, the eighteenth and nineteenth centuries saw European-inspired liberal political and social thought flourish in the Middle East.

The colonial era of the late nineteenth and early twentieth centuries raised hopes of British friendship that were to be disappointed, but still Arab elites remained fascinated with the West. Future kings and generals attended Victoria College in Alexandria, learning the speech and manners of British gentlemen. Many then went on to Oxford, Cambridge, or Sandhurst—a tradition that is still maintained by Jordan's royal family, although now they go to American schools. After World War I, a new liberal age flickered briefly in the Arab world, as ideas about opening politics and society gained currency in places like Egypt, Lebanon, Iraq, and Syria. But the liberal critics of kings and aristocrats were swept away along with those old regimes. A more modern, coarser ideology of military republicanism, state socialism, and Arab nationalism came into vogue. These ideas, however, were still basically Western; the Baathists and Nasserites all wore suits and wanted to modernize their countries.

The new politics and policies of the Arab world went nowhere. For all their energy Arab regimes chose bad ideas and implemented them in worse ways. Socialism produced bureaucracy and stagnation. Rather than adjusting to the failures of central planning, the economies never really moved on. Instead of moving toward democracy, the republics calcified into dictatorships. Third World "nonalignment" became pro-Soviet propaganda. Arab unity cracked and crumbled as countries discovered their own national interests and opportunities. An Arab "Cold War" developed between the countries led by pro-Western kings (the Gulf states, Jordan) and those ruled by revolutionary generals (Syria, Iraq). Worst of all, Israel dealt the Arabs a series of humiliating defeats on the battlefield. Their swift, stunning defeat in 1967 was in some ways the turning point, revealing that behind the rhetoric and bombast lay societies that were failing. When Saddam invaded Kuwait in 1990, he destroyed the last remnants of the pan-Arab idea.

Since then things have only gotten worse. Look at Egypt today. The promise of Nasserism has turned into a quiet nightmare. The government is efficient in only one area: squashing dissent and strangling civil society. Fouad Ajami, the Lebanese-born American scholar, has lamented that Egypt, once the heart of Arab intellectual life, now produces just 375 books a year, compared with 4,000 from Israel, which has one-tenth of Egypt's population. Ajami quotes the commentator Karim Alrawi, who has warned that "the modernizing imperative that has dominated and driven Egypt since the early 1800s, after its encounter with Europe, is being reversed."[10]

Shockingly, Egypt has fared better than its Arab neighbors. Syria has become one of the world's most oppressive police states, a country where 30,000 people can be rounded up and killed by the regime with no consequences, as happened in 1982 in the city of Hama. (This in a country whose capital, Damascus, is the oldest continuously inhabited city in the world.) In thirty years Iraq too has gone from being among the most modern and secular of Arab countries—with women working, artists thriving, journalists writing—into a squalid playpen for a megalomaniac. Alone among modern dictators, Saddam has used chemical weapons against his own people (the Iraqi Kurds). Lebanon, a diverse, cosmopolitan society with a capital, Beirut, that was once called the "Paris of the East," plunged itself into an abyss of war and terror from which it is only now emerging.

All these countries had an authoritarian past, but over the past few decades traditional dictatorship has been wedded to new technologies and methods of control to produce governments that control every aspect of their societies. As the historian of Islam Bernard Lewis has pointed out, today's tin-pot dictators wield far greater powers than did the fabled emperors of yore, such as the sixteenth-century Ottoman Suleyman the Magnificent, or the eighth-century Caliph Haroun al Rashid (immortalized in *The Thousand and One Nights*). The Gulf sheikhdoms, for example, which were once ruled in a relaxed Bedouin fashion by monarchs who had limited power over their nomadic people, now are rich states that use their wealth to build police forces, armies, and intelligence agencies, all of which exercise tight control over their people. Even in the rich Gulf states one senses the frustration and anger of a populace that has been given some wealth but no voice—locked in a gilded cage. Most

Americans think that Arabs should be grateful for the U.S. role in the Gulf War, which saved Kuwait and Saudi Arabia. Most Arabs, however, think that the United States saved the Kuwaiti and Saudi royal families—a big difference.

By the late 1980s, while the rest of the world was watching old regimes from Moscow to Prague to Seoul to Johannesburg crack, the Arabs were stuck with their corrupt dictators and aging kings. Regimes that might have seemed promising in the 1960s were now exposed as tired kleptocracies, deeply unpopular and thoroughly illegitimate. In an almost unthinkable reversal of a global pattern, almost every Arab country today is less free than it was forty years ago. There are few places in the world about which one can say that.

## The Failure of Economics

At almost every meeting or seminar on terrorism organized by think tanks and universities since September 11, 2001, when someone wants to sound thoughtful and serious, he says in measured tones, "We must fight not just terrorism but also the roots of terrorism." This platitude is inevitably followed by a suggestion for a new Marshall Plan to eradicate poverty in the Muslim world. Who can be opposed to eradicating poverty? But the problem with this diagnosis is that it overlooks an inconvenient fact: the Al Qaeda terrorist network is not made up of the poor and dispossessed.

This is obviously true at the top; bin Laden was born into a family worth more than $5 billion. But it is also true of many of his key associates, such as his deputy, Zawahiri, a former surgeon in Cairo who came from the highest ranks of Egyptian society. His father was a distinguished professor at Cairo University, his grandfather the chief imam of Al Azhar (the most important center of mainstream Islam in the Arab world), and his uncle the first secretary general of the Arab League. Look further down at Mohammed Atta, the pilot of the first plane to hit the World Trade Center. He came from a modern—and moderate—Egyptian family. His father was a lawyer. He had two sisters, a professor and a doctor. Atta himself studied in Hamburg, as had several of the other terrorists. Even the lower-level Al Qaeda recruits appear to have been educated, middle-class men. In this sense, John Walker Lindh, the California kid who dropped out of American life and tuned into the Taliban, was not that different from many of his fellow fundamentalists. In fact, with his high school diploma against their engineering degrees, one could say that he was distinctly undereducated by comparison.

In fact the breeding grounds of terror have been places that have seen the greatest influx of wealth over the last thirty years. Of the nineteen hijackers on the four planes used in the September 11 attacks, fifteen were from Saudi Arabia, the world's largest petroleum exporter. It is unlikely that poverty was at the heart of their anger. Even Egypt—the other great feeder country for Al Qaeda—is not really a poor country by international standards. Its per capita income, $3,690, places it in the middle rank of nations, and it has been growing at a decent 5 percent for the last decade. That may not be enough when you take population growth into account—its population growth has been about 3 percent—but many countries around the world are doing far worse. Yet they have not spawned hordes of men who are willing to drive planes into Manhattan skyscrapers. If poverty were the source of terror, the recruits should have come from sub-Saharan Africa or South Asia, not the Middle East.

Inequality alone cannot explain it either. The standard measure of a country's income inequality is called the Gini index. A lower Gini index is better; Brazil's is 60, Belgium's is 25, and Egypt's is 28.9, lower than almost every Latin American country and most other developing countries as well. In fact it has a slightly more equal distribution of income than does France, which scores 32.7. The top 30 percent of Egypt's population accounts for 64 percent of its gross domestic product (GDP); in France the top 30 percent accounts for 65 percent of GDP. The bottom 30 percent in Egypt makes up 14.2 percent of GDP; in France the same bottom tier makes only 10 percent.[11] The Gulf states, which do not release such data, probably have higher levels of inequality but probably do not reach the levels of inequality in, say, Brazil, Colombia, and Nigeria.

There is, however, a powerful economic dimension to the crisis in the Arab world. The problem is wealth, not poverty. In Chapter 2 we saw how regimes that get rich through natural resources tend never to develop, modernize, or gain legitimacy. The Arab world is the poster child for this theory of trust-fund states. And this is true not only for the big oil producers. Consider Egypt, which is a small but significant exporter of oil and gas. It also earns $2 billion a year in transit fees paid by ships crossing the Suez Canal, and gets another $2.2 billion a year in aid from the United States. In addition, it gets large sums in remittances—money sent home—from Egyptians who work in the Gulf states. All told, it gets a hefty percent of its GDP from unearned income. Or consider Jordan, a progressive state that is liberalizing; it gets $1 billion a year in aid from the United States. Although that may seem to be a small figure, keep in mind that Jordan's GDP is only $17 billion. Almost 6 percent of its annual income is foreign aid from one country.

Easy money means little economic or political modernization. The unearned income relieves the government of the need to tax its people—and in return provide something to them in the form of accountability, transparency, even representation.[12] History shows that a government's need to tax its people forces it to become more responsive and representative of its people. Middle Eastern regimes ask little of their people and, in return, give little to them. Another bad effect of natural-resource-derived wealth is that it makes the government rich enough to become repressive. There is always money enough for the police and the army. Saudi Arabia, for example, spends 13 percent of its annual GDP on the military, as does Oman. Kuwait spends around 8 percent. Various estimates of Iraqi military spending before the Gulf War have put its military spending at somewhere between 25 and 40 percent of annual GDP, an unusually high rate no doubt sustained, in part, by the Iran-Iraq War, but also by the massive internal intelligence network maintained by Saddam and his Baath Party.

For years many in the oil-rich states argued that their enormous wealth would bring modernization. They pointed to the impressive appetites of Saudis and Kuwaitis for things Western, from McDonald's hamburgers to Rolex watches to Cadillac limousines. But importing Western goods is easy; importing the inner stuffing of modern society—a free market, political parties, accountability, the rule of law—is difficult and even dangerous for the ruling elites. The Gulf states, for example, have gotten a bastardized version of modernization, with the goods and even the workers imported from abroad. Little of their modernness is homegrown; if the oil evaporated tomorrow, these states would have little to show for decades of wealth except, perhaps, an overdeveloped capacity for leisure.

## Fear of Westernization

About a decade ago, in a casual conversation with an elderly Arab intellectual, I expressed my frustration that governments in the Middle East had been unable to liberalize their economies and societies in the way that the East Asians had. "Look at Singapore, Hong Kong, and Seoul," I said, pointing to their extraordinary economic achievements. The man, a gentle, charming, erudite, and pro-Western journalist, straightened up and replied sharply, "Look at them. They have simply aped the West. Their cities are cheap copies of Houston and Dallas. That may be all right for fishing villages, but we are heirs to one of the great civilizations of the world. We cannot become slums of the West."

This sense of pride and fall is at the heart of the Arab problem. It makes economic advance impossible and political progress fraught with difficulty. America thinks of modernity as all good—and it has been almost all good for America. But for the Arab world, modernity has been one failure after another. Each path followed—socialism, secularism, nationalism—has turned into a dead end. People often wonder why the Arab countries will not try secularism. In fact, for most of the last century, most of them did. Now people associate the failure of their governments with the failure of secularism and of the Western path. The Arab world is disillusioned with the West when it should be disillusioned with its own leaders.

The new, accelerated globalization that flourished in the 1990s has hit the Arab world in a strange way. Its societies are open enough to be disrupted by modernity, but not so open that they can ride the wave. Arabs see the television shows, eat the fast foods, and drink the sodas, but they don't see genuine liberalization in their societies, with increased opportunities and greater openness. They don't see economic opportunities and dynamism, just the same elites controlling things. Globalization in the Arab world is the critic's caricature of globalization, a slew of Western products and billboards with little else. For the elites in Arab societies it means more things to buy. But for some of them it is also an unsettling phenomenon that threatens their comfortable base of power.

This mixture of fascination and repulsion with the West—with modernity—has utterly disoriented the Arab world. Young men, often better educated than their parents, leave their traditional villages to find work. They arrive in the noisy, crowded cities of Cairo, Beirut, Damascus or go to work in the oil states. (Almost 10 percent of Egypt's working population worked in the Gulf states at one point.) In their new world they see great disparities of wealth and the disorienting effects of modernity; most unsettlingly, they see women, unveiled and in public places, taking buses, eating in cafes, and working alongside them. They come face to face with the contradictions of modern life, seeking the wealth of the new world but the tradition and certainty of the old.

Globalization has caught the Arab world at a bad demographic moment. Its societies are going through a massive youth bulge; more than half of the Arab world is under the age of twenty-five. Fully 75 percent of Saudi Arabia is under the age of thirty. A bulge of restless young men in any country is bad news. Almost all crime in every society is committed by men between the ages of fifteen and twenty-five. Lock all young men up, one social scientist pointed out, and violent crime will drop by more than 95 percent. (That is why the socialization of young men—in schools, colleges, and camps—has been one of the chief challenges for civilized societies.) When accompanied by even small economic and social change, a youth bulge produces a new politics of protest. In the past, societies in these circumstances have fallen prey to a search for revolutionary solutions. France went through a youth bulge just before the French Revolution in 1789, as did Iran before its revolution in 1979. Even the United States had a youth bulge that peaked in 1968, the year of the country's strongest social protests since the Great Depression. In the case of the Arab world, this upheaval has taken the form of a religious resurgence.

## The Rise of Religion

Nasser was a reasonably devout Muslim, but he had no interest in mixing religion with politics, which struck him as moving backward. This became painfully apparent to the small Islamic parties that supported Nasser's rise to power. The most important one, the Muslim Brotherhood, began opposing him vigorously, often violently, by the early 1950s. Nasser cracked down on it ferociously, imprisoning more than a thousand of its leaders and executing six in 1954. One of those jailed was Sayyid Qutb, a frail man with a fiery pen, who wrote a book in prison called *Signposts on the Road*, which in some ways marks the beginnings of modern political Islam or what is often called Islamic fundamentalism.*

In his book, Qutb condemned Nasser as an impious Muslim and his regime as un-Islamic. Indeed, he went on, almost every modern Arab regime was similarly flawed. Qutb envisioned a better, more

---

*In many ways the original fundamentalist is Qutb's contemporary, the Pakistani scholar Abul Ala Maududi. Qutb was an admirer of Maududi and translated his writings into Arabic. But it is Qutb who is read throughout the Islamic world today.

virtuous polity based on strict Islamic principles, a core goal of orthodox Muslims since the 1880s.[13] As the regimes of the Middle East grew more distant, oppressive, and hollow in the decades following Nasser, fundamentalism's appeal grew. It flourished because the Muslim Brotherhood and organizations like it at least tried to give people a sense of meaning and purpose in a changing world, something no leader in the Middle East tried to do. In his seminal work, *The Arab Predicament*, which best explains the fracture of Arab political culture, Fouad Ajami explains, "The fundamentalist call has resonance because it invited men to participate . . . [in] contrast to a political culture that reduces citizens to spectators and asks them to leave things to their rulers. At a time when the future is uncertain, it connects them to a tradition that reduces bewilderment." Fundamentalism gave Arabs who were dissatisfied with their lot a powerful language of opposition.

On that score, Islam had little competition. The Arab world is a political desert with no real political parties, no free press, and few pathways for dissent. As a result, the mosque became the place to discuss politics. As the only place that cannot be banned in Muslim societies, it is where all the hate and opposition toward the regimes collected and grew. The language of opposition became, in these lands, the language of religion. This combination of religion and politics has proven to be combustible. Religion, at least the religion of the Abrahamic traditions (Judaism, Christianity, and Islam), stresses moral absolutes. But politics is all about compromise. The result has been a ruthless, winner-take-all attitude toward political life.

Fundamentalist organizations have done more than talk. From the Muslim Brotherhood to Hamas to Hizbullah, they actively provide social services, medical assistance, counseling, and temporary housing. For those who treasure civil society, it is disturbing to see that in the Middle East these illiberal groups *are* civil society. Sheri Berman, a scholar who studies the rise of fascist parties in Europe, has drawn an interesting parallel. "Fascists were often very effective at providing social services," she pointed out.

When the state or political parties collapse, in that they fail to provide a sense of legitimacy or purpose or basic services, other organizations have often been able to step into the void. In Islamic countries there is a ready-made source of legitimacy in the religion. So it's not surprising that this is the foundation on which these groups have flourished. The particular form—Islamic fundamentalism—is specific to this region, but the basic dynamic is similar to the rise of Nazism, fascism and even populism in the United States.

If there is one great cause of the rise of Islamic fundamentalism, it is the total failure of political institutions in the Arab world.

Islamic fundamentalism got a tremendous boost in 1979 when Ayatollah Ruhollah Khomeini toppled the staunchly pro-American shah of Iran. The Iranian Revolution demonstrated that a powerful ruler could be taken on by groups within society. It also revealed how in a developing society even seemingly benign forces of progress—for example, education—can add to the turmoil. Until the 1970s most Muslims in the Middle East were illiterate and lived in villages and towns. They practiced a kind of village Islam that had adapted itself to local cultures and to normal human desires. Pluralistic and tolerant, these villagers often worshiped saints, went to shrines, sang religious hymns, and cherished art—all technically disallowed in Islam. By the 1970s, however, these societies were being urbanized. People had begun moving out of the villages to search for jobs in towns and cities. Their religious experience was no longer rooted in a specific place with local customs and traditions. At the same time they were learning to read and they discovered that a new Islam was being preached by a new generation of writers, preachers, and teachers. This was an abstract faith not rooted in historical experience but literal and puritanical—Islam of the high church as opposed to Islam of the street fair.

In Iran, Ayatollah Khomeini used a powerful technology: the audiocassette. Even when he was exiled in Paris in the 1970s, his sermons were distributed throughout Iran and became the vehicle of opposition to the shah's repressive regime. But they also taught people a new, angry, austere Islam in which the West is evil, America is the "Great Satan," and the unbeliever is to be fought. Khomeini was not alone in using the language of Islam as a political tool. Intellectuals, disillusioned by the half-baked or overly rapid modernization that was throwing their world into turmoil, were writing books against "Westoxification" and calling the modern Iranian man—half Western, half Eastern—"rootless." Fashionable intellectuals, often writing from the comfort of London or Paris, would criticize American secularism and consumerism and endorse an Islamic alternative. As theories like these spread across the Arab world, they appealed not to the poorest of the poor, for whom Westernization was magical, since it meant food and medicine. Rather, they appealed to the educated hordes entering the cities of the Middle East or seeking education and jobs in the West. They were disoriented and ready to be taught that their disorientation would be solved by recourse to a new, true Islam.

In the Sunni world, the rise of Islamic fundamentalism was shaped and quickened by the fact that Islam is a highly egalitarian religion. This for most of its history has proved an empowering call for people who felt powerless. But it also means that no Muslim really has the authority to question whether someone is a "proper Muslim." In the Middle Ages there was an informal understanding that a trained scholarly-clerical community, the *ulama*, had the authority to pronounce on such matters.[14] But fundamentalist thinkers, from the Pakistani Maulana Maududi and Qutb to their followers, have muscled in on that territory. They loudly and continuously pronounce judgment as to whether people are "good Muslims." In effect they excommunicate those whose Islam does not match their own. This process has terrified the Muslim world. Leaders dare not take on the rising tide of Islamists. Intellectual and social elites, widely discredited by their slavish support of the official government line, are also scared to speak out against a genuinely free-thinking clergy. As a result, moderate Muslims are loath to criticize or debunk the fanaticism of the fundamentalists. Some worry, like the moderates in Northern Ireland, about their safety if they speak their mind. Even as venerated a figure as Naguib Mahfouz was stabbed in Egypt for his mildly critical comments about the Islamists. Most are simply cowed into silence. I have watched this transformation in India, where I grew up. The rich, colorful, pluralistic, and easygoing Islam of my youth is turning into a dour, puritanical faith, policed by petty theocrats and religious commissars.

Nowhere is this more true than in the moderate monarchies of the Persian Gulf, particularly Saudi Arabia. The Saudi regime has played a dangerous game: it has tried to deflect attention from its spotty economic and political record by allowing free reign to its most extreme clerics, hoping to gain legitimacy by association. Saudi Arabia's educational system is run by medieval-minded religious bureaucrats. Over the past three decades, the Saudis—mostly through private trusts—have funded religious schools (madrasas) and centers that spread Wahhabism (a rigid, desert variant of Islam that is the template for most Islamic fundamentalists) around the world. In the past thirty years Saudi-funded madrasas have churned out tens of thousands of half-educated, fanatical Muslims who view the modern world and non-Muslims with great suspicion. America in this worldview is almost always uniquely evil.

This exported fundamentalism has infected not just other Arab societies but countries outside the Arab world. It often carries with it a distinctly parochial Arab political program. Thus Indonesian Muslims, who twenty years ago did not know where Palestine was, are today militant in their support of its cause. The Arab influence extends even into the realm of architecture. In its buildings the Islamic world has always mixed Arabic influences with local ones— Hindu, Javan, Russian. But local cultures are now being ignored in places such as Indonesia and Malaysia because they are seen as insufficiently Islamic (meaning Arab).

Pakistan has had a particularly bad experience with exported fundamentalism. During the 11-year reign of General Zia ul-Haq during the 1980s, the dictator decided that he needed allies, since he had squashed political dissent and opposition parties. He found them in the local fundamentalists, who became his political allies. With the aid of Saudi financiers and functionaries, he set up scores of *madrasas* throughout the country. The Afghan war attracted religious zealots, eager to fight godless communism. These "jihadis" came mostly from Arabia. Without Saudi money and men, the Taliban would not have existed, nor would Pakistan have become the hotbed of fundamentalism it is today. Zia's embrace of Islam brought him a kind of legitimacy, but it has eroded the social fabric of Pakistan. The country is now full of armed radicals, who first supported the Taliban, then joined in the struggle in Kashmir, and are now trying to undermine the secular regime of General Pervez Musharraf. They have infected the legal and political system with medieval ideas of blasphemy, the subordinate role of women, and the evils of modern banking.

Pakistan is not alone. A similar process has been at work in countries as diverse as Yemen, Indonesia, and the Philippines. During the 1980s and 1990s, a kind of competition emerged between Iran and Saudi Arabia, the two most religious states in the Middle East, to see who would be the greater religious power in the Islamic world. As a result, what were once small, extreme strains of Islam, limited to parts of the Middle East, have taken root around the world—in the globalization of radical Islam.

## An Islamic Reformation

Even if it is the Arab world and not Islam that is the problem, for some Islam can be the solution. Many Westerners and some Muslims have argued that what Islam needs is a clean break between church and state, its own version of the Reformation that will do for Islam what it did for the West. The magic that these great processes worked in the lands of Christendom amounted to what some have called "the renunciation of certainty." No longer could a gang of priests decree what ordinary men could and could not do. The Reformation broke the back of priestly authority and power. In particular, it ended the pope's sole dominion over Christianity.

But in Islam, there was never any one universally obeyed priestly hierarchy from whom the masses required liberation. Islam does not have a clergy, nor a religious hierarchy as do Catholicism and some Protestant sects. The mosque in Islam is simply a place to pray—not, like the church, a theological institution. The person who leads the prayer in many congregations, standing alongside all others, is often the one who best knows the prayer. With no central religious authority, the supremacy of state over church—which arose in Europe as a result of religious wars—has always existed in the lands of Islam. The Muslim caliph was first and foremost a prince; he was not a pope, and he did not have to contend with one. He could build mosques and patronize religious scholars, but he was not a religious authority. (In one of the hadith quoted above the prophet declared that the only thing a ruler needs to do to maintain legitimacy is facilitate prayers.) It makes little sense, then, to argue that Muslims need to undergo a historical process to solve a problem they never had.

Actually this very fact—that Muslims never had a pope to rebel against—is the very source of the quandary. In the Islamic world, since temporal authority was always dominant over spiritual authority,* the issue of separating the two never came up. This meant that rulers and those who opposed them could manipulate the faith in order to serve their own ends. Rulers could always find some priest to legitimate them, and rebels could find inspiration in the words of others. The Saudi king has his clerics; bin Laden has his.

There is one exception to this rule, and it is Iran. The Shia tradition, dominant in Iran, does have a clerical establishment; expanded after Khomeini's revolution, it now has an elaborate hierarchy and a

*After the Prophet Mohammed, who combined both temporal and spiritual authority.

pope-like figure at the top. Bernard Lewis considers how this might lead to an Iranian reformation:

> Khomeini during his rule seems to have effected a kind of "Christianization" of Iran's Islamic institutions, with himself as an infallible pope, and with the functional equivalent of a hierarchy of archbishops, bishops, and priests. All of this was totally alien to Islamic tradition, and thus constituted an "Islamic revolution" in a sense quite different from the one usually conveyed by references to Khomeini's legacy. . . . It may be that Muslims, having contracted a Christian illness, will consider a Christian remedy, that is to say, the separation of religion and state.[15]

Paradoxically Iran's theocracy might provide a path toward greater reform. It is not unthinkable that the country that led the Middle East into Islamic fundamentalism might eventually lead it out. But Iran might move toward modernity not because it is, as the regime claims, a democracy, for Iran's democracy is highly restricted. Candidates are vetted by the mullahs before they can run for office, the free press has been shut down, student protests have been muzzled. The clergy holds all power, while the elected president, Mohammed Khatami, an erudite philosopher-priest, makes well-meaning but ineffectual speeches and statements. Khatami's reformist rhetoric and election by a large majority are important, of course. Iran will evolve into a secular democracy in a process that mixes reform and revolution. The reasons are obvious: the regime has mismanaged the economy, is repressive politically, and faces millions of alienated young men and women. Most important, in Iran theocracy has been discredited. The Islamists have lost their trump card. Everywhere else in the Middle East and North Africa they are the alluring, mythical alternative to the wretched reality in which people live. In Iran fundamentalism *is* the wretched reality under which people live. The next time a mullah comes knocking on an Iranian's door he will turn his back: "Been there, done that."

The Iranian example has led many to wonder if the Islamists must come to power in other countries in the Middle East so that they can be discredited. According to this reasoning, the mullahs are needed to cause a rebellion, which might even trigger an Islamic Reformation, and then real democracy. But that reasoning makes the mistake of generalizing from the unique experiences of Shia Iran onto the whole Sunni world of Islam. Besides, Iran has gone through hell over the last twenty-five years. Its once-vibrant culture has been silenced and its economy has plummeted along with living standards. It is not much of a solution to recommend that other countries descend into the abyss so that they can eventually escape from it, if they are lucky.

It is true that wherever Muslim fundamentalists have been involved in day-to-day politics—Bangladesh, Pakistan, Turkey, Iran—their luster has worn off. They routinely poll well below traditional political parties. People have realized that the streets still have to be cleaned, government finances have to be managed and education attended to. The mullahs can preach, but they cannot rule. But that is not reason enough to risk having Egypt and Saudi Arabia go through regime change that takes them on a roller-coaster for twenty years. If these regimes would open up *some* political space and force their fundamentalist foes to grapple with practical realities rather than just spin dreams, they would quickly dull the extremists' allure. This does not have to mean a move to democracy overnight. But Egypt, for example, is ripe for significant political reform. It has a per capita income of almost $4,000, within the zone of transition. It has a middle class and a developed civil society. Yet it will not allow Muslim fundamentalists to run for election to its utterly powerless parliament. The war on the regime's political opponents, liberal and Islamic alike, has benefited the extremists. The few Arab regimes that have tried a different approach—such as Jordan and Morocco—allowing some dissent within the system, are faring better. If countries do more to include the fundamentalists in the system, they will stop being seen as distant heroes and will be viewed instead as local politicians.

As this suggests, the key is not religious reform, but political and economic reform. The entire emphasis on a transformation of Islam is misplaced. The key to making Christianity compatible with modernity was not to get the church to suddenly accept liberal interpretations of theology. It was to modernize society until the churches had to adapt to the world around them. After all, many of the anti-modern prejudices in Islam exist in Christianity as well. The Quranic condemnations of usury and gambling, the dietary restrictions, the requirement for fasting—are all similar to precepts in the Bible. But Christians live in societies that modernized politically, economically, and socially, and, along the way, adapted their faith. Religion in the Western world is now a source of spiritual inspiration and not a template for day-to-day living. The Bible still condemns masturbation, usury, and the wearing of woven cloth; Christian societies just no longer see it as an authority on these matters.

To those who say Islam is different I can respond only, of course. But is it so different that if it existed within a modern, capitalist, democratic society it would not change? Again, if we move from the realm of theory to fact we have some evidence on the ground. Turkey, Bosnia, Malaysia, and to a lesser extent South Asia have somewhat modern Muslim communities. Perhaps most important, the United States, Canada, and Europe have large Muslim communities. In all these places Islam is adapting to modern life without a grand Reformation. In all these countries the majority of believers—though not all—have found ways to be devout without being obscurantist, and pious without embracing fury. The lesson of the varied paths to modernity discussed in the previous chapters—Protestant, Catholic, Orthodox, Confucian, Latin—is that if you get the politics and economics right, culture will follow.

## The Road to Democracy

For the most part, this task of reform in the Middle East must fall to the peoples of the region. No one can make democracy, liberalism, or secularism take root in these societies without their own search, efforts, and achievements. But the Western world in general, and the United States in particular, can help enormously. The United States is the dominant power in the Middle East; every country views its relations with Washington as the most critical tie they have. Oil, strategic ties, and the unique U.S. relationship with Israel ensure American involvement. Washington will continue to aid the Egyptian regime, protect the Saudi monarchy, broker negotiations between Israel and the Palestinians. The question really is, Should it not ask for something in return? By not pushing these regimes, the United States would be making a conscious decision to let things stay as they are—to opt for stability. It is a worthwhile goal except that the current situation in the Middle East is highly unstable. Even if viewed from a strategic perspective, it is in America's immediate security interests to try to make the regimes of the Middle East less prone to breed fanatical and terrorist opposition movements.

At the start the West must recognize that it does not seek democracy in the Middle East—at least not yet. We seek first constitutional liberalism, which is very different. Clarifying our immediate goals actually makes them more easily attainable. The regimes in the Middle East will be delighted to learn that we will not try to force them to hold elections tomorrow. They will be less pleased to know that we will continually press them on a whole array of other issues. The Saudi monarchy must do more to end its governmental and nongovernmental support for extremist Islam, which is now the kingdom's second largest export to the rest of the world. If this offends advocates of pure free speech, so be it. It must rein in its religious and educational leaders and force them to stop flirting with fanaticism. In Egypt, we must ask President Mubarak to insist that the state-owned press drop its anti-American and anti-Semitic rants and begin opening itself up to other voices in the country. Some of them will be worse than what we hear now, but some will be better. Most important, people in these countries will begin to speak about what truly concerns them—not only the status of Jerusalem or American policies in the Gulf but also the regimes they live under and the politics they confront.

Israel has become the great excuse for much of the Arab world, the way for regimes to deflect attention from their own failures. Other countries have foreign policy disagreements with one another—think of Japan and China—but they do not have the sometimes poisonous quality of the Israeli-Arab divide. Israel's occupation of the West Bank and the Gaza Strip has turned into the great cause of the Arab world. But even if fomented by cynical Arab rulers, this cause is now a reality that cannot be ignored. There is a new Arab street in the Middle East, built on Al-Jazeera and Internet chat sites. And the talk is all about the plight of the Palestinians. If unaddressed, this issue will only grow in importance, infecting America's relations with the entire Muslim world and ensuring permanent insecurity for Israel. The United States should maintain its unyielding support for the security of Israel. But it should also do what is in the best interests of itself, Israel, and the Palestinians, which is to press hard to broker a settlement that provides Israel with security and the Palestinians a viable state. Peace between the Israelis and Palestinians will not solve the problems of Arab dysfunction, but it would ease some of the high tensions between the Arab world and the West.

The more lasting solution is economic and political reform. Economic reforms must come first, for they are fundamental. Even though the problems the Middle East faces are not purely economic, their solution may lie in economics. Moving toward capitalism, as we have seen, is the surest path to creating a limited, accountable state and a genuine middle class. And just as in Spain, Portugal, Chile, Taiwan, South Korea, and Mexico, economic reform can produce political effects in the Middle East. Economic reform means the beginnings of a genuine rule of law (capitalism needs contracts), openness to the world, access to information, and, perhaps most important, the development of a business class. If you talk with Arab businessmen and women, they want the old system to change. They have a stake in openness, in rules, and in stability. They want their societies to modernize and move forward rather than stay trapped in factionalism and war. Instead of the romance of ideology, they seek the reality of material progress. In the Middle East today there are too many people consumed by political dreams and too few interested in practical plans. That is why, to paraphrase Winston Churchill's line about the Balkans, the region produces more history than it consumes.

There is a dominant business class in the Middle East, but it owes its position to oil or to connections to the ruling families.* Its wealth is that of feudalism, not capitalism, and its political effects remain feudal as well. A genuinely entrepreneurial business class would be the single most important force for change in the Middle East, pulling along all others in its wake. If culture matters, this is one place it would help. Arab culture for thousands of years has been full of traders, merchants, and businessmen. The bazaar is probably the oldest institution in the Middle East. And Islam was historically highly receptive to business—Mohammed himself was a businessman. Ultimately, the battle for reform is one Middle Easterners will have to fight, which is why there needs to be some group within these societies that advocates and benefits from economic and political reform.

This is not as fantastic an idea as it might sound. Already stirrings of genuine economic activity can be seen in parts of the Middle East. Jordan has become a member of the World Trade Organization (WTO), signed a free-trade pact with the United States, privatized key industries, and even encouraged cross-border business ventures with Israel. Saudi Arabia is seeking WTO membership. Egypt has made some small progress on the road to reform. Among the oil-rich countries, Bahrain and the United Arab Emirates are trying to wean themselves of their dependence on oil. Dubai, part of the United Arab Emirates, has already gotten oil down to merely 8 percent of its GDP and publicly announces its intention to become a trading and

---

*There are some exceptions to this rule in Gulf states such as Dubai, Bahrain, and even Saudi Arabia.

banking center—the "Singapore of the Middle East." (It would do well to emulate Singapore's tolerance of its ethnic and religious minorities.) Even Saudi Arabia recognizes that its oil economy can provide only one job for every three of its young men coming into the work force. In Algeria, President Abdelaziz Bouteflika desperately wants foreign investment to repair his tattered economy.

If we could choose one place to press hardest to reform, it should be Egypt. Although Jordan has a more progressive ruler, and Saudi Arabia is more critical because of its oil, Egypt is the intellectual soul of the Arab world. If it were to progress economically and politically, it would demonstrate more powerfully than any essay or speech that Islam is compatible with modernity, and that Arabs can thrive in today's world. In East Asia, Japan's economic success proved a powerful example that others in the region looked to and followed. The Middle East needs one such homegrown success story.

There is another possible candidate for this role: Iraq. Before it became a playpen for Saddam's megalomania, Iraq was one of the most advanced, literate, and secular countries of the region. It has oil, but, more important, water. Iraq is the land of one of the oldest river-valley civilizations of the world. Its capital, Baghdad, is 50 kilometers north of one of the wonders of the ancient world, the Hanging Gardens of Babylon, and has been an important city for thousands of years. Iraq in the 1950s was a country with a highly developed civil society, with engineers, doctors, and architects, many of whom were women. Were the United States to dislodge Saddam and—far more important— engage in a serious, long-term project of nation-building, Iraq could well become the first major Arab country to combine Arab culture with economic dynamism, religious tolerance, liberal politics, and a modern outlook on the world. And success is infectious.

The consummate politician, former Speaker of the House Thomas P. "Tip" O'Neill, once said that all politics is local. So is the politics of rage. The frustrations of ordinary Arabs are not about the clash of civilizations or the rise of McDonald's or the imperial foreign policy of the United States. They are a response to living under wretched, repressive regimes with no political voice. And they blame America for supporting these regimes.

For those who think that this problem is unique to the Arab world or that Arabs will never change, recall that twenty-five years ago the most virulent anti-American protests took place in countries such as Chile, Mexico, and South Korea. The reasons were the same: people disliked the regimes that ruled them and they saw the United States as the benefactor of those regimes. Then these dictatorships liberalized, people's lives improved, economic reforms took place, followed by democratic openings. The result: anti-U.S. sentiment has quieted down to the usual protests against the Americanization of their culture. If in the future street demonstrations against McDonald's are the only kind of anti-Americanism we have to worry about, the Middle East will have made progress indeed.

## The Majestic Clockwork

Spreading democracy is tough. But that does not mean that the West—in particular the United States—should stop trying to assist the forces of liberal democracy. Nor does it imply accepting blindly authoritarian regimes as the least bad alternative. It does, however, suggest a certain sophistication. The haste to press countries into elections over the last decade has been, in many cases, counterproductive. In countries such as Bosnia, which went to the polls within a year of the Dayton peace accords, elections only made more powerful precisely the kinds of ugly ethnic forces that have made it more difficult to build genuine liberal democracy there. The ethnic thugs stayed in power, kept the courts packed and the police well fed. The old system has stayed in place, delaying real change for years, perhaps decades. In East Timor and Afghanistan, a longer period of state-building has proved useful. In general, a five-year period of transition, political reform, and institutional development should precede national multiparty elections. In a country with strong regional, ethnic, or religious divisions—like Iraq—this is crucial. It ensures that elections are held after civic institutions, courts, political parties, and the economy have all begun to function. As with everything in life, timing matters.

Although it is easy to impose elections on a country, it is more difficult to push constitutional liberalism on a society. The process of genuine liberalization and democratization, in which an election is only one step, is gradual and long-term. Recognizing this, governments and nongovernmental organizations are increasingly promoting a wide array of measures designed to bolster constitutional liberalism in developing countries. The National Endowment for Democracy promotes free markets, independent labor movements, and political parties. The U.S. Agency for International Development funds independent judiciaries. In the end, however, elections trump everything. If a country holds elections, Washington and the world will tolerate a great deal from the resulting government, as they did with Russia's Boris Yeltsin, Kyrgystan's Askar Akayev, and Argentina's Carlos Menem. In an age of images and symbols, elections are easy to capture on film. But how do you televise the rule of law? Yet there is life after elections, especially for the people who live there.

Conversely, the absence of free and fair elections should be viewed as one flaw, not the definition of tyranny. Elections are an important virtue of governance, but they are not the only virtue. It is more important that governments be judged by yardsticks related to constitutional liberalism. Economic, civil, and religious liberties are at the core of human autonomy and dignity. If a government with limited democracy steadily expands these freedoms, it should not be branded a dictatorship. Despite the limited political choice they offer, countries such as Singapore, Malaysia, Jordan, and Morocco provide a better environment for the life, liberty, and happiness of their citizens than do the dictatorships in Iraq and Libya or the illiberal democracies of Venezuela, Russia, or Ghana. And the pressures of global capitalism can push the process of liberalization forward as they have in China. Markets and morals can work together.

The most difficult task economically is reforming the trust-fund states. It has proved nearly impossible to wean them of their easy money. In 2002 the World Bank began experimenting with a potentially pathbreaking model in the central African country of Chad. Chad has major oil fields, but foreign companies were wary of major investments to extract and transport the oil because of the country's history of political instability. The World Bank agreed to step in, bless the project, and loan the government money to partner with a multinational consortium—led by ExxonMobil—to get the oil flowing. But it also put in place certain conditions. Chad's parliament had to pass a law guaranteeing that 80 percent of the oil revenues would be spent on health, education, and rural infrastructure, 5 percent would be spent on locals near the oil fields, and 10 percent would be put into an escrow account for future generations. That leaves the government 5 percent to spend as it wishes. To ensure that the system works in practice as well as in theory, the bank required that all oil revenues be deposited in an offshore account that is managed by an independent oversight committee (made up of some of Chad's leading citizens). It is too soon to tell if this model works, but if it does, it could be copied elsewhere. Even in countries that do not need the World Bank's help, it could have a demonstration effect. The Chad model provides a method by which natural-resource revenues can become a blessing for countries rather than the curse they currently are.

Finally, we need to revive constitutionalism. One effect of the overemphasis on pure democracy is that little effort is given to creating imaginative constitutions for transitional countries. Constitutionalism, as it was understood by its greatest eighteenth-century exponents, such as Montesquieu and Madison, is a complicated system of checks and balances designed to prevent the accumulation of power and the abuse of office. This is accomplished not by simply writing up a list of rights but by constructing a system in which government will not violate those rights. Various groups must be included and empowered because, as Madison explained, "ambition must be made to counteract ambition."

Constitutions were also meant to tame the passions of the public, creating not simply democratic but also deliberative government. The South African constitution is an example of an unusually crafted, somewhat undemocratic structure. It secures power for minorities, both those regionally based such as the Zulus and those that are dispersed, such as the whites. In doing so it has increased that country's chances of success as a democracy, despite its poverty and harrowing social catastrophes.

Unfortunately, the rich variety of unelected bodies, indirect voting, federal arrangements, and checks and balances that characterized so many of the formal and informal constitutions of Europe are now regarded with suspicion. What could be called the Weimar syndrome—named after interwar Germany's beautifully constructed constitution, which nevertheless failed to avert fascism—has made people regard constitutions as simply paperwork that cannot make much difference (as if any political system in Germany would have easily weathered military defeat, social revolution, the Great Depression, and hyperinflation). Procedures that inhibit direct democracy are seen as inauthentic, muzzling the voice of the people. Today around the world we see variations on the same majoritarian theme. But the trouble with these winner-take-all systems is that, in most democratizing countries, the winner really does take all.

Of course, cultures vary, and different societies will require different frameworks of government. This is a plea not for the wholesale adoption of any one model of government but rather for a more variegated conception of liberal democracy, one that emphasizes both words in that phrase. Genuine democracy is a fragile system that balances not just these two but other forces—what Tocqueville called "intermediate associations"—to create, in the end, a majestic clockwork. Understanding this system requires an intellectual task of recovering the constitutional liberal tradition, central to the Western experience and to the development of good government throughout the world.

This recovery will be incomplete if we limit it in our minds to what is happening in faraway countries that are troubled and poor and utterly different from the prosperous, democratic West. Democracy is a work in progress, abroad as well as at home. The tension between democracy and liberalism is one that flourished in the West's own past. In a very different form, it still exists and is growing in the Western world. It is most widely prevalent in one country in particular: the United States of America.

## CHAPTER 5

# Too Much of a Good Thing

THEY SAY THAT money can't buy happiness, but you would think $5 trillion would make a dent. In the last quarter-century the United States has added just that amount to its real gross domestic product,[1] and yet every survey and measure that psychologists use suggests that Americans are no happier than they were twenty-five years ago. Not only is the country richer, it is in better shape in almost every way. Most Americans barely remember how broken their country seemed in the early 1970s. Battered by the humiliation of Vietnam, it was struggling with stagflation, oil crises, race riots, and rising crime. But over the next two decades, the U.S. economy boomed almost uninterruptedly,* per capita income rose by 50 percent, crime declined, race relations improved, cities began thriving again, and every component of the so-called misery index dropped. Internationally the change was even more dramatic. By the

---

*Of course there were recessions and business downturns during this period, but in historical perspective the 1980s and 1990s will be remembered as a long period of peacetime expansion. Even median incomes, which had stagnated during the 1970s and 1980s, rose during the 1990s for every group of Americans, from the very rich to the very poor.

early 1990s the Cold War was won, communism was destroyed, socialism discredited, and America towered above the world politically, economically, militarily, and culturally. You would think that such success would cheer anyone up.

Except that Americans don't quite see it that way. Despite progress on all these fronts, they think that something has gone fundamentally wrong with their country—specifically, with their political system. Simply put, most Americans have lost faith in their democracy. If you examine what lies underneath America's disquiet, you will find that the troubles of American democracy are similar to those being experienced by countries across the globe. The democratic wave has hit America hard, perhaps harder than any other Western country. Founded as a republic that believed in a balance between the will of the majority and the rights of the minority—or, more broadly, between liberty and democracy—America is increasingly embracing a simple-minded populism that values popularity and openness as the key measures of legitimacy. This ideology has necessitated the destruction of old institutions, the undermining of traditional authority, and the triumph of organized interest groups, all in the name of "the people." The result is a deep imbalance in the American system, more democracy but less liberty.

A foreigner might think it odd to be told that the world's most powerful democracy is experiencing a crisis of faith, but it is. If this sounds extreme, consider the simplest and most compelling statistic, the decline in trust toward the nation's capital, the symbol of its political system. In the early 1960s the vast majority of Americans—more than 70 percent—agreed with the statement, "You can trust government in Washington to do what is right all or most of the time." After thirty years of slippage, that number is now close to thirty percent. Survey respondents did show increased trust in Washington right after September 11, 2001: a Gallup poll in October 2001 found 60 percent trusting Washington all or most of the time, but that figure returned to pre–September 11 levels by June of 2002. Even with the renewed sense of urgency that the battle against terrorism has evoked, there is little prospect that the "trust numbers" will return to the levels of the 1940s, 1950s, and 1960s. It's not just that one statistic. Responses to the statement "Public officials don't care what people like me think" show virtually the same spiral downward since 1960. The Harris poll's "Alienation Index" went from an average of 34 percent in the 1960s to an average of 63 percent in the 1990s. And on and on. Every measure of public trust points in the same dismal direction.[2]

Voting levels (in presidential elections) have dropped almost 20 percent since 1960. The decline is even more dramatic among whites because there has been a surge in African American voting since the 1960s, when the Jim Crow laws that disenfranchised Southern blacks were dismantled. And this decline has occurred even though the last two decades have seen strenuous efforts to get people to vote through "motor-voter laws."[3] Some argue that low voter turnouts are a sign of contentment, so don't worry, be happy. But that would imply that when turnout rates were higher in the past—say, in the 1950s—people were in a revolutionary mood, which is not true. In any event, whatever the virtues of voting, such a serious decline is worth exploring.

Voting is not only the one universal act of citizenship in a free society but also one of the least demanding. All you have to do is show up at a polling booth every few years. Other civic duties requiring greater commitment—such as membership in a political party or on a school council—have collapsed even more sharply. Using an impressive array of data, the political scientist Robert Putnam calculated that engagement in public and civic affairs generally has declined by 40 percent since the middle 1960s.[4]

Disenchantment with their political system is palpable in the way Americans vote, respond to public opinion polls, write letters to the editor, talk on television, and indeed express themselves anywhere in any form. Consider the titles of some of the more important studies of American politics during the roaring 1990s: *Why Americans Hate Politics; Slouching toward Gomorrah; Arrogant Capital; The Betrayal of Democracy; Democracy on Trial; Running Scared; Dirty Politics; Demosclerosis.* There are literally dozens more, all just as gloomy about the state of American democracy. The former president of Harvard University, Derek Bok, titled his recent comprehensive study of American democracy *The Trouble with Government.* Even after September 11, the spate of new patriotism has tended to celebrate the country, its ideals, its people, but rarely its politics or political system. If anything, many of the tracts continue the now-established tradition of establishment-bashing. When you consider that public attitudes toward government have shifted from positive to negative during three decades of extraordinary economic growth and social stability, the puzzle deepens, and it becomes difficult not to conclude that something has gone seriously wrong with American democracy.

Explanations for this plunge. Some blame it on Vietnam and Watergate, others on government's ever-expanding appetite, still others on the decline in the quality of politicians. Yet a careful study by scholars at Harvard's Kennedy School of Government concluded that none of the usual suspects was guilty, at least not wholly guilty.[5] For example, although Vietnam and Watergate obviously cast a shadow on the government, the decline in public attitudes began before the Vietnam War turned sour and continued well after Vietnam and Watergate had faded from memory. Similar, but smaller, declines in public trust have taken place in most countries in the industrialized world, so the cause of this phenomenon is unlikely to be uniquely American (like Watergate). As for the rise of big government, although the number of employees and agencies in Washington expanded greatly during the 1960s and early 1970s, as a percentage of the total economy the federal government has stayed roughly the same size for almost a quarter of a century now. The biggest growth in government came from the expansion of entitlements such as Social Security and Medicare, which are wildly popular.

Let us begin by keeping in mind that the World War II era and its aftermath were periods of unusual patriotism, cooperation, and civic spirit. All institutions—family, church, even corporations—have declined in standing from their lofty 1950s peaks. This trend is part of a broad movement away from the stable, collective order of the post–World War II era and toward a fast-paced, competitive, individualistic society with a distrust of hierarchy and stability. Despite a genuine revival of patriotism, September 11 will not alter this long-term shift.

The idea that the quality of political leadership has declined since those halcyon days occupies a powerful place in the public imagination. A scholar in his eighties put it to me eloquently: "In my youth, when I looked toward Washington, I saw world historical figures—Roosevelt, Marshall, Eisenhower, MacArthur, Truman, Acheson. Today I see Richard Gephardt, Dennis Hastert, and George W. Bush." (We were having lunch in the paneled dining room of one of New York City's grand clubs, a perfect setting for misty nostalgia.) But his youth, in the 1930s and 1940s, was dominated by the Great Depression and World War II. Difficult times bring out great leaders. In fact, they bring out the best in most of us. Consider how September 11 transformed George W. Bush and much of the country. The much-celebrated "greatest generation" of Americans came of age in times that called for sustained service and sacrifice. Today's war against terrorism echoes those calls for sacrifice, but for most Americans it has not required much in the way of actual service—yet. Those who were called on to perform—Mayor Rudolph Giuliani, the police officers and firefighters of New York City, the Rangers in Afghanistan—performed heroically.

From a broader historical perspective, the notion that today's politicians are any worse than the norm is silly. Few people pine for the good old days when Rutherford B. Hayes or Millard Fillmore was president. Through most of its history, America's politicians have been normal, competitive creatures trying to survive and flourish within the system. When he was president of Harvard, Bok asked the longtime Speaker of the House of Representatives, Thomas P.

O'Neill, if he thought the quality of people elected to Congress over thirty years had gotten better or worse. "Tip" thought for a minute and replied, "The quality is clearly better, much better. But the results are definitely worse." During his quixotic run for the presidency, the bizarre billionaire Ross Perot said something similar about his experiences in dealing with Washington. "Good people, bad system," he observed.

So what has made the system decline? The timing of the shift in public trust is an important clue. Why do public attitudes turn around the middle 1960s and keep sinking? One big change began during this period and has continued unabated: the democratization of politics. It might seem strange to speak of the democratization of a democracy, but the phenomenon is best described by that phrase. Since the 1960s most aspects of American politics—political parties, legislatures, administrative agencies, and even courts—have opened themselves up to greater public contact and influence in a conscious effort to become more democratic in structure and spirit. And curiously, more than any other, this change seems to coincide with the decline in standing of these very institutions.

This is not how most Americans see the issue. Their complaint is often couched in precisely the opposite language: "Nobody listens to people like me." There is truth in these observations, in the sense that organized groups—special interests—now run Washington, but what Americans often do not realize is that this is a direct consequence of the changes of the last few decades. The more open a system becomes, the more easily it can be penetrated by money, lobbyists, and fanatics. What has changed in Washington is not that politicians have closed themselves off from the American people and are unwilling to hear their pleas. It is that they do scarcely anything but listen to the American people.

Washington today is organized around the pursuit of public opinion. It employs armies of people to continually check the pulse of the American people on every conceivable matter. It hires others to determine the intensity of their feelings on these issues. It pays still others to guess what people might think tomorrow. Lobbyists, activists, consultants, and politicians all use this information as the basis for their actions. And through this whole process everyone keeps praising the wisdom, courage, rectitude, and all-round greatness of the American people.

The only reassuring aspect of this sorry spectacle is that, as the pandering has gone up, the public's attitude toward politicians has gone down. During World War II, Britain's prime minister, Winston Churchill, was advised by a colleague in Parliament to "keep his ear to the ground." He responded by pointing out that "the British nation will find it very hard to look up to leaders who are detected in this position." The American people have watched their leaders bow and scrape before them for the last three decades—and they are repulsed by it. Perhaps they sense that this is not what democracy is all about.

## Indirect Democracy

Democracy in America—as in most of the Western world—has historically been one element of a complex political structure. Within a democratic framework, the United States has a rich diversity of institutions and processes, many of which, as we saw in Chapter 1, precede democracy and are distinctly undemocratic. The most obvious example is the court system, where enormous power is exercised by unelected men and women with life tenure. But a rich array of nongovernmental institutions and political parties also mediates between the individual and the state. And most of these institutions, until recently, were organized undemocratically. Take political parties, in which candidates and platforms were chosen by tightly controlled party hierarchies (a system now characterized solely by the image of the "smoke-filled room," the worst possible insult in our health-conscious times). Parties, of course, needed to appeal to the public, so they assembled their candidates and platforms with that in mind. But the selection of candidates was done internally before going to the public for approval. Legislatures also used to function in a hierarchical and closed manner. Representatives and senators met in committees to trade, barter, and compromise on issues. Their votes on the final bill were public, but the internal committee votes and discussions were secret. The idea was to let these institutions function— and then have the public render a judgment on the results.

A legislature best represents the idea of indirect democracy. The American people choose who will legislate for them; they do not themselves write or pass bills. For precisely this reason James Madison, author of the Constitution, did not really regard America as a democracy. Democracies were governed directly, through popular assemblies, like the city states of ancient Greece—which Madison and many other American founders regarded as turbulent, illiberal, and unstable. For Madison, America was better termed a republic, in which the citizenry delegates the task of governing to its representatives. In the founders' views, representative, republican democracy provided the right balance of popular control and deliberative decision-making.

Many of the great theorists of democracy would have agreed. The most famous expression of the Madisonian view comes from an Englishman, the Whig politician and philosopher Edmund Burke, who famously told his constituents in Bristol during a campaign, "Your representative owes you, not his industry only, but his judgment; and he betrays instead of serving you if he sacrifices it to your opinion. . . . You choose a member indeed; but when you have chosen him, he is not a member of Bristol, but he is a Member of Parliament."[6]

In 1956 Senator John Kennedy published a book, *Profiles in Courage*, in which he praised eight American statesmen for their principled embrace of unpopular positions. Kennedy dismissed the notion that as a senator his job was simply to mirror his constituents' positions:

[Such] a view assumes that the people of Massachusetts sent me to Washington to serve merely as a seismograph to record shifts in public opinion. . . . The voters selected us because they had confidence in our judgment and our ability to exercise judgment from a position where we could determine what were their own best interests, as part of the nation's interests. This may mean that we must on occasion lead, inform, correct, and sometimes even ignore public opinion for which we were elected.

Whether or not Kennedy practiced what he preached, the more important point is that the book was instantly venerated. It won the Pulitzer Prize and became a best-seller. Today such views probably would still be praised but would also be regarded with amusement as quaint expressions of a world gone by. When he was retiring from the Senate, Bill Bradley recalled that by the end of his career, if a politician adopted a policy without regard for its popularity, he was considered not brave but stupid: "It meant you didn't understand politics." Over the last thirty years the Senate has been populated by many decent and honorable people. But they are politicians, not saints. They must survive and flourish within the political system, and that system has changed radically in recent years. That is why so many of the best in the Senate have left voluntarily in the last decade. Almost all of them have left saying that the political system has gotten out of control. Ironically, for all their wisdom most of these men and women voted for the changes that turned American politics into the hyper-responsive, poll-driven system that it has become. They did so under the banner of democracy, in a classic case of good intentions gone haywire.

## Open for Business

The late 1960s and early 1970s were a time of attacks on much more than the old political parties. Not since the Great Depression had the basic legitimacy of the American system been under such an assault. From the civil rights movement through Vietnam, Watergate, and the "long, hot summer" of urban violence, many Americans challenged the very premises of their government. As the revolutionary fervor subsided by the early 1970s, scholars and politicians began to discuss ways to address the critics. If the system were not fixed, many feared, it would lose its basic legitimacy. And fixing, as is often the case in America, meant democratizing.

Congress, the most responsive branch of government, was among the first to change. Considered—with reason—too closed and hier-archical, beginning in 1970, it transformed the way it did business, moving power out of the hands of the leadership into the entire body of members. It opened itself up to greater scrutiny and made itself more accountable in various ways. It changed the laws govern-ing campaign contributions. In sum, it democratized itself and thus the American political system.

Three decades later, almost everyone associated with these reforms—politicians, journalists, activists, scholars—believe that they have made matters worse. "We were going to reform the system. But we created more problems than we solved," said Senator Joseph Biden, who entered the House in 1973. "The campaign finance laws, the Indepen-dent Counsel statute—nothing turned out the way it was supposed to." The old system was far from perfect. The Senate, at its oligarchical worst, was the principal obstacle to civil rights legislation for almost a century. But the new system has crippling problems of its own.

The House of Representatives' class of 1974—the Watergate babies—democratized the method of choosing committee chairs, using internal party elections rather than seniority. Committee chairs' powers were also curtailed. For example, whereas once they could refuse to even consider legislation proposed by subcommittees, they were now required to do so. The number of subcommittees was expanded almost 50 percent, to give all members opportunities to leg-islate. The rules were also changed to allow unlimited numbers of new bills and amendments, coming from any member of the House, whether or not he or she was on the relevant committee. To allow this more democratic system to work, congressional staffs grew by almost 50 percent during the 1970s. Moreover, they were now appointed by (and therefore beholden to) individual members, not committee chairs.

From an institution dominated by 20 or so powerful leaders, Congress has evolved into a collection of 535 independent political entrepreneurs who run the system with their individual interests uppermost—i.e., to get re-elected. By any measure—bills, amendments, suspension bills—the system is far more responsive to each individual member's whim. It is also far more responsive to nonmembers. Among the most consequential reforms of the 1970s was the move toward open committee meetings and recorded votes. Committee chairs used to run meetings at which legislation was "marked up" behind closed doors. Only members and a handful of senior staff were present. By 1973 not only were the meetings open to anyone, but every vote was formally recorded. Before this, in voting on amendments members would walk down aisles for the ayes and nays. The final count would be recorded but not the stand of each individual member. Now each member has to vote publicly on every amendment. The purpose of these changes was to make Congress more open and responsive. And so it has become—to money, lobbyists, and special interests.

Most Americans have neither the time, the interest, nor the inclination to monitor Congress on a day-to-day basis. But lobbyists and activists do, and they can use the information and access to ensure that the groups they represent are well taken care of in the federal budget and the legal code. This is true not only for lobbies that want money. On any number of issues, from tort law to American policy toward Cuba to quotas, well-organized interest groups—no matter how small their constituencies—can ensure that government bends to their will. Reforms designed to produce majority rule have produced minority rule.

Robert Packwood, who served in the Senate from 1969 until his ouster in 1995, recalled that the reforms made it far more difficult for members to vote on the merits of a bill.

Most members genuinely want[ed] to do what they thought was in the national interest if they could. That wasn't always easy to do, however. But it was easier to do before the passage of the Sunshine laws [which required that public business be conducted in the open].

When an interest group came in, you would say, "Gosh darn, I tried to support you. I really did. The chairman bent my arm." Then, to protect yourself, you would tell the chairman that when those guys came in, to tell them that you really fought hard on their issue.

But once lobbyists knew your every vote, they used it as ammunition. Former senator Dale Bumpers pointed out that

> these groups developed very harsh methods of dealing with those who crossed them. Suddenly every vote began to have political consequences. Congress began to finesse the tough issues and tended to straddle every fence it couldn't burrow under. . . . It isn't that these groups don't have a legitimate interest but they distort the process by wrangling over the smallest issues, leaving Congress paralyzed, the public disgusted, and the outcome a crapshoot.[7]

One of the few instances in recent memory when Congress withstood special-interest pressure—and tons of it—was in 1986 when it passed, with strong bipartisan support, sweeping tax reforms that eliminated hundreds of loopholes and hidden subsidies. One of its architects, former representative Dan Rostenkowski, who was chairman of the House Ways and Means Committee, argued that it was possible only because he insisted on closed hearings during the markup of the bill. "It's not that you want to ignore the public. It's just that the lobbyists, the pressure groups, the trade associations—they all have their pet projects. If you put something together in public, the Members are looking over at the lobbyists and the lobbyists are giving the 'yes' and 'no' signs."*

---

*Of course, after the markup sessions, the lobbying began in full force, though with limited effect. The political scientist James Thurber remembers watching the lobbyists with their cell phones at a congressional hearing on the 1986 tax reform: "They started dialing the instant anyone in that room even thought about changing a tax break. Their calls alerted interested parties and brought a deluge of protest borne by phone, letter or fax. There is no buffer allowing Representatives to think about what's going on. In the old days you had a few months or weeks, at least a few days. Now you may have a few seconds before the wave hits."

## Frozen in the Past

As the U.S. government has become larger and more open, groups that petition it—lobbyists—have become Washington's greatest growth industry. As with all the other changes relating to this topic, the expansion of lobbying began in the 1960s and has continued ever since. In the mid-1950s there were 5,000 registered lobbyists in Washington; they doubled by 1970, then doubled again by 1990. Like a never-ending spiral, every new piece of proposed legislation generates new lobbies designed to procure or protect some slice of the federal budget. Jonathan Rauch, one of the best journalists in Washington, reported that in 1979 there were 117 health groups in Washington. By 1993, with President Bill Clinton proposing sweeping changes in this area, that number had jumped sevenfold. Of course, even after Clinton's health-care bill failed, almost all the new groups stayed on, pressuring Congress on their pet issues.

In his important book *Demosclerosis*, Rauch applies and extends the insights of the economist Mancur Olson to argue that the rise of interest groups has made American government utterly dysfunctional. Washington is unable to trim back—let alone eliminate—virtually any government program, no matter how obviously obsolete. The classic example Rauch provides is the mohair subsidy.* In 1954, wool was deemed a "vital strategic commodity" because of its use in military uniforms. As a result the government subsidized wool producers, providing over $100 million in handouts to ranchers, 1 percent of whom got half the total subsidy. Like most of these kinds of subsidies, this one did not really work and made the industry less efficient. But that is only the beginning of the story. Six years later synthetic fibers such as Dacron had knocked wool off the Pentagon's strategic commodities list. But the wool lobby got to work and convinced Congress to keep the money flowing. Three decades later, a

*Mohair is a kind of wool, from Angora goats.

subsidy that had lost all justification for its existence in 1960 was still fully intact. Finally, in 1993 Congress, embarrassed by this highly publicized piece of wasteful spending, killed the program. But it could not kill the lobby. In a few years the lobby's hard work paid off and, to no one's surprise, the mohair subsidy is back. It is smaller and has to be renewed every year, but that does not seem to bother the wool lobbyists. After all, it gives them something to do.

Multiply this example by 100,000 and you have some sense of why American government has become, in Rauch's words, "a giant frozen mass of ossified programs trapped in a perpetual cash crunch." The mohair subsidy is in one sense an atypical example because it did finally get killed and then trimmed. Cotton growers have been more effective. There are only 25,000 cotton growers in the United States, with an average net worth of $800,000. They receive $2 billion in government subsidies. Most government programs are now eternal. Maritime subsidies have been in place for more than 200 years, even though the Pentagon now owns and operates its own fleet. Agricultural subsidies, put in place as a temporary relief measure during the Great Depression, are so intricate and absurd that farmers are paid to grow crops and then destroy them. In a recent act of bipartisanship, the free-market administration of President George W. Bush and the fiscally responsible Congress voted to expand these subsidies substantially, despite budgetary and trade pressures to cut them.

Lobbies have existed for most of American history in some form or another, and presidents from Grover Cleveland to Calvin Coolidge have railed against them. Their explosion in number and effectiveness since the early 1960s is in part due to government's becoming so much bigger in the last three or four decades; the money to be made through effective lobbying has increased enormously. Equally important, Congress can now be monitored and influenced as never before. As a result, lobbies, which do most of the monitoring and influencing, have gained power compared with the target of their efforts— the government.

Whether you are a liberal or a conservative this condition should dismay you. For conservatives it means that the goal of reducing federal spending has become a hopeless cause. Since the early 1980s, three Republican presidents (Ronald Reagan, George H. W. Bush, and George W. Bush), one Republican Speaker (Newt Gingrich), and one Democratic president (Bill Clinton) have tried to pare down government spending. But they bumped up against the reality of interest-group power. As a result, in eight years Reagan was able to close exactly four government programs of any note. David Stockman, Reagan's budget director who was messianic about the need to rationalize the federal budget, concluded in despair that, by 1984, "the Reagan White House was nearly bereft of any consistent anti-spending policy principles." On succeeding Reagan in 1989, Bush senior tried a different tactic and proposed killing 246 smaller programs. The savings would have been tiny: about $3.5 billion, or .25 percent of federal spending. Still, he turned out to be far too ambitious. Once Congress was through with his proposals, only eight programs were killed, amounting to a grand savings of $58 million. Similarly Clinton's landmark budget deal of 1994 killed forty-one small programs, totaling .01 percent of the federal budget.

The 1994 Republican revolution was the critical test of Rauch's theory. Newt Gingrich and his freshman horde came to power on a platform dedicated to changing the way Washington worked and, specifically, to killing wasteful subsidies. Four years later, the Republican revolution was in shambles. Gingrich had resigned as Speaker and even as a member of the House. Once the most powerful politician in America, he is now an analyst for Fox News. And although he certainly made many political errors, Gingrich and the Republicans found that changing Washington was not nearly as easy as it had seemed.

The Republicans began in 1995 with a budget proposal that would have eliminated about 300 programs, mostly "corporate welfare," saving more than $15 billion. Then the lobbying began. Constituencies for every item of "wasteful spending" in the federal budget began fighting for their lives—or rather their livelihoods. By contrast, few people flooded congressional offices with faxes urging them to trim spending. It turned out that most Americans wanted smaller government in the abstract, but they were not the ones calling their Congressmen. The beneficiaries of government subsidies did so, however—and in droves. A few months later the Republicans ended up passing a budget with total reductions of $1.5 billion, only one-tenth of what they had planned, and totaling only .001 percent of the overall budget. Since then, Congress has fared little better, having saved the government a couple of billion dollars (out of a $1.8 trillion federal budget). When unexpected economic growth produced record-level surpluses, people began to believe that controlling spending was unnecessary. In the new economy, money would just pour into government coffers. George W. Bush came into office in 2000 with two fiscal promises: to cut taxes and to cut spending. As ever, it proved easier to deliver on the first than on the second. Since he took office, spending has shot up as a percentage of GDP, even when the post–September 11 increased defense spending is excluded. The federal government spent, in the first two years of the Bush presidency, more than it spent in the first five years of the Clinton presidency. "They said it would starve the beast," said Kevin Hassett of the American Enterprise Institute about the Bush tax cut, "but we have a hungry beast who is somehow finding food anyway."[8]

For liberals this failure means that spending real money on new problems or opportunities in America has become close to impossible. Raising taxes is not an option because, when you add in state, local, and payroll taxes, Americans believe (not unreasonably) that they are overtaxed. Thus, every dollar that goes to subsidize the production of mohair or the study of asparagus competitiveness (another federal grant) is in effect one less dollar for education, food stamps, or new infrastructure. Moreover, since everybody understands that new programs never die, the threshold for creating them gets higher and higher. Franklin Roosevelt believed that government should engage in "bold and persistent experimentation." But, as Rauch pointed out, in his day—with only a handful of interest groups banging at his door—Roosevelt could start so many new programs because he could also shut down those that did not work. In today's government, trial and error becomes impossible because the errors get set in stone. The federal government gets frozen into its role as perpetual defender of the status quo. The industries, problems, and opportunities of the future do not have lobbies; those of the past do.

When government seems unable to apply any kind of reason or logic to its priorities and spending, people lose faith in its ability to solve new problems. One of the most significant changes in the past few decades has been the widespread belief among the young that effective social change can best come from outside the government, through nongovernmental organizations, think tanks, the press, or even private business. Government in America today is seen as a cumbersome dinosaur, trapped by its history and unable to respond to the problems of tomorrow. Is it any wonder that bright, young, energetic people shy away from it?

Rauch himself is resigned to the belief that "the American government probably has evolved into about what it will remain: a sprawling, largely self-organizing structure that is 10% to 20% under the control of the politicians and voters and 80% to 90% under the control of the countless thousands of client groups. It will change only at the margins, in ways that generally accord with the clients' wishes, but not systematically or in ways that threaten more than a few clients' franchises." This is the heart of America's dilemma today. The American people believe that they have no real control over government. What they do not realize is that the politicians have no control, either. Most representatives and senators believe that they operate in a political system in which any serious attempts at change produce instant, well-organized opposition from the small minority who are hurt by the change. And it is these minorities who really run Washington.

## The Mischiefs of Faction

That small, dedicated minorities would hijack politics worried the American founders greatly. Identifying precisely this problem, which he called "the mischiefs of faction," Madison blamed it for "the instability, injustice, and confusion . . . [that] have, in truth, been the mortal diseases under which popular governments have everywhere perished." In his famous essay, Federalist Paper 51, he argued that the only effective solution to this problem would be to curtail the freedom of association and expression that allow such groups to form ("Liberty is to faction what air is to fire"). But the cure would be worse than the disease, and Madison quickly rejected it.

Instead Madison placed his faith in the size and complexity of America. First, he argued, factions that were minorities would not be able to have their way because the other factions—outnumbering the minority—would rise and thwart them. Even if the factions were strong, in the vast and variegated country that was America competing factions would spring up and they would all cancel each other out. Alas, on this crucial point Madison was wrong. Perhaps he did not imagine that government would ever have such large coffers that it would attract droves of fanatically self-interested groups. But there is also a theoretical problem with Madison's reasoning. Olson has pointed out that it is much easier for narrow interest groups to form, since their members stand to gain much and the rest of the country loses little. This is part of what he terms "the logic of collective action." If a group of 100 farmers got together to petition the government to give them $10 million, the benefit to each farmer is $100,000. The cost to the rest of the country is about 4 cents per person. Who is more likely to form a lobby, them or us? Multiply this example by thousands and you understand the central problem of American democracy today.

Also, factions do not in fact cancel each other out. Most interest groups are happy to see others flourish. When asked whether he would favor cutting his competitors' subsidies, Bog Bergland of the National Rural Electric Cooperative said, "We think a good argument can be made for more support of all sides."[9] It helps the argument of any one group to point out that other groups are being funded—so why discriminate against them? The more the merrier. After all, it is easier to get a special tax loophole for yourself if you advocate them for others as well. As a result, government policy has become not the sum of interest groups canceling each other out and arriving at a rational mean, as Madison posited, but rather the accumulation of giveaways, one after the other in a ruinous downward spiral. It is the path of least resistance, in politics, that is the road most often taken.

This holds true even for policies that do not involve money. Consider the U.S. policy toward Cuba. Ten years after the end of the Cold War, two things should be obvious. First, Cuban communism no longer poses even the remotest geopolitical threat to the U.S. Second, however much we may disdain Fidel Castro's abuse of human rights, imposing economic isolation through sanctions clearly only tightens his grip on the country by giving him something to mobilize his people against. As historical experience shows, the best thing we can do to push Cuba along on the road to liberal democracy is open it up to the world of commerce and contact. And a substantial majority of Americans agree with this approach. It is how the United States dealt with two other communist regimes, China and Vietnam. So why not Cuba? The answer is faction. Anti-Castro Cuban Americans have controlled the issue because they are more determined about it than anyone else and live in two electorally significant states, Florida and New Jersey. Although a majority of Americans may have a different opinion, only Cuban Americans organize, donate, and vote on it. Thus a handful of Americans in two states have been able to dictate American foreign policy. As with other issues on which a vocal minority overwhelms a silent majority, the cost to the public interest is small. But it adds up.

The chief institution that until relatively recently stood as a buffer between such groups and politicians was the political party. Strong political parties could mediate between various interest groups and, by bringing them all under a general umbrella, force a position that reflected the breadth of feeling in the party as a whole. These positions could change, but any changes would have to be negotiated within the party, where trade-offs were discussed and where the more general interests of the party were considered. That is why Clinton Rossiter, the eminent scholar of American politics, opined, as quoted before, "No America without democracy, no democracy without politics, no politics without parties." Of course, this is not always how they functioned, but for more than two centuries parties did very well at channeling public passions and interests into a workable system of democratic politics. And they could do so in the future as America proceeds through the big technological, economic, and demographic changes that are upon us—except for the fact that political parties do not really exist in America anymore.

## The Decline of Parties

In December 2000, a few days after the Florida recount battles had ended, I asked George Stephanopoulos, the broadcast journalist and former political strategist, whether he thought the Democratic Party would nominate former vice president Al Gore to run for president in 2004. The newspapers that week had been full of speculation that leading figures in the party wanted to dump Gore. Stephanopoulos's answer was clarifying: "There is no Democratic Party," he said. "If Gore wants to run, he has to raise the money, get good publicity, and move up in the polls, which will get him more money and better press. What party elders think is irrelevant because there is no party anymore. Those who style themselves as 'elders' are just old pols looking for something to do."

Political parties have no real significance in America today. Over the last generation the parties have become so open and decentralized that nobody controls them. The machines and their bosses, the party organization, the volunteer cadres, and party elders have all withered in significance. The party is, at most, a fund-raising vehicle for a telegenic candidate. If a candidate is popular and wins the nomination, the party becomes supportive. That candidate then benefits slightly by getting more resources, organizational support, and new lists of potential donors. In fact, primary candidates find it useful to run against the party establishment. It gives their campaigns freshness and the appeal of the underdog battling the machine—an approach that worked for George McGovern, Ronald Reagan, and Jimmy Carter. Today, however, this strategy is more difficult because there is no longer an establishment to run against. Who was the Democratic establishment's candidate in 1992? Bill Clinton, Bob Kerry, or Paul Tsongas? None of the above.* The success of George W. Bush was due not to his being the candidate of the establishment but to his being the candidate of his family; he had the two things you need in a partyless system—name recognition and a fund-raising machine. Anyone who has both, whether they have any experience in politics or not, is now at a huge advantage. Thus, in this new, more "democratic" system, we have seen many more political dynasties, celebrity officials, and billionaire politicians than before. And this is only the beginning. As the political party declines further, being rich and/or famous will become the routine path to high elected office.

For most of American history, presidential candidates were reflections of their political parties. Today, parties are reflections of their candidates. If the candidate moves to the center, the party moves to the center. If the candidate bucks left, the party bucks left. Once Clinton was elected as a "New Democrat" it became difficult to find any old Democrats in Washington. And when George W. Bush announced that he was a compassionate conservative, the rest of the Republican Party discovered that was what they had been all along.

*The exception that proves this rule is Senator Robert Dole, who was granted the Republican nomination in 1996 almost as a gift for his years of service to the party.

The political party today is an empty vessel, waiting to be filled by a popular leader.

The bullet that killed the American political party was the primary election. Parties exist to compete in general elections. So choosing a candidate is the most important decision a party makes. Once that process was taken out of the hands of the party organization and given over to the voter, the party organization became a shell. That is why no political parties in other democracies have abdicated their involvement in selecting candidates. The primary is a uniquely American and recent phenomenon. Why and how it emerged is an interesting story. But to say that the American political party was killed is inaccurate; it actually committed suicide.[10]

Direct primaries began cropping up in large numbers in the first quarter of the twentieth century, as part of the Progressive era's assault on corrupt party machines. ("Let voters not bosses decide!") They also appealed to the American desire for "more" democracy. But the first push toward primaries did not change the character of the party system. Between 1912 and 1968 the winner of the direct primaries became the party nominee only 10 out of 23 times (this excludes sitting presidents, who were always renominated by the party). In 1960 only 16 states held Democratic primaries and 15 held Republican primaries. Primary elections chose just 38 percent of the delegates to the national political convention. The active leadership of the party—elected officials, local and regional party bosses, and organizers—retained a majority of the votes and clout. Primaries existed as a way of testing a particular candidate's marketability to the general voter. When John Kennedy won West Virginia, he proved that a Catholic could fare well in the South. Estes Kefauver, however, won many of the primaries and was still denied the Democratic nomination in 1952 because Adlai Stevenson was favored by the party machine. Wendell Wilkie did not even enter the primaries in 1940 and yet was nominated by the Republican Party.

One of the persistent themes of the protests of the 1960s—in the civil rights movement, the Vietnam demonstrations, the chaos outside the 1968 Democratic convention in Chicago, and even at Wood-stock—was the need for more participatory politics. Seeking to respond to these demands, the Democratic Party decided to make itself more democratic: it fundamentally changed its method for picking candidates. The primary quickly replaced every other means of selecting delegates to the national convention, and by 1980 more than 70 percent of delegates were chosen in open primaries. The Republicans followed the Democrats' lead: by 1980, 75 percent of Republican delegates were chosen through primaries. Today that fig-ure is over 80 percent for both parties, and the remaining percentage usually votes for the person who wins the primaries. (In fact, it would be considered a scandal if these delegates-at-large were to exercise their judgment on the merits of the candidates.)

Primary voters do not constitute anything close to a majority of the party, let alone of the American people. (In the last presidential election, only 23 percent of registered voters voted in the pri-maries, roughly 18 percent of the voting-age population). As a result, the delegates to both party conventions tend to be more extreme than their average members. This stands to reason, since the delegates do not reflect the average party member but rather the average active, primary-voting party member. (Think of how many people you know who are active party volunteers and vote in all primaries.) For example, only 10 percent of Republican dele-gates in 2000 thought the budget surplus should be used to pre-serve Medicare and Social Security, compared to 46 percent of all Republican voters. Only 24 percent of Republican delegates thought soft money should be banned, even though 60 percent of voters thought it should. Similarly, only 10 percent of Democratic delegates supported school vouchers, while 41 percent of Demo-cratic voters did. Only 20 percent of Democratic delegates sup-ported the death penalty, while 46 percent of Democratic voters did.[11] Among both parties and across almost every issue the gulf between delegates and voters repeats itself. Ironically, the old elites were far more representative of the rank and file of the party—and the country—than are the professional activists of today. The new political "base" turns out to be very narrow.

Presidential elections are mainstream events, and the candidates chosen to compete in them invariably come from the political center. But other politicians are elected and influenced by their active primary electorate. Thus the parties reflect less of the ideas of their mainstream policy-makers and officials and more of the views of their strongest activist groups and organizers—the ones who mobilize votes during the primary. In that sense the "democratizing" reforms have not eliminated elites, just replaced them, and not demonstrably for the better. The old party was rooted in neighborhoods, local government, and broad-based organizations such as unions and business associations. The new party is dominated by Washington professionals—activists, ideologues, fund raisers, and pollsters. This is why Washington remains so much more polarized than the country at large, and why making deals and compromises across party lines has become so much harder. The political system today prefers deadlock to dealmaking; it's better for fund-raising.

## The Money Machine

The primary system produced the democratic paradox that recurs through the recent history of reforms, in which majority rule turns into minority rule. It reappears in the case of campaign finance reform. Finance reforms of the 1970s were supposed to make the system accessible to more people. Seeking to end politicians' reliance on a few large contributors, the new measures imposed a $1,000 per person limit on contributions to a single candidate. Political parties could contribute only $5,000 per candidate. They also provided for the formation of corporate political action committees (PACs), which allowed small contributors to pool their resources to advance a common policy objective. No single contribution to a PAC could exceed $5,000. Yet despite these reforms, PACs are now seen as symbols of everything that is wrong with America's present-day campaign finance system.

The democratization of campaign finance has changed the nature of American politics, and not for the better. Rather than being able to rely on a few large donors for cash—whose names were always well publicized and scrutinized—candidates must now raise money in small increments from tens of thousands of contributors and PACs, whose agendas are less well publicized and less scrutinized. And it has produced a new group of power brokers: fundraisers. As journalist and former White House speechwriter David Frum explained:

> With an individual-donor limit of $1,000 and a spending limit of $36 million, it no longer suffices to locate a few eccentric millionaires. A candidate must spend the now-all-important year before the primaries winning the support of thousands of affluent contributors. It's like filling a bathtub with a tablespoon. And since not even the most grimly determined candidate can woo so many people one by one, he or she must first win the support of the few hundred maestros of the Rolodex who have proved their ability and willingness to sponsor the fund-raising galas, cocktail parties, breakfast meetings, and intimate suppers necessary to extract the requisite quota of funds from each major region's check-writing Democrats and Republicans.[12]

As a result, raising money has become the fundamental activity of a political campaign, and performing well at a fundraiser the first, indispensable skill for a modern American politician. If there are party elders, they are now the "masters of the Rolodex," without whom no campaign can get off the ground. All these changes have contributed to the weakening of political parties. The most recent burst of campaign finance reform will only deepen that trend, since it weakens political parties even more. The only remaining currency that parties had was the so-called soft money that they could spend in support of a candidate. Now that money will be spent—

for it *will* be spent—not by parties but shadowy groups and organizations that are less public and less accountable. The masters of the Rolodex have become even more crucial to the political life of the country.

The most pernicious effect of these changes to the campaign finance system is that they have made politicians more vulnerable. Politicians should have a healthy fear of being voted out of office. That is what democracy is all about—up to a point. But today politicians have an obsessive, all-consuming, permanent paranoia about always being one step away from defeat. Having lost the umbrella support and cover of parties, American politicians "walk the electoral world alone," in British political scientist Anthony King's words. Candidates used to gain their strength from their standing within their parties, their substantive accomplishments, and their political skills with party elders. Now they gain it from their own entrepreneurial skills in polling, constituent service, managing special interests, and fund raising. But that also means that they are alone and always one misstep away from going bankrupt and thereby losing power. If they do something unpopular, the party no longer protects them, Congress no longer protects them, the media no longer protect them. As King wrote, "they can be picked off one by one; they know it; they adjust their behavior accordingly."[13]

The prospect of an election concentrates the mind of a politician. And American politicians are now single-mindedly focused on winning the next election to the exclusion of all else, not because they are worse human beings than their predecessors were but because the system pushes them in this direction. Hence the sad spectacle of modern American politics, in which politicians ceaselessly appease lobbies, poll voters, genuflect before special interests, and raise money. Of course this does not produce good government—quite the contrary—and so the search for good government continues. In America that means the search for "more" democracy, this time through referendums.

## Direct Democracy

The idea of taking government directly to the people is as old as the United States of America. Actually, older: the first referendum was held in 1640 in the Massachusetts Bay Colony. And throughout the late eighteenth and nineteenth centuries, federal and state constitutions were presented to the people for ratification. But once these constitutions were adopted, creating a system of government, referendums died out. Throughout the nineteenth century courts routinely ruled that referendums were unconstitutional, citing the long-established doctrine that once the people had delegated legislative powers, they could not selectively take them back—*delgeta postesta non potest delgari*. Representative democracy, in the nineteenth-century view, could not function if there were end runs around it.

All this changed, starting in South Dakota in 1898. The Gilded Age of the late nineteenth century produced great fortunes and firms. Big business—particularly the railroads—often had strong ties within state legislatures, creating a cozy relationship between money and politics. (Decades later, Americans were shocked to discover similar arrangements in the emerging economies of Asia and denounced them as crony capitalism.) Progressive reformers were appalled and frustrated by this well-entrenched corruption and decided to bypass the legislatures altogether, taking public policy directly to the people. They pushed through amendments to state constitutions that allowed for referendums, initiatives, and recalls—all designed to give the public the ability to override the power of the special interests who ran the legislatures. (The other important Progressive reform was the constitutional amendment establishing the direct election of senators, who until the early 1910s were elected by state legislatures.) Progressives believed that they would return politics to a purer, uncorrupted state, since the common man, and not the wealthy few, would rule. At the heart of these reforms, the historian Richard Hofstadter wrote, "was the Man of Good Will. . . . He would think and act as a public-spirited individual, unlike all the groups of vested interests that were ready to prey on him. . . . Far from joining organizations to advance his own interests, he would . . . address himself directly and high-mindedly to the problems of government."

By the 1920s most states had established laws allowing for some form of direct democracy. But as politics was cleaned up and the Progressive era waned, so did the zeal for referendums. From the 1930s to the early 1960s they declined in frequency and import. But in the late 1960s, as attacks mounted against the "establishment" and rhetoric soared about participatory democracy, the idea of going directly to the people was revived, most vigorously by the left wing of the Democratic Party. Although its intellectual proponents were mostly on the left, however, the initiative movement got its most powerful boost a decade later from the right. In 1978 Howard Jarvis organized California's Proposition 13 and in so doing, the legend goes, changed the course of American history.

Proposition 13 mixed two quite separate issues: taxes and referendums. Taxes of all kinds had risen all through the late 1960s and 1970s, as Lyndon Johnson's Great Society, entitlement spending, and new urban initiatives all blossomed. (In the 1960s you got elected, believe it or not, by promising to raise people's taxes and spend them on grandiose public schemes.) In California, a housing boom in the 1970s had caused property taxes to skyrocket, and the state legislature seemed unwilling to cut taxes even as surpluses swelled into billions of dollars. Proposition 13 proposed a massive rollback, pushing taxes back to their 1975 levels and setting limits on how much they could be raised.

Despite much public anger about high taxes, Proposition 13 was not expected to pass. Jarvis was viewed as a crank. The *San Francisco Chronicle* described him as "a choleric seventy-five-year-old gadfly who saw taxes as government-licensed theft."[14] California's leading political figures all opposed it, including the state's foremost conservative, former governor Reagan, who thought it too extreme. Polls a month before the election showed that supporters and opponents of the initiative were in a statistical dead heat and almost 20 percent of voters were still undecided. Then, three weeks before the June vote, the Los Angeles County assessor released his annual report showing a staggering increase in property taxes. The story hit at precisely the right moment and, riding on a wave of indignation, Proposition 13 passed with 65 percent of the vote.

After the election results the establishment jumped kangaroo-style on the bandwagon. Jarvis the buffoon became Jarvis the political genius, appearing on the covers of *Time* and *Newsweek* and meeting with foreign leaders such as Margaret Thatcher and Jacques Chirac. A few weeks after the vote Reagan urged Republicans to "use the California vote on Proposition 13 to light a prairie fire of opposition to costly and overpowering government." They did. Proposition 13 put tax-cutting at the heart of the Republican Party agenda. Many Democrats embraced its message, as well. California's liberal governor, Jerry Brown, declared himself a "born again" convert on the issue. Politicians around the country began drawing up tax-cutting plans. New Jersey's Democratic Senate candidate, Bill Bradley, campaigned on a pledge to help reduce federal taxes by $25 billion. Five months after Proposition 13's passage, in November 1978, sixteen states held referendums on tax policy.

But there was another, more powerful legacy of Proposition 13, which was the first referendum in four years on the California ballot. It provided a new, magically simple way around the cumbersome process of changing public policy. Instead of voting scores of legislators out of office or lobbying them to vote on bills, why not pass laws directly? The number of referendums had already grown by the 1970s, but after 1978 they spread like Reagan's prairie fire. In the 1960s voters across the country were asked to legislate on 88 issues. That number grew to 181 in the 1970s and 257 in the 1980s. By the 1990s, the number of initiatives had almost quintupled, to 378. In 2000 alone, voters decided on 204 pieces of legislation, concerning everything from health care and education reform to gay rights and physician-assisted suicide.

Has it worked? The last two decades saw a sustained experiment with the mechanisms of referendum, initiative, and recall.[15] It is, of course, easy to look at any one issue on which the public voted correctly—in one's view—and say, "This system is much better because it produced a good result; the legislature would never have passed this law." This explains why the right has been so enamored with initiatives over the past few decades. How can one look a tax cut in the mouth? But the results of one piece of legislation are a short-sighted way to judge systemic change. After all, voters may also vote in favor of many things of which one strongly disapproves. As the left has gained ground and won referendums on its own causes, conservatives have shifted their attitudes about California in a comical about-face. Ever since the Richard Nixon and Reagan years brought triumph to conservatism in that state, it was axiomatic on the right that California was the national bellwether. Its referendums pointed to the future. But now, as California's liberal majorities have begun to pass their favored policies, conservatives have decided that the nation's most populous state is in fact a weird, atypical la-la land, out of touch with America. Now, for conservatives, its referendums are symbols of the past.[16] As liberal victories grow in other states, however, conservatives might wonder why they liked this strange initiative process in the first place. Liberals, on the other hand, who had long grumbled about populist lawmaking, are rediscovering their love of the referendum. Until of course, the tide turns once again.

Some might argue that referendums at least put new issues on the table that political elites refused to discuss. Not really. Take taxes, for example. Proposition 13 probably accelerated the rise of tax cuts on the national agenda. But the trend was already in the air and politicians were latching on to it. By the late 1970s, Americans were showing signs of disenchantment with big government and had been voting conservative politicians into office at all levels. More than gas lines and stagflation, more than the cultural rebellions of the 1960s, more even than Soviet expansion, taxes were the big issue of American politics in the late 1970s. Pollster Richard Wirthlin said, "You have to go back to the Vietnam war to find such a focus on an issue."[17] Although Proposition 13 gave a powerful push to the tax-cutting cause, the Republican Party had already embraced it, the Democrats were running scared, and public opinion on the issue was overwhelmingly clear. If Proposition 13 had not happened, tax cuts would likely have moved forward just as fast.

The better yardstick by which to judge initiatives is whether law-making by plebiscite has advantages over lawmaking by legislature. And what are the effects of this new system of direct democracy? The best place to search for an answer is in California. In many ways California is the poster child for direct democracy, having experimented most comprehensively with referendums on scores of issues, big and small. California also may well be a herald of what lies ahead. It is America's most populous state, with an economy that mixes farming, the new economy, and old defense industries. Its population is multi-ethnic, multiracial, multireligious, even multilingual. Most important, California has often led the country, indeed the world, in technology, consumption, trends, lifestyles, and of course, mass entertainment. It is where the car found its earliest and fullest expression, where suburbs blossomed, where going to the gym replaced going to church, where goat-cheese pizza was invented. And the technological and ideological forces that lead so many to assume that direct democracy is the wave of the future—declining political parties, telecommuting, new tech-nology, the Internet generation—are all most well developed in this vast land. Outside of Switzerland—which is an oddity, not a trendset-ter—California is the fullest manifestation of direct democracy in the world today. And if California truly is the wave of tomorrow, then we have seen the future, and it does not work.

## California Dreaming

No one disputes the facts. In the 1950s and early 1960s California had an enviable reputation as one of the best-run states in the union. "No. 1 State," said a *Newsweek* cover from 1962, "Booming, Beautiful California." *Time* agreed; its title read "California: A State of Excitement." There was much to be excited about. The state's economy was booming, and with moderate tax rates it had built extraordinary and expanding public resources, from advanced highways and irrigation systems to well-run police forces to breathtaking parks and zoos. The state's crowning achievement was its world-class public-education system, which started in kindergarten and ended with the prestigious University of California campuses. Californians seemed blissfully content, annoying intellectuals in the cold, damp Northeast to no end. ("All those dumb, happy people," said Woody Allen.) But for the rest of the world, sunny, prosperous, well-managed California symbolized the dazzling promise of the United States. California was the American dream.

California today is another story. In the spring of 2001 California was plunged into blackouts and electricity shortages that reminded me of India. (In fact they were worse than anything I experienced growing up.) Sure, California is home to Silicon Valley and Hollywood, two of the greatest centers of American industry and creativity. But that is its private sector. Its public sector—indeed its public life—is an unmitigated mess. The state and local governments struggle each year to avoid fiscal crises. Highways that were once models for the world are literally falling apart, and traffic has become both a nightmare and an expensive drag on productivity. In the 1950s California spent 22 percent of its budget on infrastructure; today it spends barely 5 percent. Public parks now survive only by charging hefty admission fees. The state's education system has collapsed; its schools now rank toward the bottom in the nation when measured by spending or test scores or student skills.

The University of California system has not built a new campus in three decades, despite the fact that the state's population has doubled. And yet, as the veteran journalist Peter Schrag points out in his penetrating book *Paradise Lost*, it has had to build twenty new prisons in the last two decades. In 1993 the *Economist* concluded that the state's "whole system of government was a shambles." Three years later the bipartisan Business–Higher Education Forum, which includes corporate executives and education leaders, reported that without major change "the quality of life will continue to decline in California with increasing transportation problems, rising crime and social unrest, and continued out-migration of business." And this was written at a time when the U.S. economy was at a thirty-year high. The best evidence of California's dismal condition is that on this one issue, both right and left agree. Echoing Schrag, who is a liberal, conservative commentator Fred Barnes explained in a cover story for the *Weekly Standard* that the state's government had stopped working: "California has lost its lofty position as the state universally envied for its effective government, top-notch schools, and auto-friendly transportation system."[18]

Not all California's problems can be traced to its experiment with referendums and initiatives. But much of the state's mess is a result of its extreme form of open, non-hierarchical, non–party based, initiative-friendly democracy. California has produced a political system that is as close to anarchy as any civilized society has seen. Consider the effects of the recent spate of initiatives. After Proposition 13 passed, the state passed dozens of other initiatives, among them Proposition 4 (which limited the growth of state spending to a certain percentage), Proposition 62 (which requires supermajorities in order to raise taxes), Proposition 98 (which requires that 40 percent of the state budget be spent on education), and Proposition 218 (which applied to local fees and taxes the restrictions of Proposition 13). Yet the state legislature has no power over funds either, since it is mandated to spend them as referendums and federal law require. Today 85 percent of the California state budget is outside of the legislature's or the governor's control—a situation unique in the United States and probably the world. The vast majority of the state's budget is "pre-assigned." The legislature squabbles over the remaining 15 percent. In California today real power resides nowhere. It has dissipated into the atmosphere, since most government is made via abstract laws and formulas. The hope appears to be that government can be run, in Schrag's words, like "a Newtonian machine immune to any significant control or judgment by elected representatives. This not only turns democracy into some fun-house contortion of the ideal but makes it nearly impossible to govern at all."[19]

Even with referendums dictating what they do, politicians are still required to translate these airy mandates into reality. The initiatives have simply made this process dysfunctional by giving politicians responsibility but no power. Experiences with referendums in places far from California confirm that this is not a problem unique to the golden state. The Connecticut Conference of Municipalities (CCM) determined that 72 of the state's 169 municipalities held referendums to approve the budgets proposed by their city executive. Of those 72, 52 had to hold additional referendums, often more than once, because the proposed budgets were rejected. Most of these referendums required local officials to cut taxes and yet improve services. "You have to be a magician to accomplish those dual purposes," complained James J. Finley, the CCM's legislative services director.[20]

The flurry of ever-increasing commandments from the people has created a jumble of laws, often contradictory, without any of the debate, deliberation, and compromise that characterize legislation. The stark "up or down" nature of initiatives does not allow for much nuance or accommodation with reality. If in a given year it would be more sensible to spend 36 percent of the California budget on schools instead of the mandated 40 percent, too bad.

As another unintended consequence, the initiative movement has also broken the logic of accountability that once existed between politicians and public policy. By creating a Byzantine assortment of restrictions over the process of taxing and spending, the voters of California have obscured their own ability to judge the performance of their politicians. When funds run out for a particular program, was it that the legislature allocated too little money, or that local communities spent too much, or that statewide initiatives tied their hands? You can imagine the orgy of buck-passing that must ensue, given California's 58 counties, 447 cities, and over 5,000 special districts. Lack of power and responsibility inevitably produces a lack of respect. California's state government and its legislature have among the lowest public-approval ratings among American states. Having thoroughly emasculated their elected leaders, Californians are shocked that they do so little about the state's problems.

Consider, for example, the difference between California's attempts to tackle illegal immigration and affirmative action, both of which were handled through plebiscite, and the national government's tackling of welfare reform, which was done through legislation. Unquestionably, the path of welfare reform looked longer and more arduous. Its proponents had to launch a national debate, muster enough votes in both houses of Congress, and then convince President Clinton to sign it, which he finally did the third time a bill was sent to him. But in that process of debate, back-and-forth, and compromise, a bipartisan solution was arrived at that addressed some of the concerns of both sides. That solution was also phased in gradually, as befits any major legislative change in a large country. As a result, welfare reform had broad political support, was viewed as legitimate, was given the time and the resources to work, and was implemented in a manner that did not spark a backlash. It is now widely regarded as a success, and congressional Republicans and Clinton both cite it as one of their proudest accomplishments.

Contrast this with Propositions 187 (on immigration) and 209 (on affirmative action). Organized groups, with the backing of some politicians, took the issue outside the political parties and the legislature, outside of the normal political process, and waged a costly television campaign. They won, and both propositions became law. But because there had been no legislative process, no compromise, no vetting of any kind, both propositions created enormous ill will and hostility. In the case of Proposition 187, the Republican victory backfired completely, since it branded them as mean spirited, anti-immigrant, and antiminority—the latter a bad label to be stuck with in California—and, increasingly, in the rest of the country. The propositions were also badly written, so that most of 187 has since been knocked down by courts. The chief architect of 209, Ward Connerly, now acknowledges that the abolition of affirmative action should have been phased in so as to create less of a shock to the system. Even if one were in favor of both propositions, the manner in which they were enacted into law was crude and counterproductive. The centuries-old method of lawmaking by legislature requires debate and deliberation, takes opposition views into account, crafts compromises, and thus produces laws that are regarded as legitimate even by people who disagree with them. Politics did not work well when kings ruled by fiat and it does not work well when the people do the same.

Perhaps the greatest paradox of the initiative and referendum movement has been its unexpected relationship to money in politics. Initially devised to remove public policy from the improper influence of big business, direct democracy has become an arena in which only the wealthiest of individuals and interest groups get to play. Like politicians, successful ballot measures must run for office. First they need to be packaged, which usually requires political consultants, focus groups, and a team of lawyers. Then they have to get on the ballot. To do that they need large numbers of signatures collected within a relatively short period of time, which almost always requires the services of professional signature-gathering firms (referred to only half-jokingly as the "initiative-industrial complex"). Next they need to be sold to the public, requiring another enormous expenditure on advertising. As a result, the sums of money spent promoting and attacking ballot measures rival those spent on the putatively more corruptible campaigns of legislative candidates. In his book *Democracy Derailed: Initiative Campaigns and the Power of Money*, David Broder reported that in the 1997–98 legislative cycle, more than $257 million was spent on initiatives nationwide, which came to more than a third of the $740 million spent by all of the candidates for the House and Senate put together. In California, in 1996 alone, more than $141 million was spent on initiatives, which was 33 percent more than was spent by the much-maligned candidates for the state legislature.

The consequence of large amounts of money entering the initiative process is depressingly similar to what happens in today's legislatures: well-organized and well-funded interest groups use the easy access to protect their turf. For example, when business groups put "paycheck protection" on the ballots, California unions were able to circle the wagons and defeat it. So far, teachers unions have been able to defeat every single school-voucher initiative, including three well-funded attempts in 2000. In Missouri and Oregon, business coalitions armed with cash and calling themselves "No Tax Dollars for Politicians" and "No Taxpayer Handouts for Politicians," respectively, defeated campaign finance initiatives by large margins. But there is a wrinkle in this story. While it seems clear that well-funded interest groups will continue to thrive in the age of direct democracy, the initiative process has introduced an unexpected player to the political scene: the billionaire policy-entrepreneur. The financier George Soros, Amway co-founder Richard DeVos, venture capitalist Timothy Draper, Microsoft co-founder Paul Allen, and many more have used the initiative process to promote their pet issues all over the map. In a sense it is hard to blame them: like everyone else, they have political views and they are doing what they believe is right. But a century ago, when the leaders of the Progressive movement were promoting direct democracy as a way to wrest power from the gilded age robber-barons, could they ever have imagined a system dominated by well-entrenched interest groups and politically minded billionaires?

Referendums and initiatives have accelerated the process of taking power away from politicians and giving it to "the people," but always through an ever-growing class of professional consultants, lobbyists, pollsters, and activists. In the name of democracy, we have created a new layer of enormously powerful elites. And since government has become a permanent campaign, their work—and influence—never stops. Those who have lost out as this revolution has proceeded are the institutions of representative democracy: Congress, politicians, the political parties, the administrative agencies, government itself. The new elites also have fewer checks on them than did those before them. The old party was rooted in a base, a philosophical tradition, and was visible and accountable—a quasi-public institution. Its officials were public figures who operated in the open and had to worry about their reputations. But who monitors the consultants, fundraisers, pollsters, and lobbyists who now run American politics? By declaring war on elitism, we have produced politics by a hidden elite, unaccountable, unresponsive, and often unconcerned with any larger public interest. The decline of America's traditional elites and institutions—not just political but cultural, economic, and religious—is at the heart of the transformation of American society. It is to this story that we turn next.

| CHAPTER 6 |

# The Death of Authority

I**N THE FALL** of 2000 Chase Manhattan Bank merged with J. P. Morgan. As with all mergers it was in fact an acquisition: Chase had bought Morgan. At first glance it had looked like just another corporate deal—albeit a big one—part of the background noise of those heady times. In fact it was a landmark in American capitalism, marking the final demise of the old Wall Street and the triumph of a new order.

The Morgan bank, as it was called, was the premier American bank for much of the twentieth century. During the many crises and panics of the late nineteenth and early twentieth centuries it had even stepped in as the lender of last resort for the American economy, until the U.S. Federal Reserve System took on that role in 1913. Morgan had built its business by being exceedingly selective about whom it served, catering almost exclusively to governments, large multinational corporations, and the very, very rich. "Morgan private accounts had once been tantamount to membership cards in the American aristocracy," explained Ron Chernow, who wrote a history of the bank. In fact the bank functioned very much like a club. This was not an affectation but the key to its handsome profits. Morgan's bankers cultivated close ties with the leading blue-chip firms as well as sovereign governments, maintaining strong personal relationships at every level. When questioned by a congressional committee about his way of doing business in 1912, J. Pierpont Morgan explained that he believed the cornerstone of credit was "character . . . Before money or property or anything else. . . . [A] man I do not trust could not get money from me on all the bonds in Christendom."[1]

Chase Manhattan, on the other hand, had a corporate culture that was, in the words of the *New York Times*, "drawn more from the streets of New York than of the rarefied air breathed by those at Morgan." With a respectable history of its own it had, by the 1990s, become a middling amalgam of troubled banks. Chase's focus was mostly on the low end of the market: home mortgages, car loans, small accounts. But catering to the great unwashed was increasingly where the money was. By the 1980s slicing and dicing large loans into small bits and selling them to the average investor had become a way to make big money. In this new game, the clubby approach was not very useful. J. P. Morgan tried to adjust to a world it saw coming, but in the end it failed. It became, in the words of the *Times*, "an anachronism in a financial world dominated by mass rather than class."[2] To get a sense of the magnitude of the revolution in American finance, consider that, in 1990 J. P. Morgan had the highest market valuation of any bank on Wall Street, ten times that of Citibank. Just ten years later, Morgan's market value was one-tenth of Citicorp's. Citicorp came to dominate because its chief executive officer (CEO), Sanford Weill, turned the company into a financial conglomerate that could handle not just high finance but mass finance.

In explaining how democratization has transformed American society well beyond merely the political sphere—the task of this chapter—the financial business is a good place to start. The industry has been revolutionized with consequences that have affected most Americans—and tens of millions outside America as well. Anyone with a pension account knows that the entire financial business now revolves around selling products to people like him or her. Anyone who watches CNBC, the cable network that covers financial news as a spectator sport, knows that the stock market is now geared toward everyday investors. Today the world's largest portfolio of stocks and bonds is owned not by the Saudi royal family or a Swiss bank but by TIAA-CREF, the pension fund for college professors and employees of nonprofit organizations. "Every man a king!" declared the southern populist Huey Long. That is not quite what has happened, but in the economic realm everyone, king and commoner alike, has become a capitalist.

The democratic wave has moved more broadly across American society—through business, law, medicine, culture, and even, as we shall see, religion. As with politics, this process accelerated in the late 1960s and early 1970s, and like politics it is an ongoing revolution still in its infancy. It has fueled two broad social changes. The first is the opening up of many American industries and professions to outsiders and the breakdown of old structures of power and control. The second, associated with the first, is the eclipse of the class of elites who ran these institutions. There is even a broader decline of the *idea* of elites—though not of the reality. These two changes have been part of a more general shift in American society that can be described as the decline of authority. Actually it is more of an assault. Though authority has always been suspect in America, since the 1960s it has been under unceasing attack, in different ways, from both the left and the right.

Another important reason for beginning this chapter with money is that it highlights something crucial to understanding the democratic wave. In many, many ways democratization has been an extraordinary, powerful force for good, breaking up oligarchies, revolutionizing businesses, bringing in and rewarding fresh talent, creating new industries, and perhaps most important, empowering individuals. We would not want to go back to the old, closed order. Yet having solved old problems—of access and exclusion—democratization has produced new ones. The competitiveness, energy, and dynamism of the new, open system have eroded certain guides and barriers, checks and balances. Ironically this new disorder has mostly hurt the average investor—the ordinary citizen—who is less able to navigate in uncharted and turbulent waters. One could imagine a democratized political, economic, and social system that still contained within it a few formal and informal restraints, sacrificing some energy and dynamism in favor of other virtues, such as transparency, honesty, equity, and stability. But to do so we would need to resurrect, in some form, the institutions and elites we have spent three decades tearing down.

## Show Me the Money

"America began to change on a mid-September day in 1958," writes Joseph Nocera in his fascinating book, *A Piece of the Action: How the Middle Class Joined the Money Class*. He is referring to the day when the Bank of America "dropped" 60,000 credit cards in Fresno, California, thereby creating the all-purpose credit card. It was a novel idea, in effect offering virtually anyone who wanted it a general line of credit, unsecured by collateral. In the 1950s Americans were just getting used to taking out loans to buy consumer products—cars, refrigerators, televisions. But debt was still disreputable. If you could not afford something, you squirreled away money until you could buy it. Besides, it was not easy to get a loan. Most banks thought that making small loans to the average family was not worth the time and effort. Except for the Bank of America. Its founder, A. P. Giannini, the son of an immigrant, wanted to make money available for "his people." His bank, founded in 1904 in a converted saloon, was initially called the Bank of Italy and in 1928 renamed the Bank of America. Whereas other banks passed off consumer loans to finance companies, Bank of America embraced the role of serving the broad middle class. As a result it grew to become America's largest bank by the 1970s.

Credit cards opened up the world of credit to the masses, allowing ordinary people to take out an advance on their future earnings, as the rich had always done. It is difficult today to imagine life without credit cards. And yet they were almost unknown forty years ago. What happened over those forty years, and most especially in the last twenty-five, is in many ways more revolutionary than in any comparable period in modern financial history. Capitalism was transformed into democratic capitalism.

Credit cards were just the beginning. From the 1970s, economics, technology, and government policy all pushed in the same direction—deregulating, decentralizing, and democratizing the economy. The money-market fund, introduced in the 1970s, turned stocks into a mass commodity. In 1951, 9 percent of Americans owned equities. Stocks were for the rich. Most Americans put their money in savings accounts, with interest rates fixed by law. Memories of the stock-market crash of 1929 had much to do with this, coupled with a strong belief that Wall Street—the whole system of brokers and banks—didn't care much about the little guy (which was basically true.) But perhaps more than anything else, the average person just did not expect his savings to generate high returns. His goal was to preserve money, not make more. But as inflation rose in the 1970s the middle class realized that its bank savings—with fixed rates—was actually losing value. People began searching for ways to get higher returns. They found one in money-market funds, a newly created financial product that, by exploiting a loophole in federal law, allowed people to buy mutual funds. The funds first bought Treasury bills, which had higher yields than savings accounts. Then Fidelity introduced funds with stock portfolios. They also allowed people to use their funds like regular bank accounts, writing checks and making deposits. Suddenly a steelworker who all his life had kept a simple savings account could own shares in blue-chip companies like General Electric, Ford, and IBM.

Add to this groundswell Congress's creation of the individual retirement account (IRA) and the 401(k) plan. Both allowed people to put aside pretax income into savings that would appreciate tax-free. This produced a strong incentive to put savings into financial instruments that could get higher returns. If you made an extra $1,000 at work, you paid income taxes on it. If your IRA portfolio grew by $1,000, however, you paid no taxes on it (until withdrawal). It was simple arithmetic—pretax compounding—but it turned tens of millions of savers into investors. Introduced only twenty-five years ago, IRAs and 401(k) plans are now the mechanisms through which most Americans participate in the stock and bond markets.

Then came discount brokerage. In 1975 the government forced the New York Stock Exchange to allow the free market to set the price of commissions on buying and selling stocks, ending 183 years of price-fixing. Soon it was easy for anyone to trade small quantities of stock. In 1975 the commission on a stock trade was, on average, $500 (in today's dollars). At a discount brokerage house today it would run under $20. On-line it costs $4. As a result of all these changes, by 2000 well over half of Americans owned equities. Along the way the stock market was transformed from an elite cartel into a business catering to a much broader base. If the symbol of the old order was a Wall Street club where a handful of power brokers lunched, the symbol of the new was CNBC, where CEOs vied for airtime to speak to a mass audience.[3]

An unlikely agent of this process of democratization was Michael Milken, the legendary 1980s investment banker who ended up in jail for fraud. Milken invented the "junk" bond and in doing so, opened up credit to a universe of small companies that had never had access to it. Start-ups and other small firms had always found it difficult to expand because they lacked capital and did not have the credit history that would qualify them for loans at reasonable rates. They faced a catch-22: you could not float a bond unless you had done it before. Milken did for companies what Giannini had done for people: he bet that the great many would prove about as creditworthy as the big boys. (Actually Milken had done some academic research that bore this hypothesis out.) And both had discovered that by helping people or companies with no credit history go straight to the debt markets—at slightly higher rates, of course—you could make very good money. For new companies, Milken's junk bonds were a godsend. They provided capital, which was often the one thing stopping the best of them from growing. The bonds also leveled the playing field, depriving giant companies of one of their main barriers against competition—access to capital. The 1980s saw the birth of dozens of companies such as MCI and CNN that became global giants fueled by junk-bond money. Milken's innovation spread to virtually every corner of finance, even foreign government debt. And because all financial instruments were now being broken up into small bits so that anyone could buy them—through mutual or pension funds—the result was a massive power shift. It was not only companies that faced a vast new creditor class; it was anyone who needed money, including countries. The old model was embodied in the story of British prime minister Benjamin Disraeli going to see Lord Rothschild to secure a loan that would allow the United Kingdom to own the Suez Canal. The new model is embodied in the countless tales of finance ministers telephoning dozens and dozens of mutual-fund managers, hoping to burnish their countries' fortunes. The *New York Times'* Thomas Friedman explains that by the 1990s, when a country took on debt, "instead of . . . dealing with just twenty major banks, it suddenly found itself dealing with thousands of individual investors and mutual funds."[4] This wasn't what the 1960s-era protesters on college campuses had meant, but power had moved to the people.

## More than Money

Once you start looking at it through this prism, almost every aspect of American life has been affected by the democratic wave. To get a sense of the reach of the democratic wave, take something as far removed from money and politics as possible: religion. Over the last thirty years the most important change in American religion has been the dispersion of power away from the mainstream churches— Episcopalians, Methodists, Presbyterians—to broad, evangelical groups with mass appeal. More important and less recognized is the fact that as these groups have grown they have adjusted and accommodated themselves to their vast followings. They have, in other words, democratized American Protestantism.

The high churches—Episcopalian and Presbyterian among others—that could not adapt in a populist age have withered into genteel insignificance. The priests have lost their place in the old order and lack any footing in the new. Episcopal bishops, for example, had a standing in society that is difficult to convey today. The Reverend Endicott Peabody, founder of the Groton School, was regarded as a national leader almost on par with presidents. This high status for ministers persisted until recently. Yale University, for example, had an Episcopal bishop as the head of its board of trustees in the 1970s and 1980s. Today it is inconceivable that such an important post would be handed over to a priest. Lacking democratic legitimacy and wealth (capitalist legitimacy), the traditional minister is regarded by many Americans as a quaint figure, vaguely admired but lacking much stature or power. Those who do wield power—and who are courted by presidents, governors, and talk-show hosts—are the populist priests, such as Billy Graham, who can claim to be speaking not so much for religion but for the people. Truly in this case, *vox populi vox dei*. The voice of the people is the voice of God.

This might not strike some as a recent shift. Religion in America has always been anti-authoritarian. Many European immigrants came to America as religious dissidents, fleeing religious authority. More important, the second Great Awakening, from 1780 to 1830, brought the egalitarian spirit of the American Revolution into religion. A new breed of evangelicals roamed the land, identifying with the common people in true Jeffersonian fashion. Egalitarian denominations such as the Baptist and the Methodist Churches exploded in size as the older, more hierarchical ones, such as the Congregationalist Church, withered. In 1775 there were twice as many Congregationalists as adhered to any other denomination in the country. By 1845 they had less than one-tenth as many followers as did the Methodists. Baptists and Methodists make up the majority of American Christians to this day. When touring America in the late 1820s and early 1830s, Alexis de Tocqueville noted this phenomenon, calling the Christianity he saw "a democratic and republican religion."

But Tocqueville's observation was mostly about the political organization of religion. In many cases ministers were selected by the town at large and accountable to it, in a general sense, for their actions. The structure of the church was egalitarian, with almost no layers of authority or bureaucracy. But in doctrinal terms most American sects were deeply authoritarian. Often highly literal in their interpretations of the scriptures, they were intolerant of rival sects or dissident voices.* For most churchgoers the price of free thinking was high—usually exile, imprisonment, or death. In a famous example, Anne Hutchinson, a devout Englishwoman who moved to Boston in 1634, began giving talks stressing the individual's role in reaching God. She was excommunicated and driven out of Massachusetts by the governor, John Winthrop.

American Christianity has changed greatly in the three centuries since Winthrop. But it remained doctrinally demanding until recently. After all, the publication of the Protestant *Fundamentals* in the early twentieth century—from which the term "fundamentalism" comes—was an effort to maintain scriptural purity against those who wanted to permit individuals to interpret religious texts more liberally. A few decades later the Scopes trial of 1925—centering around a community that had banned the teaching of evolution in the classroom—showed that most fundamentalist Christians were willing to defend doctrinal authority even if they were totally at odds with mainstream America. Christianity for them was not open to individual interpretation.

Today we see occasional battles over the teaching of evolution, but they mask the reality of a faith transformed. The last thirty years have

---

*Of course there were always distinctive voices of independence, such as Thomas Paine, Thomas Jefferson, Ralph Waldo Emerson, Henry David Thoreau, and Walt Whitman. But this kind of dissent was a secular, elite phenomenon.

seen the most profound changes in American religion since its seventeenth-century Great Awakening. Recent decades are often characterized as a time of heightened religiosity in America, which may be true in the sense that membership is up in some conservative churches.* But what is far more striking is that during this period American Christianity—particularly Protestantism—has become doctrinally pluralistic and highly attentive to the beliefs, desires, and wishes of its people. Fundamentalism, having lost its religious core, has become largely a political phenomenon. The average believer has become all-powerful, shaping the organization, doctrine, and beliefs of the religion. Ironically, these democratic changes are most pronounced in the sect that is often seen as reactionary: the evangelical movement. Evangelical Christianity made itself populist and democratic, in clear contradiction of its founding ideals, in large part because it was the only way to avoid the fate of the mainstream churches. Examining its transformation will give us a sense of the broader decline of religious authority in the country.

## My Church Is Your Church

In 1976 the Gallup organization shocked the nation—or, rather, its coastal elites—by revealing that 31 percent of Americans considered themselves born again, or evangelicals. Later that year Jimmy Carter freely discussed his Southern Evangelical Baptist faith during the presidential campaign. By 2000 the number of born agains and evangelicals had risen to 46 percent of Americans, which included both presidential candidates (who were both Methodists). One in particular, George W. Bush, symbolizes the change in American Christianity

---

*In fact the Gallup surveys, on which most of these claims rely, show that the percentage of Americans who go to church has been roughly constant—in the low 40s—with the exception of the 1950s, when it went up to 49 percent. By almost all other yardsticks, including other questions that Gallup has asked for decades, religion is playing a slightly smaller role in most Americans lives.

over the last few decades. Bush is a convert. His father, George H. W. Bush—like generations before him—is a blue-blooded Episcopalian. But as went the Bush family, so went the country. The old structure of religious authority has yielded to a new one.

The puzzle concerning the rise of evangelical Christianity is how, in an era pervaded by individualism and tolerance, such a strict and traditional religion came to flourish. The answer given by many, including most within the churches, is that evangelicalism thrives because of its strictness, because it offers a radical alternative to modern culture. And certainly in today's chaotic world, moral standards and strictures are a powerful psychological draw. But to accept this rationale is to ignore the profound way in which modern Protestantism has transformed itself.

The pioneer of this transformation was Billy Graham. Graham began his career in the 1940s as a graduate of Wheaton College, preaching about sin and damnation. One of the original fundamentalists, Bob Jones, Sr. (1883–1968), believed that only conservative Protestants could be saved. The rest—Jews, Catholics, Mormons—were all damned. Catholics in particular were an evil cult with a leader, the pope, who was literally the Antichrist, an institutional position that Bob Jones University held openly until 2000, when Senator John McCain brought it to national attention during the South Carolina Republican primaries. Jones believed that mainstream American culture was godless and depraved, and the country doomed—this in the 1920s. He founded his own university (in 1927) to save "true" Christians from the hell of modern America. He sought neither to change the country nor to water down his message to gain followers, believing fiercely in what he called "the soul-satisfying contentment of being a scriptural minority."

Billy Graham began his career as a preacher in this spirit, giving stern sermons condemning much of modern life as sinful. But as his audience grew larger and larger and he was beamed into mainstream homes via radio and television, his message grew softer and softer. Within a few decades he had changed his image from a fiery preacher of perdition to a benign father figure to all Americans, a position powerfully reinforced by his friendship with and counsel to every American president since Richard Nixon. It is remarkable just how forgiving Graham became: he denounced neither Nixon after Watergate nor Clinton after Monicagate. The theologian Richard John Neuhaus pointed out in 1999, "When he started out in the 1940s, Billy Graham made no bones about preaching hellfire and damnation for those who have not accepted Christ. He hasn't been featuring that for a very long time. Not to put too fine a point on it, one may assume that Mr. Graham knows what does and does not sell."

Graham's popularity also signaled the use of technology to spread a broad religious message. In so doing it replaced—displaced—personal interaction among members of local religious communities. The media ministries that followed in Graham's wake all came at the expense of local churches, whose ministers tended to be far more watchful and demanding of their congregations. This was the most marked shift from the traditional, high Episcopal style of religious authority, in which the local priest is your moral guide, to the new, evangelical model, where moral guidance is provided through a television show. It is difficult to flout moral codes while you are a member of a local parish, among friends and counselors. But if all you do is watch a preacher on television, no one is watching you.

If Billy Graham was the pioneer, Jerry Falwell was the most prominent agent of the democratization of the evangelical tradition. This might seem an odd claim, but Falwell's reputation as a reactionary was formed mostly by his political advocacy over the last twenty years, as founder of the conservative political group the Moral Majority. A look at his entire career reveals a more opportunistic figure whose chief goal was to make his church appeal to the masses. An entrepreneur who cared little for religious authority, Falwell broke with his Baptist leadership to found the Thomas Road Baptist Church in 1956, with thirty-five members. He admired businessmen—his father was one—and explained in 1971 that "the church would be wise to look at business for a prediction of future innovation." His particular observation was that "the greatest innovation in the last twenty years is the development of giant shopping centers. . . . A combination of services of two large companies with small supporting stores has been the secret of the success of shopping centers. The Thomas Road Baptist Church believes that the combined ministries of several agencies in one Church can . . . attract the masses to the gospel." It was a strategy that worked and led to the rise of the "megachurch." In a recent sermon, Falwell announced plans for a new 1,400-acre "Jerry Falwell Ministries (JFM) World Headquarters." The site will house among many other facilities: a university, several institutes, a 12,000-seat sanctuary, a 24-hour prayer call center, an adoption center, a fellowship for church planting, a "megachildren's world," indoor and outdoor athletic facilities, a state-of-the-art television production center, a recreational vehicle park, and a "futuristic" youth camp.[5]

In the process of expanding, Falwell and others like him discovered that the easiest way to attract a mass audience was to mimic mainstream culture and values, giving the people what they want, which is a less religiously demanding and more warm and service-oriented Christianity. This was, of course, a total repudiation of the original fundamentalist spirit of men like Bob Jones, Sr., and Oral Roberts. Evangelical churches are now designed to blend in perfectly with modern consumerist America. Look at "Christian rock," the music often called a sign of the rise of religion but more surely a sign of the hollowness of that rise. Christian recording companies make music in every style of pop—hard rock, heavy metal, jazz, easy listening, grunge, funk, and hip-hop, a current best-seller. The journalist Nicholas Dawidoff explains, "In each case the sound of the Christian version is virtually identical to its secular counterpart, and so are many of the trappings, from Christian mosh pits to Z music, a 24-hour cable channel that plays only Christian music videos."[6] Or consider the archconservative evangelist Pat Robertson, whose television show, The 700 Club, and its 24-hour "national counseling center" have adopted mainstream America's therapeutic attitude toward human problems. People are praised, comforted, consoled, but never condemned. You are as likely to hear Robertson berate someone for sinning as you are Oprah Winfrey. Fittingly, Robertson's program now runs on the Family Channel, sandwiched between children's shows and situation comedies.

If faith as therapy was Robertson's model, faith as hedonism was the subliminal message of the Pentecostal evangelists Jim and Tammy Faye Bakker. "Christianity should be fun, it should be joyful. . . . It's not a drag to be saved!" Bakker once exclaimed. To practice what they preached, the Bakkers built a 2,300-acre theme park, Heritage USA—proudly called a "Christian Disneyland"—with a 504-room hotel, a water park, a shopping mall, a counseling center, "a high-tech passion play in the Heritage amphitheater," and a replica of Billy Graham's boyhood home.* In 1986 Heritage USA drew 6 million visitors, making it the third largest theme park in the United States after the two Disneys. "People ask me why a Christian complex needs a water park," Bakker once admitted to the New York Times, referring to his $8 million behemoth. "Well, if the Bible says we are to be fishers of men, then a water park is just bait. . . . And I don't see anything wrong with using some pretty fancy bait."[7]

University of Virginia sociologist James Davison Hunter, who has studied the movement closely, explains in his seminal work American Evangelicalism that evangelicals learned that to gain a mass following it was important "not only to be tolerant of others' beliefs, opinions, and life-styles, but more important to be tolerable to others. The critical dogma is not to offend. . . . [This] entails a deemphasis of Evangelicalism's more offensive aspects, such as accusations of heresy, sin, immortality, paganism, and themes of judgment, divine wrath, damnation, and hell. Anything that hints of moral or religious abso-lutism and intolerance is underplayed." Another scholar of American Christianity, the University of California's Susan Friend Harding,

---

*Although not a Pentecostal himself, Graham is now seen by many evangelicals as a founder of the movement.

writes of Heritage USA—in words also true of most modern evangelical churches—that it was "a ceaseless if implicit critique of fundamentalism's restraint, its sacrificial logic, its obsession with authority, hierarchy, and rules. . . . [T]he Bakkers promised their partners material abundance and well-being but they were refining a gospel of infinite forgiveness, a folk theology that seemed almost to sanction sinning by guaranteeing God's perpetual forgiveness in advance."[8] Since authority could no longer be exercised in traditional ways, the only path to survival and success was adaptation.

The fundamentalist involvement in politics is best understood as a response to this weakening of its religious authority and base. Falwell, the pioneer in this field, was vocally nonpolitical all through the 1950s, 1960s, and early 1970s. In 1965 he published a sermon specifically devoted to this topic: "As far as the relationship of the church to the world, it can be expressed as simply as the three words which Paul gave to Timothy—'preach the Word.' . . . Nowhere are we commissioned to reform the externals. We are not told to wage wars against bootleggers, liquor stores, gamblers, murderers, prostitutes, racketeers, prejudiced persons or institutions, or any other existing evil as such."[9] He routinely deplored the involvement of priests in political battles.

In the 1950s and 1960s, political activism meant campaigns on behalf of civil rights, which neither Falwell nor his congregation was much interested in. In fact, the role of Protestant churches in the civil rights movement was a perfect example of old-fashioned religious authority being used to educate and bring along the congregations. And Falwell did not like it. But by the 1970s, Falwell's followers—particularly in the South—had gotten politicized and moved right on a host of social issues. They voted for Nixon, abandoning their traditional home in the Democratic Party. Even so, it was only in 1978, five years after the *Roe v. Wade* Supreme Court decision giving abortion constitutional protection, that Falwell founded his political advocacy and lobbying group, the Moral Majority. In doing so he again incurred the wrath of the hard-line fundamentalists. The Moral Majority explicitly sought support from

Catholics, Jews, Mormons—indeed anyone who agreed with its agenda. For this sin, Bob Jones, Jr. (the son and successor to Bob Jones, Sr.), labeled Falwell "the most dangerous man in America." One could argue that Falwell moved toward active political conservatism because religious conservatism—which required doctrinal purity, hostility toward other sects, condemnation of sins such as adultery, and an ascetic rejection of materialist culture—had become unsalable. What remains of the old Protestant fundamentalism is politics: abortion, gays, evolution. These issues are what binds the vast congregation together. But even here things have changed as Americans have become more tolerant of many of these social taboos. Today many fundamentalist churches take nominally tough positions on, say, homosexuality but increasingly do little else for fear of offending the average believer, whom one scholar calls the "unchurched Harry." All it really takes to be a fundamentalist these days is to watch the TV shows, go to the theme parks, buy Christian rock, and vote Republican. The sociologist Mark Shibley calls it the "Californication of conservative Protestantism." Having lost the enemies and causes that united and energized their flock, fundamentalists have been experimenting—in the wake of September 11—with a new enemy, Islam. Falwell, Robertson, and Franklin Graham (Billy's son) have all begun speaking of Islam in poisonous and derogatory terms, calling the religion "evil" and its founder, Mohammed, a terrorist. The language once used to describe abortionists, gays, and the ACLU has been shifted over to Muslims. It remains to be seen if this new attempt at hate-mongering will work better than past ones.

The decline of authority in American Christianity is even more pronounced when one looks beyond evangelical sects. The sociologist Alan Wolfe has pointed out that the fastest-growing American churches are the so-called new paradigm churches, which reject the idea of a headquarters for the sect. These movements are totally decentralized and democratic. Wolfe quotes a professor who notes that "Jesus and his disciples were a kind of 'hub and spoke' operation, comparable to the ones run by airlines today, as they have responded to the postmodern conditions of deregulation and intense competition." The rise of "spiritual seekers" is another manifestation of the new face of religion. Seekers believe that religion is an entirely personal matter, with no requirements or commandments, and that each individual must construct his own faith. Every man a priest, as Huey Long might have said. Seeker churches mostly resemble the one run by Reverend Jess Moody in Van Nuys, California, who has "renovated his teaching style, banning all references to hellfire and damnation from his preaching." Also missing are some of the standard terms of Christian theology. "If we use the words redemption or conversion," Moody says, "they think we're talking about bonds."[10]

Modern society is full of quests for "spiritualism" and identity, probably because it is a modern way to address the age-old urge for security and faith. But the key feature of all successful and growing mass Christian sects today is an emphasis on individual choice and democratic structures. To be sure there is a backlash against this trend in all religious communities, but these new orthodox groups together account for about 5 percent of Americans. The more striking trend is of democratization and, as a result, the loss of what Hunter calls "binding address"—the power of scripture, authority, and tradition. Over the last four decades America's most conservative social movement, evangelical Christianity, went up against modern democratic culture and found itself utterly transformed. The tale of evangelical Christianity highlights the more rapid and widespread decline of all religious authority in American life. This may be good or bad, depending on your point of view, but there is little doubt that it has happened.

## The Best That Has Been Known and Thought

Harry Scherman was a bad playwright, but he turned out to be a good businessman. After struggling with scripts for years, Scherman started something he called the Book-of-the-Month Club in 1926. His notion was simple: to expose the newly educated American middle class to the joys of great literature. It was also an attempt, explains

Janice Radway in her history of the club, to "manage the flood of books for his customers . . . [thus assuring] them that they could keep up with the tempo of modern cultural production without sacrificing their appreciation for distinction."[11] Books were selected by a five-member editorial board known as the "judges." All were respected writers; the first board comprised an English professor from Yale, a successful novelist, a Midwestern newspaper editor, and two erudite newspaper columnists. The board made its selections without concern for their commercial potential. During the 1930s and 1940s it picked books by George Orwell, Arthur Miller, Truman Capote, and Ernest Hemingway, among others. Still, the New York literati looked down at the BOMC. In his famous 1960 essay, "Masscult and Midcult," the critic Dwight McDonald scoffed that the club "since 1926 has been supplying its members with reading matter of which the best that can be said is that it could be worse." Actually it could have been a lot worse. Although never overly intellectual or academic, the BOMC found high-quality literature that could appeal to a broad audience. It believed in the democratization of culture—in fact it was spearheading it—but it did so by elevating people rather than bringing standards down.

Then came the 1960s. The assault on authority that took place in every part of society seeped into the small but influential world of the book business. "The idea of the judges of the Book-of-the-Month Club as a kind of governing literary body of the nation . . . was simply out of date," the New York Times wrote in retrospect. The club's fortunes began sagging, and in 1977 it was acquired by the media conglomerate, Time Inc. Soon the judges' autonomy was completely eroded and the club's selections—heavily influenced by Time's marketing department—became those books likely to succeed commercially. Stephen King, Tom Clancy, Michael Crichton, and Terry McMillan became familiar figures on the list. The number of book club selections was greatly expanded, almost tripling between 1980 and 1998. Anything that people were likely to buy—cookbooks, marriage guides, romance novels—was placed on the list.

It was a complete inversion of the original idea. Instead of trying to shape popular taste, the BOMC was trying to mirror it.*

The story of the Book-of-the-Month Club is the story of American culture. A onetime writer for *The New Yorker*, John Seabrook, describes this as a cultural shift "from townhouse to megastore." The townhouse, which dominated American culture until a few decades ago, is his metaphor for cultural standards set by elites whose guiding principle is quality. In today's cultural megastore, however, such ideas of taste, standards, and hierarchy are absurd. Everything goes and the only thing that matters is popularity. Whereas the townhouse was ruled by people schooled in the canon, the megastore is run by those with a feel for what will be popular—what generates "buzz." If men like *The New Yorker*'s legendary editor Harold Ross embodied the old order, pop music promoter David Geffen embodies the new. Ross, hardly a priestly intellectual, had a feel for cultural content; Geffen has a feel for mass tastes. As Seabrook put it, "The old cultural arbiters, whose job it was to decide what was 'good' in the sense of 'valuable,' were being replaced by a new type of arbiter, whose skill was to define 'good' in terms of 'popular.' This vast change in our civilization was making itself felt in virtually every museum, library, university, publishing house, magazine, newspaper, and TV in the country."[12]

A few years ago, the *New York Times* asked two of the best-known museum directors in America to list the components of a great twenty-first-century museum. Philippe de Montebello, the legendary director of New York City's Metropolitan Museum of Art, suggested great works of art, intelligent and seductive presentation, public-spirited curators, an endowment large enough to ensure integrity and independence from market-driven decisions, fully committed trustees, staff members who believe in authority and discrimination when

*This strategy failed and the BOMC is now trying to return to its roots. It has appointed a new board of judges, including some prominent writers such as Anna Quindlen, who make selections for members. That this new old model is succeeding suggests that people actually want guidance in the cultural realm after all.

presenting art, and finally "an unwavering belief in the primacy of the experience of art over that of the museum as agora." The hip director of New York's Guggenheim Museum, Thomas Krens, had a quite different list. He began with a nod to a "great collection," of course, but then went on to "great architecture, a great special exhibition, a great second special exhibition, two eating opportunities, two shopping opportunities, a high-tech interface via the internet, and economies of scale via a global network." That is a vivid picture of the difference between the old order and the new.

Krens is the leading figure of a new generation of museum directors who want to put on a show—any show—that will generate publicity and draw in the crowds. He recently opened a Guggenheim Museum at the Venetian Hotel and Casino on the Las Vegas strip. These gimmicks are flamboyant and often upstage the art itself. But then, getting people to look at the art is not the point; getting them to visit the museum is. Once there, perhaps they will avail themselves of "a shopping opportunity" or two. As the *New Republic*'s art critic, Jed Perl, wrote of Krens's most famous project, the building of a dazzling new museum in Spain designed by Frank Gehry, "Nobody goes to the Guggenheim Bilbao to see the art. Looking at art is something you remember to do while you are there, like going to the bathroom or taking your vitamins." The art on display in such museums is also of a different character. Krens has put on special exhibitions of "the art of the motorcycle" and the clothing of Giorgio Armani. One could—and should—include modern, commercial work as part of a show on modern art. But, as Perl explained, these museums are not trying to define a style or period, they are simply putting on shows of already familiar popular icons in mass culture: "They are not making taste; they are validating whatever taste currently prevails. They are not presenting ideas that graphic designers or MTV producers might later bring to a broader public [and that might prove popular or unpopular]; they are mirroring what the culture already knows, and congratulating the public for knowing it."[13] In sum, they are not leading but following.

One more thing. The motorcycle exhibition was funded by BMW, which had the largest number of bikes on display. The Armani exhibition came only eight months after Giorgio Armani himself had pledged $15 million to the Guggenheim. Art and commerce have always mixed, but the current commercialization of art is different because it is populist and consumerist. For centuries, patrons of art collected what they liked, or what they were taught to like by experts. They rarely gave a thought to whether the collection would curry favor with the public. That was part of the pleasure of being rich. But today's corporate sponsors are very different. They support art as part of a business strategy. James Twitchell, a sociologist and an inventive scholar of American marketing, points out that, as a result, they use largely "non-aesthetic criteria, resulting in shows that hit some politically correct button or, at the very least, are uncontroversial." Twitchell points out that what gets exhibited these days has a great deal to do with what can gain corporate support. The Guggenheim had to abandon plans for a show on "Picasso and the Age of Iron" because no one wanted to be associated with something as old fashioned as iron. BMW turned down an opportunity to sponsor a show on "Masterworks from Munich" because "Munich is not very sexy." An exhibition of the works of the pathbreaking seventeenth-century classicist Guido Reni was cancelled because no one saw a commercial benefit in being associated with it. Had previous patrons adopted this attitude, the history of art might have been very different.

We could pretend that "sexiness" and "buzz" have some inherent characteristics, such as novelty or originality, but they are really just proxies for popularity, which translates into profit. This cultural trend illuminates something important: the relationship between democratization and marketization. Because people now exist in large measure as consumers and exert their power through that identity, marketization has become the shadow partner of democratization. They are the twin forces propelling the democratic wave. This dual nature of democratization—empowering citizens and consumers—explains why so few dare criticize this transformation of society. For the left, it is difficult to condemn the culture of every-man. For the right, it is impossible to admit that capitalism—even in the realm of culture—can have bad consequences. Both are unwill-ing to admit that, without guidance or reference to authority, people can make bad choices. Of course, being guided requires not simply that people be willing to follow but that someone be willing to lead.

## American Aristocracy

In 1967 the president of CBS News, Bill Leonard, told a young pro-ducer named Don Hewitt that they were to start a television news-magazine called *60 Minutes*. Hewitt asked for some guidance as to what the network wanted out of this show. Leonard's requirements were simple: "Make us proud," he said. Recounting that exchange, Hewitt—still the producer of the now-legendary show—reckons that it was "the last time that anyone in television ever said to anyone else in television, 'make us proud.'"

There are dozens of stories like this one about dozens of profes-sions—journalism, publishing, law, accounting, and medicine, among others. More than simply nostalgic tales of old-timers, they actually reveal an important shift in the role of elites in American society. Thirty years ago the people who published books, produced televi-sion news, ran law firms, and headed hospitals viewed themselves as concerned partly with profit, and partly with public service. Televi-sion executives, for example, fully understood that they were required to provide some quality programming in return for their use of the public airwaves. These people thought of themselves less as business-men and more as professionals—"a body of men," in the words of the English intellectual R. H. Tawney, "who carried out their work in accordance with rules designed to enforce certain standards for the better protection of its members and for the better service of the public."[14] For much of the twentieth century, professionals formed a kind of modern aristocracy, secure in its status and concerned with the country's welfare and broader interests. They and other leading citizens took upon themselves certain broader public duties. Most of the great museums, symphonies, opera companies, public parks, and libraries in American cities and towns were built not by the state but by groups of such civic-minded individuals. Secure in their wealth or status, these people tended to take a long-term—if proprietary—interest in the health of their town, city, or country. For all the elitism and privilege that accompanies such a world, American democracy was well served by public-spirited elites.

One of the distinctive elements of Anglo-American society has been that private elites and associations have always performed public tasks. This is unusual; most countries follow the French-continental model, in which government agencies and bureaucrats are placed in charge of every aspect of economic and social life. Consider the various ways in which financial markets are regulated in America—through the New York Stock Exchange, the regional Federal Reserve banks—and you will notice that many of these agencies were, in their origins, private but with public roles. On a smaller scale, the two great parks in Manhattan, Central Park and Riverside Park, are both operated by bodies that are part public and part private. It would be inconceivable for Parisian parks to be run by private citizens. Or consider the American Bar Association and the American Medical Association, which regulate their professions—with authority granted to these private groups by the state.

This kind of partnership has deep roots in Anglo-American history. It developed with the rise of the English gentry, who—as we saw in Chapter One—came to perform governmental functions in their localities and then beyond. It was transported to the American colonies and then the republic, where men of means went into politics and government without the expectation that it would be their career. When George Washington returned to his farm after two terms as president, he was following his class instincts. He was of the Virginia landed elite, whose members were expected to serve without pay as vestrymen, justices of the peace, commanders of local militia, and delegates to the House of Burgesses. This tradition was carried forward by men such as Thomas Jefferson, James Madison, James Monroe, William Henry Harrison, John Tyler, Benjamin Harrison, and Theodore and Franklin Roosevelt, among others. Perhaps more important, beneath these storied figures, a whole world of American aristocrats took on public service as an integral part of their lives, moving in and out of government at both high and low (local) levels. Some were rich, but most were lawyers or bankers. On the continent of Europe by contrast, government became a profession, staffed at the highest levels by career civil servants. In France, for example, it is routine for well-regarded bureaucrats to move into the private sector but unheard of for a businessman to be recruited into government.

Professionals in America have always had a special status. Alexander Hamilton foresaw this at the founding when he explained in the Federalist Papers that ministers, lawyers, and professors would be the neutral and thus "imperial arbiters" between various industries and factions. They alone would be able to promote the general interests of society. Today, however, the professions are shadows of their former selves. They have been crushed by a pincer movement with the market increasing competition on one side and the state on the other taking over many of the functions of professions and private business. "The gentry saved England from the bureaucratization which has been the fate of all continental states," wrote Max Weber in 1905 in *The Protestant Ethic and the Spirit of Capitalism*. Today that distinction between the Anglo-American world and the continent is far less clear. Over the last four decades the state has taken on most of the regulatory and judicial functions of professional associations as well as much of the immense authority that private companies, public charities, and individuals exercised over a community's public life. Andrew Carnegie was devoted to education, so he helped build the public library system in America. Today any such proposal would be mired in paperwork and red tape, because the entire process is thoroughly bureaucratized. This expansion of the state has been wonderful in many respects—providing more services to more people—but it has made Americans assume that government is the proper vehicle for public action. Having made their contribution to society by paying their taxes, people feel freed of the obligations of public involvement and service. This attitude is even more widespread in continental Europe, where despite levels of wealth comparable to those in the United States, people give much less of their money and time to private charities. Even in America, actual public service, in the sense of local government or even community boards, is increasingly seen as an arena for professional politicians, not interested citizens. This shift in the relationship between elites and society affects the success of government. Major law schools and business schools report that, over the last thirty years, fewer and fewer of their most talented graduates express any intention of going into government.

Law is perhaps the best example of a private profession that historically had a public function. Even today a lawyer is considered an "officer of the court," which is more than a fancy phrase. It accurately describes the fact that lawyers have duties and responsibilities in upholding the legal system. The government requires that lawyers maintain certain professional standards and perform certain tasks in return for being given a license to practice. The profession, however, has imposed many more conditions and burdens on its members, asking them to live up to not simply legal but ethical standards as well. Codes of professional conduct enforced by organizations such as the American Bar Association were designed to hold lawyers to an internal set of standards that would make them respected and trusted professionals and not simply hustlers. Historically lawyers played the role of senior advisers—counselors—to their clients, looking out for their long-term interests. This often meant that they advised their clients not to engage in time-consuming litigation or legal maneuvers, even though such activity would have generated handsome legal fees. Elihu Root, a leader of the New York bar, who served during the early twentieth century as secretary of state, secretary of war, and senator from New York, once remarked that "half the practice of a decent lawyer consists of telling his client he's a damned fool and should stop."

The lawyer had a unique place within American society.[15] In a country without a landed aristocracy, lawyers formed a privileged but public-spirited elite. In every town and city in America they were the leading citizens who helped build the museums and hospitals, formed civic institutions, and moved in and out of government at all levels. Consider, for example, James C. Carter, a prominent New York lawyer in the late nineteenth century. He helped found the Bar of the City of New York and played a key role in reform movements in the city and the state, including the Tilden Commission, the anti-Tammany Committee, the National Municipal League, the Citizens Union, the City Club, and the Good Government Clubs. His public life, in other words, took up a good part of his work life. And he was not unusual. Scores like him could be found in New York and in every town in America. Henry Stimson, one of Root's legal protégés who went on to serve as secretary of war to both Theodore and Franklin Roosevelt and secretary of state to Herbert Hoover, noted in his memoirs that "the American lawyer should regard himself as a potential officer of his government. . . . [I]f the time should come when this tradition has faded out and the members of the bar [have] become merely the servants of business the future of liberties could be gloomy indeed." The connection Stimson drew between lawyers and liberty is not unfounded. When Tocqueville famously commented that America's aristocracy could be found "at the bar or on the bench," he meant more than that lawyers were at the top of the heap in the United States. Tocqueville's great fear about America was "the tyranny of the majority." Because the country did not have a social structure like Europe's, he worried that it lacked a class of aristocrats who could act as social stabilizers. Without such a class, he worried, the country would fall prey to demagogues, populists, and other such illiberal forces. For Tocqueville, lawyers were the natural aristocrats because, echoing Hamilton, he believed that they were not beholden to others and could look out for the public good. Lawyers, he wrote, created "[a] form of public accountability that would help preserve the blessings of democracy without allowing its untrammeled vices."

This was a somewhat idealized vision of law but it did powerfully influence the behavior of most American lawyers until about thirty years ago. The writer Michael Lewis recalled the partners at his father's firm in New Orleans: "Their lives had been premised on a frankly elitist idea: an attorney was above the fray. He possessed special knowledge. He observed a strict code of conduct. . . . The most important thing in the world to him was his stature in the community, and yet so far as anyone could determine he never devoted an ounce of his mental energy to worrying about it. Status wasn't a cause; it was an effect of the way he led his life." This cloistered world of law began to unravel with the many new entrants into the profession, the Supreme Court decision in 1977 that allowed lawyers to advertise their services, and the heightened competition for money among the major law firms. Law "succumbed to the twin American instincts to democratize and commercialize. (Often they amount to the same thing)," Lewis wrote.[16] A generation ago law was a business that was run almost like a cartel. In any city there were a limited number of firms. It was difficult to enter the market. Those who were in it made a good living but did not try to bid up business. Law was a way to make a decent and highly respectable living, not a place to get rich. They valued a stable market with steady and predictable profits. This cartel-like structure ensured that lawyers had enough free time to pursue their public interests. An elderly partner in a New York law firm said to me,

I have all these youngsters wondering how they can combine law and public service like Dean Acheson and Cyrus Vance. Well, they can't. First no lawyer who does stuff like that on the side is going to make partner. Second, no partner who does it will bill enough hours to be considered worth having. Vance spent months working on political and policy issues when he was a young lawyer. You just can't do that anymore. Law is now a business, and a damn competitive business at that.

## From Watchdogs to Lapdogs

What was true of law was true, to varying degrees, of most professions. The American Medical Association was once perhaps the most powerful modern-day guild, giving doctors status, security, and power. In return doctors were supposed to place their patients' health above all other concerns. The medical profession has always wanted to reassure its patients that they need never worry that a doctor would do a procedure or prescribe a pill for anything but the best medical reasons. (The Hippocratic oath says nothing about billing cycles.) Over the past few decades, however, as government has become the largest player in the health-care industry, as insurance companies and health maintenance organizations have tried to cut costs, and as other health-care professionals have become more powerful, the doctors have lost their privileged perch. A doctor is now just another business owner whose days are filled with cost-cutting, government mandates, worries about lawsuits, and competitive pressures. As a result, that unique relationship between doctor and patient no longer exists, except among the very rich, for whom money is not a concern. As with law, the older version of the medical profession is somewhat rose-tinted, but that does not change the fact that there has been a seismic shift in medicine over the past thirty years.

A similar tale can be told about accounting. In a congressional hearing in 1933, Representative Alben Barkley of Tennessee asked Colonel Arthur Carter, head of one of the largest accounting firms of the day, whether accountants could be trusted to keep tabs on their clients. "Who audits you?" Barkley asked. "Our conscience," Carter replied. It was more than that, of course. The industry had high standards and treasured its reputation as an honest guardian of financial records. Accountants were meant to be dull but trustworthy—not exactly the picture of accounting revealed by the Enron debacle. In trying to understand the fall of the huge accounting firm Arthur Andersen in 2002, the *Wall Street Journal* interviewed accountants who explained how the profession had changed dramatically over the last twenty years. If the decision to allow lawyers to advertise was the symbolic shift in law, for accounting it was the 1989 agreement between the Federal Trade Commission and the American Institute of Certified Public Accountants allowing accountants to charge contingent fees rather than restricting them to hourly fees. This meant that accountants could make enormous sums of money for general consultancy services. It was a move meant to reform the industry, making it more open and competitive (again, marketization and democratization worked hand in hand). But a chief result of the reforms was that accountants devised tax-avoidance schemes for companies in return for a piece of the tax savings. Anthony Rider, an accountant at Ernst & Young, recalled for the *Journal* how he was taught to sell clients new services: law, insurance, consulting, planning, anything that could make a buck. "It was like telling reporters to sell subscriptions," he recalled. "I couldn't do it. I knew my clients didn't really need it." Rider was fired, but most of his colleagues complied. Over time, accountants bent over backward to do anything their clients wanted, fundamentally changing their roles, in the *Journal*'s words, "from watchdogs to lapdogs."[17]

This kind of blurring of lines has become standard fare on Wall Street. Bankers and brokers had certain responsibilities toward their investing public, among them to maintain a clean separation between their researchers, who evaluated companies, and their bankers, who did business with those same companies. Henry Kaufman, former head of research at Salomon Brothers, recalled that until the 1980s, firms honored this separation and kept research genuinely independent. By the late 1990s, these rules were fast eroding; the internet frenzy wiped them clean. Researchers issued absurd reports touting the stocks of new technology companies, and the banks then pocketed large fees for issuing those stocks. Most of what happened was perfectly legal. In fact, the process had many of the usual benefits of deregulation, creating a more competitive market, bringing in new players, and fostering technological and managerial innovation. But it also created new problems, opening up conflicts of interest, perverse incentives, and dangers to the broader public—which was meant to be the beneficiary of all these changes. The new financial markets were now more vigorous, energetic, and open—but they were also more prone to volatility, false information, fraud, and mania. In the wake of the Internet bust, many politicians and bureaucrats began clamoring for greater oversight and regulation—to make explicit and illegal what was merely implicit and unethical before. If and when such laws are passed they will mark one more, perhaps inevitable, shift from the Anglo-American model of informal regulation to the continental one of formal regulation. A better, more flexible, and more intelligent solution might have been to have these professions police themselves, restoring some of the restraints that were tossed aside in the past few decades. But that would be trying to put Humpty Dumpty together again.

## The Suicide of the Elites

The central cultural shift that underpins all these trends in specific professions is the role of elites. Americans do not like to think or talk about elites. The word itself evokes snobbery and sounds distinctly un-American. But America has always had elites—the small percentage of the country that actually runs most major institutions. The old elites were a closed circle, based on bloodlines, birth, and ethnicity. The new system is more democratic, with people rising to the top because of money, brains, or celebrity—all in all, a much better and more open process of selection. Another great difference, however, is that the old elites were more socially responsible in part because they were utterly secure in their status. The new ones operate in a far more open and competitive world. CEOs of major companies today wield enormous power but feel insecure, pressed on all sides, and forced constantly to survive, stay ahead, and bolster the bottom line. Their interests are thus not wide-ranging but narrow; their horizon not long term but tomorrow. In sum, they do not think or act like elites, which is unfortunate, because they still are.

One of the clearest signs of this shift in the mood of elites is the kinds of causes they support. In the early twentieth century, men such as Robert Brookings established public-policy research institutes—of which the Brookings Institution (founded in 1916) was the first and leading example—that were designed to serve the country beyond partisanship and party politics. Brookings wanted an institute "free from any political or pecuniary interest . . . [to] collect, interpret and lay before the country in a coherent form the fundamental economic facts."[18] The National Bureau of Economic Research (founded in 1920) was dedicated to similar nonpartisan ends. Yet the early twentieth century was not, as is commonly assumed, a less ideological time. In fact, perhaps because of the tussles that surrounded every issue of those days—women's suffrage, tariffs, regulating business, World War I, the League of Nations—people sought to create institutions that examined public policy outside the blood-scarred arena of party politics. The Council on Foreign Relations (CFR), for example, was founded by Democrats and Republicans in 1921 to maintain bipartisan support for American engagement in the world. All this sounds so worthy and dutiful as to be incredible in today's ironic age, but these people truly believed that it was important for a democracy to have places for civil discourse on important public issues. The CFR's first honorary president was Elihu Root, a senior Republican eminence, and its first president was John W. Davis, who became the Democratic presidential candidate in 1924. The CFR strove to create a foreign-policy discussion for the country that was civil and not permeated with partisanship. The founding editor of the CFR's magazine, *Foreign Affairs*, once told his deputy that if one of them became publicly identified as a Democrat, the other should immediately start campaigning for the Republicans.

Today, when elites involve themselves in issues it is entirely from a partisan perspective, often one related to some issue that affects them. Almost every institute and think tank created in the past thirty years is deeply ideological. This was partly the result of a concerted effort by American conservatives to create a "counter-establishment" to the one epitomized by the Brookings Institution and the Council on Foreign Relations, which they believed—legitimately—had drifted leftward in the 1960s and 1970s. But rather than rectifying this tilt by creating more independent institutions, conservatives decided to create ones that pushed their own partisan line. This conservative action will inevitably produce a liberal reaction, further polarizing the world of public policy in Washington. The scholars at most public-policy institutes today (there remain important exceptions) are chosen for their views, not their expertise, and in any event, know the conclusions at which they must arrive. They are not explicitly pushed toward any views but they understand that they were not hired by these think tanks to be free-thinking intellectuals. As Burton Pines, director of research at the Heritage Foundation, openly admitted, "We're not here as some kind of Ph.D. committee giving equal time. Our role is to provide conservative public policy makers with arguments to bolster our side."[19] In an age when old ideologies are not as useful to address new problems, these litmus tests have the effect of producing lots of predictable polemics and little serious analysis.

Partisan institutes are in many ways less troubling than those that have been set up to promote not ideology but naked interest. Many of the new "institutes" and "foundations" in Washington are in fact front groups for special interests: corporations, labor unions, even foreign governments. They produce a barrage of "research" to prove that their benefactors deserve government subsidies or other kinds of favoritism. Between party lines and patronage, the space for genuinely independent evaluations of public policy has almost vanished in Washington. Washington is now divided into two ideological camps and everyone ends up living, more or less, in one or the other. A nostalgia check: public policy has never been made in a vacuum, and party politics and interest groups have influenced—and should influence—the process. But anyone who has watched Washington over the last thirty years would acknowledge that it has undergone a dramatic shift, with a steep rise in aggressive advocacy in support of narrow interests, whether by intellectuals or by lobbyists. Instead of seeking—even as a goal—to get beyond pure partisanship, Washington's new elites simply use it to their advantage.

One institution remains to play the role of mediator in American society: the press. It explains and interprets the world to its public and its public to the world. More than any institution in America today the press defines reality and determines the political agenda. Yet unlike other mediating groups, which have historically tempered public passions, the press today often inflames them. It sensationalizes, dramatizes, and trivializes news. This is most true of television and the tabloids, but the trend affects much of journalism. The reasons for it are hardly sinister. Journalism has been hit by the same forces of democratization and marketization as has every other profession. The three traditional television networks, for example, operated as a cartel until the 1980s, knowing that they had a virtually captive audience. This stronghold, coupled with certain regulations about content, made the networks view their news bureaus as loss-making outfits that burnished their brands. They spent money on foreign news, documentaries, and culture.

Then came the information revolution, lowering costs, opening up outlets, and bringing in new competition of every kind. The rise of cable television meant the end of the three-network monopoly. Today the traditional networks compete virtually minute-by-minute against dozens of other news, entertainment, and talk outlets. This competition has produced some bright personalities and sharp programming. It has sometimes given more edge to dull shows. But the overall effect has been a race to the bottom. If you cannot amuse or frighten your audience into watching your channel, he or she will flip to another. A veteran broadcast journalist said to me, "The rise of alternatives was meant to be good for viewers in giving them choice. But the truth of the matter is that it's easy to get people to watch sex and mayhem. Good programming, like good books, asks a little more of the viewer. But no executive today will risk having the viewer bored for even a minute. Everyone is terrified of that remote control." There are, of course, serious news programs that buck this trend. But most of them were started decades ago and built their audience gradually over those years.

The world of print journalism has also been battered by the many alternate ways of getting news. Many once-great newspapers have shut down; others have become shadows of their former selves. But print journalism is flourishing in the sense that a hand-ful of high-quality papers and magazines still thrive. The *New York Times*, the *Wall Street Journal*, and the *Washington Post* are all better today than they have ever been. This is because they target a much smaller audience than does television, catering to a relatively select group. But the civic role that thousands of small newspapers filled throughout America cannot be filled by these three newspapers. Another—and crucial—reason for their continuing quality is that all three are family-owned papers, run by public-spirited propri-etors who believe that they are operating not simply corporations but also national institutions. Every major newspaper that has been sold by its family owners to a large corporation has seen a dramatic decline in quality, from the *Los Angeles Times* to the *Philadelphia Inquirer*. In many cases the paper was shut down altogether. A few serious magazines flourish, but again this is because the owners of publications such as *The New Yorker* and *The Atlantic Monthly*—both catering to an even smaller audience than do quality newspapers—are willing to subsidize excellence.* But there are fewer and fewer such owners, and it shows. This is unfortunate; it is possible to have a functioning liberal democracy without high-quality journalism that reaches large audiences, but it is far from ideal. The media, after all, is the one industry explicitly protected in the U.S. Consti-tution. But its dilemmas are not unique; other professions are also important to the success of democracy, and their decline is also worrying. The writer James Fallows suggests that "there are some

---

*Newsweek*, where I work, is one of the few mass-circulation publications that still covers the news seriously and in depth. It is able to do so largely because *Newsweek* is owned by the Graham family, which also owns the *Washington Post*.

goods and services whose value to society is not fully captured by a purely commercial model—think of health-care, education, journalism, and law. Society would be worse off if their supply and character were determined entirely by the free market. You wouldn't want your child to attend a college that set its curriculum purely on the basis of market forces. Similarly, good journalism has benefits to society beyond the profits it produces." That does not imply that the government regulation must be used to protect these industries. Indeed, for law and journalism historically, the solution has been public-spirited elites. But what to do when there are fewer and fewer such elites?

It is easier to be public spirited when your perch and position in society are secure. Such was the case with America's original elite—the Protestant establishment. From the founding of the nation until the 1960s, white Anglo-Saxon Protestants (WASPs) occupied the commanding heights of American society. Presidents, secretaries of state, governors, captains of industry, leaders of the bar, and presidents of universities were all WASPs. And they had connections to one another through a network of families, schools, colleges, and clubs, forming not simply a collection of privileged individuals but a social class—an American version of European aristocracy. A sprinkling of outsiders was allowed into the club, as long as they looked, dressed, and talked like WASPs. ("Think Yiddish, dress British," went the Jewish slogan for success.) With social class came a certain set of values. WASP values were not intellectual or academically minded. The pedigreed newspaper columnist Joseph Alsop recalled an episode when he was entering Groton, the New England prep school that, in its heyday, was the premier training ground for the WASP elite. His mother mentioned to its legendary headmaster, Endicott Peabody, that young Joe was interested in books and ideas. "We'll knock that all out of him," responded Reverend Peabody. Groton sought to turn out not bright minds but "muscular Christians," men who played hard but fair, followed a moral code, and believed in public service as a responsibility that came with power. Groton's motto is *cui servire est* *regnare*—"to serve is to reign."[*][20] There were, of course, plenty of wastrels and dumb jocks who got jobs, promotions, and other privileges because they belonged to the right ethnic group. But on the whole the leadership of the WASP establishment practiced and preached public service—from the presidency to local government.

As America became more diverse, open, and inclusive over the twentieth century, the WASP establishment faced a dilemma: it could maintain its power and refuse to allow new entrants into its sanctuaries, or it could open up to the new rising non-WASP members of society. The story is a mixed one. At first, in the early years of the century, the aristocracy became a caste, restricting membership in social clubs and turning away qualified Jews from Ivy League colleges.[21] But over time, this kind of exclusion proved unsustainable. In part the mood of the times would not allow it, in part capitalist competition wanted the best and the brightest, regardless of their ethnicity. But in the end the WASPs opened the doors to their club. By the late 1960s and early 1970s, virtually all the institutions the Protestant establishment controlled were opened up to outsiders. Therein lay the seeds of the establishment's own destruction. Whether through the civil rights movement or the opening up of Ivy League colleges or white-shoe firms on Wall Street, WASPs accepted new elites—Jews, Irish Catholics, Italians, and eventually women, blacks, Hispanics, and Asians—into the corridors of power. (Pockets of this world—some small men's clubs—have remained ethnically exclusive and have become irrelevant to society at large as a consequence. Exclusive clubs do still flourish in America, but now they discriminate on the basis of money, not ethnicity.) The WASPs made this move partly because they were pushed, but also because they knew it

---

[*]This is how it is often translated. The more literal and devout translation would be, "to serve Him is to rule," but Peabody always meant the phrase to be taken in a sense that implied public service. His preferred variation, from the Book of Common Prayer, is "whose service is perfect freedom." He once remarked, "If some Groton boys do not enter public service and do something for our land, it will not be because they have not been urged."

was the right thing to do. Confronted with a choice between their privilege and their values, they chose the latter.

America's new elite is a bunch of smart college graduates. It is a much more heterogeneous, meritocratic, and dynamic elite than the old one. People within it are not self-conscious about their elite status. If anything, they deny it. For many years after he became one of the richest men in the world, Bill Gates seemed to see himself as vaguely upper-middle class. And until recently, when their wealth and power became too vast to ignore, the country saw him and the new breed of tycoons he represented the same way: as ordinary folk who just happened to have lots of money. But this image is false and damaging. A relatively small group of people—perhaps 1 million or 0.5 percent of the country—runs most of the major institutions in the United States or has influence in other ways. This state of affairs has dramatic consequences for the nation.* They wield enormous power when compared with the average American. If neither they nor the country believes that they are in any sense an elite, then neither will adjust to their status. Elites will not lack power because they go unnoticed—far from it. In the words of Rudyard Kipling, they will have power but "power without responsibility; the prerogative of the harlot through the ages."[22]

During the first Gilded Age at the end of the nineteenth century, the conspicuous consumption and ostentation rivaled anything done by today's rich. But the rich then, perhaps because of religion or a

---

*Power is not simply financial or political. The medieval theory of estates and guilds was premised on the idea that those who possessed special expertise had special responsibilities. Knowledge is power. And if that sounds old fashioned, consider what one of North America's top biologists said to me: "There are a few dozen of us who know how to make really dangerous stuff, stuff that could kill tens of thousands of people if not more. I feel kind of weird about it. I don't know what to do with this power." Neither he nor society had thought through how he should deal with his knowledge. In everyone's mind, he was just a researcher in a laboratory, not an aristocrat. And yet he has more (potential) power today than any of Europe's princes ever did.

lingering Puritanism, worried about the effects of their wealth. Consider how schools such as Groton have changed in the last three or four decades. Until the 1970s their dormitories were bare cubicles, without doors or ceilings, with few creature comforts and no stereo systems or televisions. Boys lined up in the morning to wash in metal basins and take cold showers. The boys who went to Groton in, say, the 1920s often came from immensely wealthy backgrounds and grew up in vast mansions with dozens of servants. Yet they were made to live in utterly Spartan conditions at school. The purpose, as the journalist-historian Nicholas Lemann has written, "was to prevent rich boys from turning into playboys or pantywaists. It trained them not to be prosperous (that they would be prosperous was almost certain) but to be good and useful."[24] Today, schools such as Groton and Andover and colleges such as Harvard and Yale teach their graduates to be prosperous, or at least to succeed in their careers. Training people to be good and useful would be considered intrusive, judgmental, and demanding. An old alumnus from Groton recalled a recent visit to the school: "The dorms look similar but they now have stereos and televisions and are chock full of every comfort you could want. The general impression, compared to my days there, is of a pheasant farm. We were consciously denied luxury. They are given it by the bucketful." This is not to say that schools like Groton have declined in quality. But like society at large, they focus largely on achievement and less on character.*

It is easy to mock the Anglo-American elite, with its striking air of high-minded paternalism, born of a cultural sense of superiority. But it also embodied certain values—fair play, decency, liberty, and a Protestant sense of mission—that helped set standards for society. Of course these codes were artificial, ethnocentric, and often hypocriti-

---

*This tendency might be even more pronounced in other competitive high schools, but in the case of the great New England prep schools, one can see the shift from their own past, when they did the opposite—emphasize character too much and achievement too little.

cal. They were often abused, honored more in the breach than in the observance. But so what? "Hypocrisy," as the historian John Lukacs has written, "is the cement that held civilization together." Standards represent a society's highest aspirations, not its complex realities. When powerful people acknowledge that there are certain standards for behavior, they limit their own power, however indirectly, and signal to society, "*This* is what we strive for."

A final example might explain this shift in our view of elites in America.[22] Of the many differences between the blockbuster movie *Titanic* and history, one in particular is telling. In the movie, as the ship is sinking, the first-class passengers scramble to climb into the small number of lifeboats. Only the determination of the hardy seamen, who use guns to keep the grasping plutocrats at bay, gets the women and children into the boats. In fact, according to survivors' accounts, the "women and children first" convention was observed with almost no exceptions among the upper classes. The statistics make this plain. In first class, every child was saved, as were all but 5 (of 144) women, 3 of whom chose to die with their husbands. By contrast, 70 percent of the men in first class perished. In second class, which was also inhabited by rich professional types, 80 percent of the women were saved but 90 percent of the men drowned. The men on the first-class list of the *Titanic* virtually made up the Forbes 400 of the time. John Jacob Astor, reputedly the richest man in America at the time, is said to have fought his way to a boat, put his wife in it, and then, refusing to take a seat, stepped back and waved her goodbye. Benjamin Guggenheim similarly declined a seat, yielding his place to a woman, asking only that she convey a message home: "Tell my wife . . . I played the game out straight and to the end. No woman shall be left aboard this ship because Ben Guggenheim was a coward." In other words, some of the most powerful men in the world adhered to an unwritten code of honor—even though it meant certain death.

The movie-makers altered the story for good reason: no one would believe it today. We have freed our upper classes of any sense of responsibility and they have happily reciprocated. In modern discourse they are just like any of us, regular folk. We behave as if society is so democratic and so dynamic that it doesn't actually have a governing elite. But it does. The rich and the powerful will always be with us. We can only ask that they recognize that with their privileges come responsibilities. Social conventions, professional associations, moral strictures, prep schools, the gentleman's code—all were attempts to civilize the strong. In the past, American society expected these men and women to behave themselves and in some way participate in the public life of the land.

Near East Potomac Park in Washington, D.C., stands a haunting monument, a statue of a man with arms outstretched, Christ-like, with an inscription on its pedestal: "To the brave men of the *Titanic*, who gave their lives that women and children might be saved." It was erected by voluntary donations from 25,000 women across the United States. When leaders of society lived up to their ideals they were honored. When they did not it was a matter of deep disappointment. Today, by contrast, we expect very little of those in positions of power, and they rarely disappoint us.

# The Way Out

THE TWENTIETH CENTURY was marked by two broad trends: the regulation of capitalism and the deregulation of democracy. Both experiments overreached. They were sensible solutions to the problems of the time, unregulated capitalism and oligarchy. But as Evelyn Waugh pointed out in his comic novel *Scoop*, every good idea is valid "up to a point."

In the early years of the twentieth century, free markets and free trade seemed to be the inevitable way of the future. Countries around the world were trading with one another, opening up their markets, indeed, their entire societies. Markets were on the march. But it turned out that those years before World War I, hyperinflation, and the Great Depression were a watershed for laissez faire. From then on, whenever a problem developed—economic, social, political—government intervention was the solution. Every crisis brought forth new regulations, and every regulation brought forth a new bureaucracy. As a result, for most of the twentieth century, capitalism was taxed, licensed, controlled, and even nationalized, so much so that by 1945 Britain's preeminent historian, A. J. P. Taylor, could assert, "Nobody believes in the American way of life—that is private enterprise." In 1961, when Britain's Queen Elizabeth II visited Ghana, she was hailed as "the greatest socialist monarch in the world," which even her Tory government accepted as a compliment. When the conservative Republican Richard Nixon imposed wage and price controls on the U.S. economy in 1971 and announced, "We are all Keynesians now," he was reflecting the widespread view—even in America—that capitalism had to be intrusively managed by the state.

Democracy moved in the opposite direction. "The cure for the ailments of democracy," wrote the influential American philosopher John Dewey in 1927, "is more democracy." He was prescient. Most problems faced by most democracies during the twentieth century were addressed by broadening the franchise, eliminating indirect elections, reducing the strength of elite groups, and empowering more and more people in more and more ways. The results were thrilling. In America that meant blacks and women got the right to vote, senators were directly elected, parties chose their candidates on the basis of popular votes, and clubs changed their character and rules. The political history of the twentieth century is the story of ever-greater and more direct political participation. And success kept expanding democracy's scope. Whatever the ailment, more democracy became the cure.

The regulation of capitalism had gone overboard by the 1970s, resulting in heavy tax rates and Byzantine government controls. Over the last two decades, governments all over the world, from the United States to France to India to Brazil, have been deregulating industries, privatizing companies, and lowering tariffs. As the economic boom of the late 1990s unravels, there will be need for new regulation and a renewed appreciation of the role of government in capitalism. But few countries are likely to return to the bloated practices of a generation ago. The state has retreated from the commanding heights of the economy.

The deregulation of democracy has also gone too far. It has produced an unwieldy system, unable to govern or command the respect of people. Although none would dare speak ill of present-day democracy, most people instinctively sense a problem. Public respect for politics and political systems in every advanced democracy is at an all-time low. More intriguingly, in poll after poll, when Americans are asked what public institutions they most respect, three bodies are always at the top of their list: the Supreme Court, the armed forces, and the Federal Reserve System. All three have one thing in common: they are insulated from public pressures and operate undemocratically. It would seem that Americans admire these institutions precisely because they lead rather than follow. By contrast, Congress, the most representative and reflective of political institutions, scores at the bottom of most surveys. People view the pandering and the resulting paralysis with dismay, even disgust. Of course that does not stop them from celebrating the processes that have made such pandering inevitable.

## Delegating Democracy

When the stakes are high we do not entrust day-to-day politics to ourselves. No democracy has ever conducted a war by weekly vote. The struggle against terrorism is, inevitably, being waged by governments that have been given much leeway by their societies. We now face new threats but also new and deep pressures on government. Democracies will have to demonstrate that they can cope with terrorism effectively, or else in many developing countries we will see the rise of a new authoritarianism. Developing countries, particularly in the Islamic world, will need to manage a difficult balancing act. They must remain strong enough to handle the new dangers of terrorism but yet be open and democratic enough that they don't create political opposition that morphs into extremism. In other words, they must be able to kill terrorists without breeding terrorism. When it works right, the state's power, legitimacy, and effectiveness can work together, each reinforcing the other, in a virtuous cycle. When things go awry, however, the virtuous cycle becomes vicious—and violent. Repression produces extremism, which produces more repression.

Russia's approach to Chechnya is a sorry illustration of this downward spiral.

Globalization has produced a special set of challenges. The increasingly open world economy has forced governments to adopt disciplined policies that maintain fiscal stability over the long term. When they do not, markets punish countries faster and more severely than ever before, plunging currencies and stock markets into ruin. And yet long-term policies cause short-term pain—to voters. Demographic changes are pressing Western governments to reform their welfare states, in particular their benefits for the elderly. This will prove nearly impossible because senior citizens are politically powerful; they are well organized, contribute money, lobby hard, and vote regularly. Real reform, however, will inevitably mean trimming back their benefits. Governments will have to make hard choices, resist the temptation to pander, and enact policies for the long run. The only possible way that this can be achieved in a modern democracy is by insulating some decision-makers from the intense pressures of interest groups, lobbies, and political campaigns—that is to say, from the intense pressures of democracy.

It is already happening. The rise of independent central banks, like the U.S. Federal Reserve, over the last few decades is the clearest example of this trend. In most advanced democracies, the government's most powerful economic lever is now exercised by an unelected body. And it works. Though they have their flaws, by and large independence of central banks has resulted in more responsible monetary policy. In part because of this discipline, the business cycle, which was once sharp and severe, has increasingly been smoothed out. The bust of 2000–2002, which followed the longest boom in half a century, is still (as of this writing) less extreme than many had feared.

Central banks are not the only example of this phenomenon. There is much hand-wringing in Europe about the undemocratic nature of the European Union (EU), often criticized as the ultimate example of undemocratic policy-making. But the awkward reality is that the EU has been effective precisely because it is insulated from political pressures. By the 1970s, Europe's statist economies had become dysfunctional, their governments paralyzed by powerful interest groups, most of them protectionist, all of them hostile to change. Over the last decade Europe has been able to make significant reforms—fiscal, monetary, and regulatory—only because of the power of the EU. When the EU has not changed its policies it has been because of its democratic member governments. Not one of Europe's major parties has had the courage to advocate the structural reforms that they all know are necessary for the continent's long-term prosperity. "The European Union is the chief, indeed the only, agent of free-market reform on the continent," says Joseph Joffe, editor of Germany's *Die Zeit*. "Without Brussels we would not have deregulated any of our major industries." Without the fear of missing the EU's budget targets, countries such as Italy would never have moved toward lower deficits. Without Brussels there would be no pressure to reform Europe's wasteful subsidies.

In the Anglo-American world the EU is presented as a caricature. To the extent that Americans—and Britons, who are currently agonizing over whether to adopt the European currency, the euro—have views, they are strong and simple. The EU is big, bloated, and undemocratic and is snuffing out the charming diversity of European life. ("Unelected bureaucrats in Brussels are telling English brewers how to make ale!" Never mind that many of these quaint local customs are actually protectionist barriers to competition.) The critics of Europe in the United Kingdom and the United States are most often those who fervently support capitalism and free trade. But the opponents of the EU on the European continent—where it operates most fully—are people of the opposite persuasion. Denmark is famously skeptical about the EU and the euro. But Poul Nyrup Rasmussen, an economist by training and former prime minister of Denmark, explained that most Danish opponents of the EU were "people who fear globalization: low-skilled workers, women, public employees. For them, the European Union is just part of this new world of global capitalism and free markets." That is why the EU and bodies like it are here to stay. However much one criticizes them, the reality is that in today's world countries cannot set interest rates or make antitrust policy by plebiscite. Much of what Brussels is responsible for—regulatory, trade, monetary, and antitrust policy—is insulated from political pressures in many countries, including the United Kingdom and the United States.

Institutions like the European Union that are often condemned for being all-powerful and remote, in fact are neither. To begin with, the EU's powers are vastly exaggerated. Brussels's budget is just over 1 percent of the EU's total gross national product. Andrew Moravscik, one of the best American scholars of Europe, points out that once you exclude translators and clerical workers, the European Commission employs 2,500 officials, "fewer than any moderately sized European city and less than 1 percent of the number employed by the French state alone." As for its undemocratic nature, any new law it wishes to pass needs more than 71 percent of weighted national-government votes—"a larger proportion than that required to amend the American Constitution." The European Union, Moravscik argues persuasively, should not be thought of as a superstate but rather as an international organization.[5] Like most such bodies, it reflects the wishes of its member states. And the EU is not growing in powers. On the contrary, it is mostly trimming back, rationalizing lines of authority and clarifying its relationship with its members. The trend among Europe's leaders is toward a larger but better-defined European Union that digests the tasks it has already taken on.

## The Problem of Legitimacy

The European Union's troubles, however, highlight the central problem of the advanced democracies. The pressures for good government are increasing, but in a democratic age, the bureaucracies created as a result of this imperative lack legitimacy. Populists such as Jean Marie Le Pen in France, Pat Buchanan in the United States, and Jorge Haidar in Austria rail against the distant powers of these institutions. They tap into genuine and understandable feelings of alienation. When interest rates rise, when trade deals are concluded, when industries are deregulated, populists protest that it was all done by sinister bodies, operating in the dark. And yet these institutions function well precisely because of their distance from day-to-day politics. They provide enormous benefits for the average citizen, in the form of stronger growth, greater productivity, a stable fiscal environment, and many more economic opportunities. How to resolve this problem and get effective government but also legitimate government?

Do not look for help from democratic theorists. Despite the existence of hundreds of unelected bodies that now help democratic governments make decisions, political philosophers who write about democracy today are mostly radicals in favor of total, unfettered democracy. Seemingly unaware of the problems that made these institutions necessary, blind to the fact that these bodies are responsive to their elected masters, the theorists are content to join with the street protests against world government. They sing paeans to the people and urge the ever more direct participation of the people (except in the running of universities, of course, which still run like medieval kingdoms). As a result, philosophy has little connection with reality these days.

Politicians also, by and large, have exacerbated the problem of democratic legitimacy. Happy to hand over complex problems to unelected bodies, they then grandstand by attacking these very institutions. Thus French politicians have been delighted to accept all the benefits that come from having lower budget deficits. But when they have to cut spending to achieve this goal, they remind their voters that the pain is all the fault of the evil European Union. "Don't blame me, Brussels made me do it," has become a popular excuse among Europe's governing class. One should not be surprised that the result has been a growing crisis of legitimacy for the EU.

This problem is only going to grow. The World Trade Organization (WTO) represents the latest in a series of powerful bodies with broad authority, distant from the people, that has attracted a fresh wave of criticism. Although the antiglobalization groups have many disparate and often contradictory agendas, they all agree that bodies like the WTO are ominous. Some of their concerns are valid—the proceedings of bodies such as the WTO should be made more open—but in truth the WTO works well precisely because it is insulated from public pressures. As we have seen, being open to "the people" means in practice being open to organized political interests, usually those representing small minorities. If trade negotiations allowed for constant democratic input, they would be riddled with exceptions, caveats, and shields for politically powerful groups. Agriculture in the Western world, one of the chief areas in which free-trade agreements have not made a dent, remains ruinously costly and unproductive precisely because small groups of rich farmers have used the democratic system to their benefit. More democracy in trade policy would mean more policies like agricultural subsidies.

The current system—the WTO and its precursor, the General Agreement on Tariffs and Trade—has produced extraordinary results. The expansion of trade has been the single greatest economic achievement of the world over the past fifty years, producing dramatic declines in poverty and disease around the globe. The world has made more economic progress in the last fifty years than in the previous five hundred. Do we really want to destroy the system that made this happen by making it function like the California legislature?

Instead of running it down or running away from it, Western politicians should embrace the spirit behind the WTO, the EU, the Federal Reserve System, and other such bodies. They should defend these bodies from their detractors, pointing out that they are deeply democratic in the Madisonian sense. Whatever one thinks of his solution, James Madison and his fellow Federalists were prescient in recognizing—in 1789!—that popular government would be plagued by one problem above all else: that of special interests.

Because Madison recognized that "special interests" were ultimately a form of free speech, he knew that there was no simple way to ban them. Madison ultimately placed his greatest hope in the structure of American government itself. For him, that America was a republic and not a pure democracy was its greatest strength. It meant that public policy would not be made directly, emotionally, or for narrow concerns. By the "delegation of government" to a group of citizens elected by the rest, it would be possible to "refine and enlarge the public views, by passing them through the medium of a chosen body of citizens, whose wisdom may best discern the true interest of their country, and whose patriotism and love of justice will be least likely to sacrifice it to temporary or partial considerations."

His words may sound old-fashioned, but they represent a remarkably modern idea: delegation. The more specialized life gets, the more we delegate. Delegation is, after all, how modern business is run. Shareholders own companies but hand over their management to people who can devote time and energy to it and who have expertise in the field. Shareholders retain ultimate control but recognize that they cannot run the companies themselves. This is not to say that some executives will not abuse the authority given to them, but when they do shareholders can punish them and often do.

Delegated democracy, in the view of many of America's founders, would produce better government because it would be exercised by people interested and experienced in public affairs and still accountable to the people. Above all, for Madison, it was a mechanism by which to temper narrow interests and short-term perspectives—precisely the problem we face today. But whereas in the rest of life delegation and specialization increase, in politics the trend is in the opposite direction. If you were to argue in the business world that any amateur could run a large company because experience in business has no bearing on one's ability to do the job, you would be ridiculed. Say that about government and you are a sage. We have decided that although we cannot file our tax forms, write our wills, or configure our computers, we can pass laws ourselves.

## Less Is More

What we need in politics today is not more democracy but less. By this I do not mean we should embrace strongmen and dictators but rather that we should ask why certain institutions within our society—such as the Federal Reserve and the Supreme Court—function so well and why others—such as legislatures—function poorly. As it happens, Alan Blinder, a Princeton professor, pondered just this question in a fascinating essay in *Foreign Affairs* magazine in 1997.[1] Blinder had completed two stints in government, first at the White House on the Council of Economic Advisers and then at the Federal Reserve, where he served as vice chairman. He noted in his essay that policy-making at the White House was dominated by short-term political and electoral considerations, whereas policy-making at the Federal Reserve was concerned largely with a policy's social, economic, and legal merits. This difference in large part accounted for the consistently high quality of decision-making at the Fed.

Blinder argued that Federal Reserve decision-making was insulated from politics for three good reasons. First, interest rates are a technical subject that specialists are better equipped to handle than amateurs. Second, monetary policy takes a long time to work and so requires patience and a steady hand. Finally, the pain of fighting inflation (higher unemployment) comes well before the benefits (permanently lower costs of goods, lower interest rates, etc.). As a result, good interest-rate policy cannot be made in an atmosphere dominated by short-term considerations. But then Blinder admitted that "a nasty little thought kept creeping through my head: the argument for the Fed's independence applies just as forcefully to many other areas of government. Many policy decisions require complex technical judgments and have consequences that stretch into the distant future." He cited health care, environmental policy, and tax policy as just such cases.

Consider the U.S. federal income tax. In its first incarnation in 1914, the entire tax code was 14 pages long, and individuals' tax returns fit on a single page. Today the tax code runs over 2,000 pages, with 6,000 pages of regulations and tens of thousands of pages of rulings and interpretations. The Internal Revenue Service publishes 480 tax forms and 280 forms to explain them. It is unclear exactly how much it costs Americans to comply with these Byzantine rules; estimates go as high as $600 billion per year, but most scholars place the number at about $100 billion, or about 15 percent of income-tax revenue (about $375 to $450 per person per year). Dale Jorgenson, chairman of the Economics Department at Harvard, calculates that moving to a flat-rate tax on consumption would raise as much revenue as the current income-tax system while increasing economic growth by more than $200 billion a year.

The tax code has become time-consuming, complex, and expensive for a simple reason: democratic politics. It presents a golden opportunity for politicians to fund their favorite programs, groups, and companies without attracting much attention. An outright grant would be noticed; a small change in tax law will not. Corporations with very similar balance sheets can pay widely differing taxes, depending on whether they have effective lobbyists who can bully Congress into rewriting the code to their benefit. Often a new law is so narrowly written as to be in effect a subsidy to one particular company. Although each tax break might seem small, the overall cost is staggering, totaling more than $550 billion in forgone revenue for the federal government in 2001. Some of these "tax expenditures" are designed to support programs with broad public approval, but others—such as narrowly targeted tax breaks for industry—can only be described as corporate welfare.

Americans of all political stripes agree that the tax code is unwieldy, inefficient, and unfair. Yet no one believes it will ever be reformed, because it is embedded in democratic politics. Blinder points out that the three reasons that the Federal Reserve is independent all apply particularly strongly to tax policy. He proposes the creation of an independent federal tax authority, much like the Federal Reserve. Congress would give it broad directions and guidelines, and on this basis it would prepare tax legislation. Congress would then vote on the bill but no amendments would be allowed. Although hardly flawless, such a system would undoubtedly produce a better tax code than the one we have now.

The United States government already experiments with this kind of delegation in some areas. The president is usually given the authority to negotiate trade agreements, which are then presented to Congress as a complete package. Congress votes on the bill as a whole with no amendments allowed. Congress used a similar procedure in the early 1990s, when it needed to close dozens of military bases as the country demobilized after the Cold War. Faced with a crisis, legislators realized that the only way to arrive at a fair outcome was to take politics out of the process. Otherwise members of Congress would all be strongly in favor of closing bases, just not the ones in their districts. They delegated the task of determining which bases should be closed to a nonpartisan commission. The final list was presented to Congress for a single vote, up or down, with no changes permitted. These processes have all worked well, combining effective government with democratic control.

Delegation is the modern-day equivalent of the strategy that Homer's wandering hero, Ulysses, used as he sailed past the Sirens, whose singing made men cast themselves into the sea. Ulysses had his sailors fill their ears with wax so that they could not hear the Sirens' calls. For his part, he wanted to hear the music, so he had himself bound tightly to the mast of his ship and told his men that no matter what he said, they were not to untie him. As they passed the treacherous waters, Ulysses was seduced by the music and begged to be released. But the system worked. His men held to his initial orders and kept him bound. As a result, the boat and its sailors emerged safely from their trial. Politicians today should bind themselves more often to the ship of state as they pass through turbulent political waters.

## The Highest Stakes

In developing countries the need for delegation is even greater because the stakes are often higher. Governments must demonstrate deep commitment and discipline in their policies or else markets quickly lose faith in them. They must focus on the long-term with regard to urban development, education, and health care, or their societies will slowly descend into stagnation or even anarchy. Far-sighted policies pay huge dividends; short-term patronage politics have immense costs.

In general dictators have not done better at these policies than democrats—far from it. Most dictators have ravaged their countries for personal gain. Scholars have asked whether democracy helps or hurts the economic growth of poor countries and, despite many surveys, have come to no conclusive answer.[2] But over the past fifty years almost every success story in the developing world has taken place under a liberal authoritarian regime. Whether in Taiwan, South Korea, Singapore, Chile, Indonesia, or even China, governments that were able to make shrewd choices for the long term were rewarded with strong economic growth and rising levels of literacy, life expectancy, and education. It is difficult to think of a Third World democracy that has achieved sustained growth rates like those of the countries listed above. Those that have gone down the path of reform are quickly stymied by the need to maintain subsidies for politically powerful groups. India has been unable to engage in sustained reform largely because its politicians will not inflict any pain—however temporary—on their constituents. As a result, for all its democratic glories, the country has slipped further and further behind on almost every measure of human development: life expectancy, infant mortality, health, literacy, education. It now ranks a shocking 124 (out of 173) on the United Nations 2002 human development index, behind China, of course, but even behind Guatemala, Bolivia, and Syria, and well behind Cuba. Surely it is time to ask whether democracies such as India, so lauded by Western intellectuals, are working for their people.

The solution is not to scuttle democracy in the Third World. Democracy has immense benefits regardless of its effects on development and growth. It also has real economic virtues. Although it does not achieve the best results, it usually protects against the worst. You may not get a Lee Kuan Yew through elections, but you will not get a Mobutu Sese Seko either. Yet cheerleading about democracy will not solve its problems. There must be a way to make democratic systems work so that they do not perennially produce short-term policies with dismal results. The stakes in poor countries are just too high.

Some form of delegation might be one solution. Central banks should become more powerful, a process that is already under way. Judges should have similar independent standing. In order to strengthen the judiciary and fight corruption, justice ministries and law-enforcement authorities should also be given more independence. Many American institutions, such as the Federal Reserve System, the Securities and Exchange Commission, and the Federal Bureau of Investigation, have their leaders appointed to long terms (7–10 years) that do not coincide with the electoral cycle. This is done deliberately, to give them some distance from politics.

A crucial area in which a creative new arrangement might be possible is in the economic realm. Decision-making in this arena should be distanced from day-to-day politics. The finance minister in a Third World country should have the ability to present his annual budget as a package that cannot be amended, only approved or denied as a whole. (The United Kingdom, because of its parliamentary system and tight party discipline, does this informally, and as a result has a reputation for being able to enact effective fiscal policy.) One might even go further and allow the economics minister to be appointed to a longer term than the norm—as with the head of the Federal Reserve—so that when a political crisis triggers the fall of a government it does not automatically result in the collapse of economic reform. None of these measures will take politics out of the process entirely. Nor should they. Politics is healthy; it is how people assert their power in a democracy. You need political support for any policy, reformist or otherwise. Instead, the goal is simply to weaken the intense pressure of politics on public policy in the stressed circumstances of the Third World, to shift the balance somewhat to make the system work better. It will not always work better. Some ministers and bureaucrats will abuse the greater authority they are given. Others will pursue well-intentioned but foolish policies. But it will probably work better than the system now prevalent in most developing democracies, which has delivered so little to its people.

It is important to emphasize that these changes are utterly compatible with democracy. They delegate authority to institutions, but ultimate power rests with the people through their elected representatives. This check should be strengthened. Two-thirds majorities in legislatures should be able to override most of the special protections outlined above. Parliamentary committees should regularly oversee the work of all unelected bodies. In a sense these new arrangements are simply an extension of the way an administrative department, say the Department of Health and Human Services, works in the United States. It formulates and implements policies based on broad guidelines handed down by Congress. The legislature exercises ultimate control but leaves much of the policy to unelected bureaucrats. If it works for welfare policy, why not for taxes? Most of all politicians should defend these systems to the public, explaining that delegation can produce a reasonable balance between good government and democratic control. Given their appreciation (in the West, at least) of courts and central banks, clearly people understand this argument.

Delegation is not simply a phenomenon that exists in the political realm. In many other areas we face the same choice. Do we want to go down the path of loosening controls, bypassing mediators, and breaking down old standards—in economics and culture, for example—or do we want instead to retain and reshape some of the guides and buffers that have traditionally been part of our society? Technology has combined with ideology to offer the alluring prospect of a world without mediation. You can become your own stockbroker, newspaper editor, lawyer, and doctor. But do you want to? Attitudes on this matter are less giddy than they were during the boom years of the 1990s. People have begun to recognize that perhaps there is a reason that mediators have existed in so many different areas in so many ages. It turns out that most investors would gladly pay slightly higher fees for the proper execution of stock trades, for financial and investment advice, and even for old-fashioned hand-holding. Those with legal complaints and medical problems realized that self-diagnosis—by reading internet sites and participating in chat groups—is only so useful. In the world of journalism, the personal Web site ("blog") was hailed as the killer of the traditional media. In fact it has become something quite different. Far from replacing newspapers and magazines, the best blogs—and the best are very clever—have become guides to them, pointing to unusual sources and commenting on familiar ones. They have become new mediators for the informed public. Although the creators of blogs think of themselves as radical democrats, they are in fact a new Tocquevillean elite. Much of the Web has moved in this direction because the wilder, bigger, and more chaotic it becomes, the more people will need help navigating it.

## Onward and Downward

But for all these encouraging signs, the broad trends still move us toward the unceasing democratization of society. Politics becomes more and more permeable, European societies become "Americanized," old institutions open up, professions and guilds die out, and technology continues to threaten most intermediaries. All of which will result in much good, as it has in the past. But it will also destroy parts of the fabric of our culture. The institutions and attitudes that have preserved liberal democratic capitalism in the West were built over centuries. They are being destroyed in decades. Once torn down they will not be so easy to repair. We watch this destruction without really being able to stop it—that would be undemocratic.

But it will leave its mark on our politics, economics, and culture, all of which will increasingly be dominated by short-term interests and enthusiasms. Edmund Burke once described society as a partnership between the dead, the living, and the yet unborn. It is difficult to see in the evolving system who will speak for the yet unborn, for the future.

Meanwhile, public dissatisfaction with the effects of all these changes will continue to grow. If these problems build, eventually people will define democracy by what it has become: a system, open and accessible in theory, but ruled in reality by organized or rich or fanatical minorities, protecting themselves for the present and sacrificing the future. This is a very different vision from that of the enthusiasts of direct democracy, who say that the liberating new world we will live in will harken back to the city-states of ancient Greece. I leave it to the reader to judge whether Californian politics today resembles Athenian democracy in its prime. In any event, it is worth remembering that direct democracy was tried only in a few small cities in ancient Greece where a few thousand men were allowed to vote. It is also worth remembering that within a hundred years all those democracies collapsed into tyranny or chaos—frequently both.

Such gloom may seem far-fetched, but if current trends continue, democracy will undoubtedly face a crisis of legitimacy, which could prove crippling. Legitimacy is the elixir of political power. "The strongest is never strong enough to be the master," Jean-Jacques Rousseau observed, "unless he translates strength into right and obedience into duty." Only democracy has that authority in the world today. But it can lose its hold on our loyalties. The greatest danger of unfettered and dysfunctional democracy is that it will discredit democracy itself, casting all popular governance into a shadowy light. This would not be unprecedented. Every wave of democracy has been followed by setbacks in which the system is seen as inadequate and new alternatives have been proposed by ambitious leaders and welcomed by frustrated people. The last such period of disenchantment, in Europe during the interwar years, was seized upon by demagogues, many of whom capitalized on the public's disenchantment with democracy. It is worth remembering that the embrace of communism and fascism in the 1930s did not seem as crazy at the time as it does now. While the democracies were mired in depression and gloom, authoritarian states had mobilized their societies and were on the march.

Modern democracies will face difficult new challenges—fighting terrorism, adjusting to globalization, adapting to an aging society—and they will have to make their system work much better than it currently does. That means making democratic decision-making effective, reintegrating constitutional liberalism into the practice of democracy, rebuilding broken political institutions and civic associations. Perhaps most difficult of all, it requires that those with immense power in our societies embrace their responsibilities, lead, and set standards that are not only legal, but moral. Without this inner stuffing, democracy will become an empty shell, not simply inadequate but potentially dangerous, bringing with it the erosion of liberty, the manipulation of freedom, and the decay of a common life.

This would be a tragedy because democracy, with all its flaws, represents the "last best hope" for people around the world. But it needs to be secured and strengthened for our times. Eighty years ago, Woodrow Wilson took America into the twentieth century with a challenge to make the world safe for democracy. As we enter the twenty-first century, our task is to make democracy safe for the world.

# Afterword

George W. Bush's second Inaugural Address was the culmination, in style and substance, of a position he had been veering toward ever since September 11, 2001—that the purpose of American foreign policy must be the expansion of democracy. It is not a new theme for an American president. Woodrow Wilson, Franklin Roosevelt, John Kennedy, and Ronald Reagan all spoke in similar tones and terms. Bush, however, has brought to the cause the passion of the convert. In short declarative sentences, in almost biblical language, Bush used virtually his entire speech to set out his worldview: that "the best hope for peace in our world is the expansion of freedom in all the world."

To borrow an old saw about the mission of journalism, Bush's words "comforted the afflicted and afflicted the comfortable." He surely hoped that democratic reformers around the world would take heart. Dictators would nervously ponder what it all meant. This, too, was in a great American tradition. When Wilson and Roosevelt spoke out against empires, it rattled Europe's great powers. When Kennedy and Reagan spoke about freedom, it worried the juntas of Latin America and the despots of East Asia. When the Carter administration began issuing annual reports on human rights, it unnerved regimes across the world. In speaking directly about the importance and universality of freedom, America—and, to be fair, Europe—have made a difference.

In doing so, however, Bush also pushed higher on the agenda the question of American hypocrisy. I often argue with an Indian businessman friend of mine that America is unfairly singled out for scrutiny abroad. "Why didn't anyone criticize the French or Chinese for their meager response to the tsunami?" I asked. His response was simple. "America positions itself as the moral arbiter of the world, it pronounces on the virtues of all other regimes, it tells the rest of the world whether they are good or evil," he said. "No one else does that. America singles itself out. And so the gap between what it says and what it does is blindingly obvious—and for most of us, extremely annoying." By the time Bush made his speech in 2005 that gap was gargantuan.

In 1947, Harry Truman announced the "Truman Doctrine," which turned into the containment of the Soviet Union by saying, "I believe that it must be the policy of the United States to support free peoples who are resisting attempted subjugation by armed minorities or by outside pressures." Echoing that formulation, Bush declared, "So it is the policy of the United States to seek and support the growth of democratic movements and institutions in every nation and culture, with the ultimate goal of ending tyranny in our world." The president went on to outline various stances that the United States will adopt in the future, all suggesting a broad shift in American policy.

The chasm between rhetoric and reality, while inevitable, is striking. The Bush administration was particularly vocal in holding dictators to account—and yet it does business with Vladimir Putin, who resided over the most significant reversal of freedoms across the globe. Bush even sided with Putin in his interpretation of the Chechen war as a defensive action against terrorists. In fact, while it is a complicated story, the Russian Army has killed about 100,000 Chechen civilians in a brutal campaign to deny them the right to secede.

The president promised the world's democrats, "When you stand for your liberty, we will stand with you." But when democratic Taiwan stood up to communist China in 2004, Bush publicly admonished it, siding with Beijing. When brave dissidents in Saudi Arabia were jailed for proposing the possibility of a constitutional monarchy in that country, the administration barely mentioned it. Saudi Arabia's King Abdullah, who rules one of the eight most repressive countries in the world (according to Freedom House), is one of a handful of leaders to have been invited to the president's ranch in Crawford, Texas. (The elected leaders of, say, India, France, Turkey, and Indonesia have never been accorded this courtesy.) The president has met with and given aid to Islam Karimov, the dictator of Uzbekistan, who presides over one of the nastiest regimes in the world today, far more repressive than Iran's, to take just one example. Pervez Musharraf, the general who rules Pakistan, is greeted as a good friend by the White House.

I do not mean to suggest that in all these cases the president should invade non-democracies or break ranks with or even condemn these leaders. In many cases the broader interests of peace and stability are served by amicable relations with these countries. But President Bush suggested in his speech that there is no conflict between America's ideals and its interests. The record of his own administration—in line with all previous ones—highlights the opposite.

The president and his administration speak constantly about the "freedom agenda" and interpret global events largely in such terms. During the summer of 2006, as missiles, car bombs, and IEDs exploded across Lebanon, Gaza, and Iraq, Condoleezza Rice described the violence as the "birth pangs" of a new, democratic Middle East. Her optimism stood in sharp contrast to the 2006 annual survey of "freedom in the world" released by Freedom House, a nonprofit that is engaged in promoting democracy around the globe. The report points out that it was a bad year for liberty, under attack from creeping authoritarianism in Venezuela and Russia, a coup in Thailand, massive corruption in Africa, and a host of more subtle reversals.

"The percentage of countries designated as free has failed to increase for nearly a decade and suggests that these trends may be contributing to a developing freedom stagnation," wrote Freedom House director of research Arch Puddington in an essay released with the rankings. Puddington also called attention to the "pushback" against democracy. Regimes across the world are closing down non-governmental organizations, newspapers, and other groups that advocate for human rights. What is most striking is that these efforts are not being met with enormous criticism. Democracy proponents are on the defensive in many places.

What explains this paradox—of freedom's retreat, even with a U.S. administration vociferous in its promotion of democracy? Some part of the explanation lies in the global antipathy to the U.S. president. "We have all been hurt by the association with the Bush administration," Saad Eddin Ibrahim, the Egyptian human rights activist, told me. "Bush's arrogance has turned people off the idea of democracy," says Larry Diamond, coeditor of the *Journal of Democracy*. Bush mixed together the issue of democracy, liberty, American arrogance, and nationalism in toxic ways.

The administration sees itself as giving voice to the hundreds of millions who are oppressed around the world. And yet the prevailing image of the United States in those lands is not at all as a beacon of liberty. Widespread public sentiment sees the United States as self-interested and arrogant.

Why? Well, consider Vice President Cheney's speech on May 4, 2006, in Lithuania, in which he accused Russia of backpedaling on democracy. Cheney was correct in his specific criticisms, but to speak as Cheney did misunderstands the reality in Russia and squanders America's ability to have an impact in it.

In Cheney's narrative, Russia was a blooming democracy during the 1990s, but in recent years it has turned into a sinister dictatorship where people live in fear. In castigating Vladimir Putin, Cheney believes that he is speaking for the Russian masses. He fancies himself as Reagan at the Berlin wall. Except he isn't. Had Cheney done his homework and consulted a few opinion polls, which are extensive and reliable in Russia, he would have discovered that Putin has had high approval ratings for most of his tenure, often approaching 75 percent.

Most Russians see recent history differently. They remember Russia in the 1990s as a country of instability, lawlessness, and banditry. They believe that Boris Yeltsin bankrupted the country, handed its assets over to his cronies, and spent most of his time drunk and dysfunctional. Yeltsin's approval ratings by 1994 were below 20 percent and in 1996 he actually went into the single digits for a while. Russians see Putin, on the other hand, as having restored order, revived growth, and reasserted national pride.

For the average Russian per capita GDP went from $600 to $5,000 during Putin's reign, much, though not all, of which was related to oil prices. The poverty rolls fell from 42 million to 26 million. College graduates increased by 50 percent and a middle class emerged in Russia's cities. The backsliding that Cheney described is quite true, but the truth is that even so, Russia today is a strange mixture of freedom and unfreedom. The country publishes 90,000 books a year, espousing all political views.

Polls in Russia show that people still rate democracy as something they value. But in the wake of the 1990s, they value more urgently conditions that will allow them to lead decent civic and economic lives. For most people in Russia—and Iraq and elsewhere—order is the basis of their lives and livelihood. Without it, freedom is a farce.

Or consider Nigeria. American officials insisted that its elected president, Olusegun Obasanjo, not run for a third term (which would have required amending election laws). This drama was largely irrelevant to what is really happening in Nigeria. Over the last 25 years, the country has gone into free fall. Its per capita GDP collapsed from $1,000 to $390. It ranks below Haiti and Bangladesh on the Human Development Index. In 2004 the World Bank estimated that 80 percent of Nigeria's oil wealth goes to 1 percent of its people. Sectarian tensions are rising, particularly between Muslims and Christians, and 12 of the country's 36 provinces have imposed *sharia*. Violent conflict permeates the country, with 10,000 people dead over the last eight years. But all Washington seemed concerned about was electoral procedures.

"We need to face up to the fact that in many developing countries democracy is not working very well," writes Larry Diamond, one of the leading experts on democratization, pointing to several countries where ostensibly free and fair elections have been followed by governmental paralysis, corruption, and ethnic warfare. The new Freedom House survey rates Haiti higher now because it held elections last year. But does anyone believe that those polls will change the essential reality in Haiti—that it is a failed state?

The basic problem confronting the developing world today is not an absence of democracy but an absence of governance. From Iraq to the Palestinian territories to Nigeria to Haiti, this is the cancer that is eating away at the lives of people across the globe, plunging countries into chaos, putting citizens' lives and livelihoods at risk. It is what American foreign policy should be focused on. But the president's freedom agenda sees the entire complex process of political and economic development through one simple lens, which produces bad analysis and bad outcomes.

The administration now rewards democracies with aid. But why not have a more meaningful measure? Why not reward countries when they protect human rights, reduce corruption, and increase the quality of governance? "Our aid should be conditional on absolute standards," says Diamond. "The European Union has forced change on countries that want to join it by demanding real progress on tough issues." Europe has been less grandiose than America in its rhetoric but has achieved more practical results on the ground.

It is easier to imagine liberal democracy than to achieve it. During his presidency, Ronald Reagan imagined a Soviet Union that was politically and economically free. Twenty years later, except for the Baltic states and Georgia, none of the countries of the former Soviet Union has achieved that. There have been more than fifty elections in Africa in the past 15 years—some as moving as those in Iraq, had we bothered to notice them—but only a few of those countries can be described as free. Haiti has had elections and American intervention, and still has foreign troops stationed there. Yet only a few of these elections have led to successful and free societies.

Every country, culture, and people yearns for freedom. But building real, sustainable democracy with rights and protections is complex.

The place where the president was right to assert the convergence of interests and ideals was the Middle East. Bush never accepted the view that Islamic terrorism had its roots in religion or culture or the Arab-Israeli conflict. Instead he veered toward the analysis that the region was breeding terror because it had developed deep dysfunctions caused by decades of repression and an almost total lack of political, economic, and social modernization. The Arab world, in this analysis, was almost unique in that over the past three decades it had become increasingly unfree, even as the rest of the world was opening up. His solution, therefore, was to push for reform.

The theory did not originate with Bush's administration. Others had made this case: scholars like Bernard Lewis and Fouad Ajami, Thomas Friedman of the *New York Times*, the Arab intellectuals who wrote the United Nations' now famous "Arab Human Development Report." These ideas were gaining some ground in the Arab world, especially after 9/11, but Bush's adoption of them was important because he had the power to pressure the region's regimes. Efforts to change the dynamics of the Middle East had always collapsed in the past as its wily rulers would delay, obstruct, and obfuscate.

In Lebanon the absence of Syria did not mean the presence of a stable democracy. It was the collapse of Lebanon's internal political order that triggered the Syrian intervention in 1976. That problem will have to be solved, even though Syrian forces have gone home. In Jordan the unelected monarch is more liberal, more open, and more progressive than most of the elected democrats, many of whom are deeply reactionary. The United Arab Emirates is rated one of the least free countries in the world, yet its biggest city, Dubai, run by fiat by an unelected monarch, is quickly becoming an open, free-market haven with surprising openness in other realms as well.

The Middle East needs incremental but persistent reform like that taking place today in Jordan, Qatar, Dubai, and perhaps even Egypt. But in the past, small, gradual reforms have been a smoke screen for doing nothing. Genuine economic reforms are the most crucial because they modernize the whole society. These reforms are also the most difficult to achieve because they threaten the power and wealth of deeply entrenched oligarchies. So far there has been more talk than action on this front, more dreams of democracy than reforms that would lay its groundwork.

This lack of attention to the long, hard slog of actually promoting democracy might explain why things have gone so poorly in the most important practical application of the Bush Doctrine so far—Iraq. Convinced that bringing freedom to a country meant simply getting rid of the tyrant, the Bush administration seems to have done virtually no serious postwar planning to keep law and order, let alone to build the institutions of a democratic state. If this sounds like an exaggeration, consider the extraordinary words in the "after-action report" of the most important division of the American Army in Iraq, the Third Infantry Division. It reads: "Higher headquarters did not provide the Third Infantry Division (Mechanized) with a plan for Phase IV [the postwar phase]. As a result, Third Infantry Division transitioned into Phase IV in the absence of guidance."

The chaos in Iraq was not inevitable. In the months after the American invasion, support for the Coalition Provisional Authority topped 70 percent. This was so even among Iraq's Sunni Arabs. In the first months of the insurgency, only 14 percent of them approved of attacks on U.S. troops. That number rose to 70 percent after a year of disorder, looting, and mass unemployment. The rebellious area in those early months was not Sunni Fallujah but Shiite Najaf.

During those crucial first months, Washington disbanded the Iraqi

Army, fired 50,000 bureaucrats, and shut down the government-owned enterprises that employed most Iraqis. In effect, the United States dismantled the Iraqi state, creating a deep security vacuum, administrative chaos, and soaring unemployment. Iraq's Sunni elites read this as not just a regime change but a revolution in which they had become the new underclass. For them, the new Iraq looked like a new dictatorship.

The administration has never fully understood the sectarian impact of its policies, which were less "nation building" than they were "nation busting" in their effects. It kept insisting that it was building a national army and police force when it was blatantly obvious that the new forces were overwhelmingly Shiite and Kurdish, mostly drawn from militias with stronger loyalties to political parties than to the state. The answer to these fundamentally political problems was technocratic: more training. In reality, a stronger Shiite Army made—makes—the Sunni populace more insecure and willing to support the insurgency.

Iraq's Sunnis are not the good guys in this story. They have mostly behaved like self-defeating thugs and the minority of Sunnis who support Al Qaeda have been truly barbarous. The point, however, is not their vices but our stupidity. We summarily deposed not just Saddam Hussein but a centuries-old ruling elite and then were stunned that they reacted poorly. In contrast, on coming into power in South Africa, Nelson Mandela did not fire a single white bureaucrat or soldier—and not because he thought that they had been kind to his people. He correctly saw the strategy as the way to prevent an Afrikaner rebellion. Alas, there has been no Iraqi Mandela.

It has now become fashionable among Washington neoconservatives to blame the Iraqis for everything that has happened to their country. "We have given the Iraqis a republic and they do not appear able to keep it," laments Charles Krauthammer. Others invoke anthropologists to explain the terrible dysfunctions of Iraqi culture. There may be some truth to all these claims—Iraq is a tough place—but the Bush administration is not so blameless. It thoughtlessly engineered a political and social revolution as intense as the French or Iranian ones and then seemed surprised that Iraq could not digest it happily, peaceably, and quickly. We did not give them a republic. We gave them a civil war.

If there is to be any hope for the future of the country, Iraq must first fulfill three conditions to become a functioning liberal democracy.

First, avoid major ethnic or religious strife. In almost any "divided" society, elections can exacerbate group tensions unless there is a strong effort to make a deal between the groups, getting all to buy into the new order. "The one precondition for democracy to work is a consensus among major ethnic, regional, or religious groups," argues Larry Diamond. This, of course, did not happen. Instead the Shia, Sunnis, and Kurds are increasingly wary of one another and are thinking along purely sectarian lines. This "groupism" also overemphasizes the religious voices in these communities and gives rise to a less secular, less liberal kind of politics.

Second, create a non–oil-based economy and government. When a government has easy access to money, it doesn't need to create a real economy. In fact, it doesn't need its citizens because it doesn't tax them. The result is a royal court, distant and detached from its society.

Iraq's oil revenues were supposed to be managed well, going into a specially earmarked development fund rather than used to finance general government activities. The Coalition Provisional Authority (CPA) steered this process reasonably well, though its auditors gave it a less-than-glowing review. Since the transfer of power to the Iraqi provisional government, Iraq's oil revenues have been managed in an opaque manner. "There is little doubt that Iraq is now using its oil wealth for general revenues," says Isam al Khafaji, who worked for the CPA briefly and now runs the Iraq Revenue Watch for the Open Society Institute. "Plus, the Iraqi government now has two sources of easy money. If the oil revenues aren't enough, there's Uncle Sam. The United States is spending its money extremely unwisely in Iraq."

This is a common complaint. America is spending billions of dollars in Iraq and getting very little for it in terms of improvements on the ground, let alone the goodwill of the people. "Most of the money is being spent for reasons of political patronage, not creating the basis for a real economy," says al Khafaji. Most of it is spent on Americans, no matter what the cost. According to al Khafaji, the rest goes to favored Iraqis. "We have studied this and I can say with certainty that [as of 2005] not a single Iraqi contractor . . . received his contract through a bidding process that was open and transparent."

The rule of law is the final, crucial condition. Without it, little else can work. America's "Viceroy," Paul Bremer, actually did a good job building institutional safeguards for the new Iraq, creating a public-integrity commission, an election commission, a human-rights commission, and inspectors general in each bureaucratic government department. Some of these safeguards have survived, but most have been shelved, corrupted, or marginalized. The courts are in better shape but could well follow the same sad fate of these other building blocks of liberal democracy. Iraq's police are routinely accused of torture and abuse of authority.

There is real pluralism and openness in Iraq, more so than in most of the Middle East. Perhaps some of the negative trends can be reversed, but Iraqi democracy is now at the mercy of the Shia majority, who we must hope will listen to their better angels. That is not a sign of success. "If men were angels," James Madison once wrote, "no government would be necessary."

From Versailles to Vietnam, this has always been the danger of American idealism. Not that the ideals were wrong or dangerous, but rather that, satisfied by the virtues of their grand goals, American policy makers lost sight of the practical realities on the ground.

In Iraq, the administration is tackling the right problems—of repression, rebellion, and political dysfunction—even if it has not been adept at constructing a solution. Outside of the Middle East, however, is the problem of tyranny the "calling of our time"? Is it the dominating issue for the world at large today?

Bush has self-consciously echoed one Inaugural Address more than any other: John Kennedy's 1961 speech, which JFK also addressed mostly to the world, promising to "pay any price, bear any burden . . . to assure the survival and the success of liberty." When John Kennedy was speaking, the vast majority of the world was unfree. Some of the largest and most productive regions of the world were ruled by powerful, totalitarian regimes that controlled every aspect of their subjects' lives and threatened the free world with armed might. Today, we live in a world that is mostly free. In 1972, when Freedom House began its practice of ranking countries on a scale of free and unfree, it placed 54 of the world's 149 in the unfree category, with scores of 6 or more (a score of 7 being the most unfree). Today only 25 of the world's 192 countries score 6 or higher. Condoleezza Rice listed some of this ragtag bunch in Senate testimony on January 18, 2005: Cuba, Burma, North Korea, Iran, Belarus, and Zimbabwe. Is ending Burmese tyranny the urgent requirement of America's security? Is battling Cuba's decrepit regime the calling of our time?

We live in a democratic age. Many countries that are not liberal democracies are often strange mixtures of freedom and unfreedom. Putin's Russia, for all its faults, is a far more open society and economy than any communist country ever was. China, often described as a totalitarian state, is actually a similar kind of mixture: a country in which people can increasingly live, work, travel, buy, sell, trade, and even worship where they want, but without any political freedom. Talk to a young Chinese official, and he will tell you that his country will loosen up those restrictions over time. This does not make Russia or China free, but neither are they the totalitarian tyrannies of old.

In this book I spoke of the intellectual contest between Russia and China, pointing out that Russia—a democracy—was becoming more illiberal by the day and that China—an autocratic regime—was becoming more open and liberal. That trend has continued, and today the more interesting intellectual contest is now between India and China and regards the age-old challenge of democracy and development.

India has weathered rather well the temptations of xenophobia and hypernationalism. Its democracy has balanced and rebalanced those forces so that while Hindu fundamentalism and fanaticism remain a troubling trend, it is not the dominant force it was when I wrote this book. In another respect, Indian democracy has been depressingly predictable. It has been trapped by a cycle of competitive populism, which has ensured that even a reform-minded government such as the one headed by Manmohan Singh has been unable to undertake much reform. The Indian government cannot spend money on education and health care for all, especially the poor, because it is busy spending money on well-organized and relatively affluent groups. Often the system of government in India seems a vast scheme to transfer money to rich farmers.

So far, China's government—cushioned from the need to entice voters—has been able to make better long-term investments in the future. It is now the world's fourth largest economy and it is growing more than four times as fast as the next two countries on the list (Germany and Japan) and more than twice as fast as number one, the United States. This explosive growth has allowed the Beijing regime to spend more money on the poor in recent years. What remains to be seen is whether a political system that is closed and authoritarian can keep governing a country that is increasingly open, messy, and diverse. Dictatorships have tended over time to become arrogant and corrupt. Can China escape the fate of other autocracies and keep up its extraordinary track record? If it does, it will be seen by many countries around the world as a viable model for modernization, one that rivals the American-centric model that speaks of democracy and economic freedom as intertwined.

China attracts attention in much of the world because the problem for many countries is not the will for democracy but the capacity to build and sustain a stable, effective, and decent government. Pakistan, for example, has not lacked a will for democracy; it established one in 1947. Since then, because of weak social structures, economic stagnation, and political crises, it has often veered toward dictatorship and, even worse, collapse. Recently, while democratic, it was careening toward an almost-failed-state status. The United States has tried to bring democracy to Haiti almost a dozen times, in different ways. None of them has stuck.

For much of the world, the great challenge today is civil strife, extreme poverty, and disease, which overwhelm not only democracy but order itself. It is not that such societies are unconcerned about freedom. Everyone, everywhere, would choose to control his own destiny. This simply does not mean as much when the basic order that precedes civilized life is threatened, and disease and death are the most pressing daily concern. Much of Africa is reasonably free, holds elections, and is far more open than ever before. The great challenge in, say, Senegal and Namibia is not freedom but an effective state. James Madison wrote in The Federalist Papers that "in framing a government which is to be administered by men over men, the great difficulty lies in this: you must first enable the government to control the governed; and in the next place oblige it to control itself." Order and then liberty—we might have remembered this in Iraq.

The dominant negative trends in much of the developing world today are toward disorder, crime, plague, and poverty. These are the forces threatening the success of these societies. These are evils that sap human beings of their potential for life, liberty, and the pursuit of happiness. And an American president should one day give an eloquent inaugural speech explaining that he or she will lead the world in taking on this great cause.

New York City
June 2007

# Notes

## A Note on the Notes

This is not a work of historical scholarship. This book's contribution to the debate is in its ideas and argument. Thus the endnotes are mostly meant to identify a striking piece of information, or provide the reference for an unusual quotation. The rule of thumb I used was, if I thought a general reader might wonder, "Where did that come from?" I've provided the answer. If I have relied on a secondary source for general insights I have usually mentioned it in the text, but I may have also cited it here.

Many of the historical interpretations I have adopted are what is sometimes called the "traditional interpretation" of events or the first set of explanations for a complex historical phenomenon. For example, on the progress of English liberalism in general and parliamentary power in particular I have taken what is sometimes called "the Whig interpretation." This is not because I deny important revisionist claims—indeed I have found E. J. Hobsbawm's work invaluable to this study—but they strike me as just that, revisions not rewritings of the traditional account. Harvard's great historian of Russia, Richard Pipes, has observed, "the trouble with revisionism is that it treats deviations and exceptions not as shadings of phenomena but as their essence." Thus J. P. Keynon, a revisionist historian, agrees that while the Whig interpretation of British history might have some flaws, no more plausible general account has replaced it. Pipes explains that revisionist claims are often exaggerated for reasons of careerism: "Each generation of historians establishes its claims to the originality of which modern reputations rest by casting doubt on the work of its predecessors usually stressing exceptions and nuances. . . . It is for this reason that the last word on any given historical subject is often the first" (Richard Pipes, *Property and Freedom* [New York: Alfred Knopf, 1999], 122 n, 149).

## Chapter 1

1 Jacob Burckhardt, *The Age of Constantine the Great*, tr. Moses Hadas (Berkeley: University of California Press, 1983), 351.

2 Benjamin Constant, "The Liberty of the Ancients Compared with That of the Moderns"(1819), in *Benjamin Constant: Political Writings*, Biancamaria Fontana, ed. (New York: Cambridge University Press, 1988).

3 Herbert Asquith, "Introduction," in Ernest Barker, *The Legacy of Rome* (Oxford, Clarendon Press, 1923), vii.

4 Quoted in David Gress, *From Plato to NATO: The Idea of the West and Its Opponents* (New York: Free Press, 1998), 125. I am particularly indebted to this fascinating and important book for its discussion of Rome and the Catholic Church.

5 Edward Gibbon, *The Decline and Fall of the Roman Empire*, vol. 3, chapter 27, part 4. Again, thanks to David Gress for this story and source.

6 E. L. Jones, *The European Miracle: Environments, Economies, and Geopolitics in the History of Europe and Asia* (New York: Cambridge University Press, 1981). This is a wonderfully broad and suggestive book, but Jones places greater weight on culture than I do.

7 Guido de Ruggiero, *The History of European Liberalism* (Oxford: Oxford University Press, 1927). A wonderful book that deserves to be a classic.

8 Daniel A. Baugh, ed., *Aristocratic Government and Society in Eighteenth Century England* (New York: New Viewpoints, 1975).

9 Paul Johnson, "Laying Down the Law," *Wall Street Journal*, March 10, 1999.

10 In the historian J. H. Plumb's words, "the Revolution of 1688 was a monument raised by the gentry to its own sense of independence." J. H. Plumb, *The Growth of Political Stability in England, 1675–1725* (London: Macmillan, 1967), 29–30.

11 Jacques Barzun, *From Dawn to Decadence: 1500 to the Present* (New York: HarperCollins, 2000), 287–89.

12 Judith Shklar, *Montesquieu* (New York: Oxford University Press, 1987), 121.

13 Douglass North and Robert Thomas, *The Rise of the Western World: A New Economic History* (Cambridge: Cambridge University Press, 1973), x.

14 Richard Pipes, *Property and Freedom* (New York: Knopf, 1999), 111.

15 Mildred Campbell, *The English Yeomen under Elizabeth and the Early Stuarts* (New York: A. M. Kelley, 1968), cited in Barrington Moore, *Social Orgins of Dictatorship and Democracy: Lord and Peasant in the Making of the Modern World* (Boston: Beacon Press, 1966).

16 Moore, *Social Orgins*, 418. The original says "bourgeois" not "bourgeoisie," but it is often quoted as the latter, which is what I have done.

17 J. M. Roberts, *The Penguin History of the World* (New York: Penguin, 1997), 553.

18 E. J. Hobsbawm, *Industry and Empire* (New York: Penguin, 1969), 26.

19 Hobsbawm, *Industry*, 48.

20 Richard Hofstadter, *America at 1750: A Social Portrait* (New York: Knopf, 1971), 131.

21 Gordon Wood, *The Radicalism of the American Revolution* (New York: Random House, 1993), p. 348.

22 Voting percentages calculated using B. R. Mitchell, *Abstract of British Historical Statistics* (Cambridge: Cambridge University Press, 1962); The Great Britain Historical G.I.S., University of Essex, available at www.geog.port.ac.uk/gbhgis/db; and E. J. Evans, *The Forging of the Modern Industrial State: Early Industrial Britain, 1783–1870* (New York: Longman, 1983). Also see Gertrude Himmelfarb, "The Politics of Democracy: The English Reform Act of 1867," *Journal of British Studies* 6 (1966).

23 Max Weber, *The Protestant Ethic and the Spirit of Capitalism* (New York: Scribner's, 1958).

24 Minxin Pei, "Constructing the Political Foundations for Rapid Economic Growth," in Henry Rowen, ed., *Behind East Asia's Growth: The Political and Social Foundations of an Economic Miracle* (London: Routledge, 1997), 39–59.

25 Myron Weiner, "Empirical Democratic Theory," in Myron Weiner and Ergun Ozbudun, eds., *Competitive Elections in Developing Countries* (Durham, N.C.: Duke University Press, 1987), 20.

## Chapter 2

1 This account, and the discussion of Lueger that follows, is largely drawn from Carl Schorske's brilliant book *Fin-de-Siecle Vienna: Politics and Culture* (New York: Vintage, 1981).

2 The 1933 election took place in an atmosphere of national hysteria, which the Nazis partly created and fully exploited. Still the reality of public support for them cannot be denied. The figures for the elections are as follows:

| Party | 1930 | 1932 (July) | 1932 (November) | 1933 |
|---|---|---|---|---|
| National Socialists | 107 | 230 | 196 | 288 |
| Social Democrats | 143 | 133 | 121 | 120 |
| Communists | 77 | 89 | 100 | 81 |
| Center (Catholics) | 68 | 97 | 70 | 73 |

3 Jack Snyder, *From Voting to Violence: Democratization and Nationalist Conflict* (New York: Norton, 2000), 118. Also on the Weimar Republic, see Sheri Berman's fine essay "Civil Society and the Collapse of the Weimar Republic," *World Politics* 49, no. 3 (April 1997).

4 On France see Phillip Nord, *The Republican Moment: Struggles for Democracy in Nineteenth-Century France* (Cambridge, Mass.: Harvard University Press, 1995). On the United Kingdom, few accounts surpass George Dangerfield's classic *The Strange Death of Liberal England* (New York: Capricorn Books, 1961). But also see Eric Hobsbawm, *The Age of Empire* (New York: Vintage, 1989).

5 Sheri Berman, "Modernization in Historical Perspective: The Case of Imperial Germany," *World Politics* 53, no. 3 (April 2001). A very persuasive essay.

6 Ralf Dahrendorf, *Society and Democracy in Germany* (New York: Doubleday, 1969). Germany's political development is an immense, complex topic, but Dahrendorf's answer to his question—which is also mine—is the best simple one. For more complex analysis of German development see David Blackbourne and Geoff Eley, *The Peculiarities of German History* (New York: Oxford University Press, 1984).

7 Karl Marx, "The Bourgeosie and the Counter-Revolution," *Neue Rheinische Zeitung*, December 1848, reprinted in Marx and Engels, Collected Works, volume 8, 154–79, available at www.marx.org/archive/marx/works/cw/volume08/.

8 Blackbourne and Eley, *Peculiarities,* 244.

9 E. E. Rich and C. H. Wilson, dirs., *Cambridge Economic History of Europe*, Vol. 5, *The Economic Organization of Early Modern Europe* (Cambridge: Cambridge University Press, 1977), 583.

10 Jacob L. Talmon, *The Origins of Totalitarian Democracy* (London: Secker and Warburg, 1955).

11 Woodrow Wilson "The Study of Administration," in Arthur S. Link, ed., *The Papers of Woodrow Wilson,* Vol. 5 (Princeton: Princeton University Press, 1968), 365–67.

12 Mark Lilla, "The Other Velvet Revolution: Continental Liberalism and Its Discontents," *Daedalus* 123, no. 2 (Spring 1994).

13 Seymour Martin Lipset, "Some Social Requisites of Democracy: Economic Development and Political Legitimacy," *American Political Science Review* 53 (March 1959).

14. Adam Przeworski and Fernando Limongi, "Modernization: Theories and Facts," *World Politics,* 49, no. 2 (January 1997). I have roughly adjusted for inflation to update the figures to 2000 purchasing power parity (PPP) in U.S. dollars. PPP is a now widely used system that weighs currencies by their domestic purchasing power rather than by exchange value and thus more accurately reflects differences in living standards. Przeworski and Limongi's original data was in 1985 U.S. dollars.

15 Angus Maddison, "The World Economy: A Millennial Perspective," Organization for Economic Co-operation and Development, 2001. I have roughly adjusted Maddison's figures for inflation to match the data in 2000 U.S. dollars.

16 Robert Kagan, "What Korea Teaches," *New Republic,* March 9, 1998.

17 Minxin Pei, "Constructing the Political Foundations for Rapid Economic Growth," in Henry Rowen, ed., *Behind East Asia's Growth: The Political and Social Foundations of an Economic Miracle* (London: Routledge, 1997), 39–59.

18 Philip Nord, *The Republican Moment: Struggles for Democracy in Nineteenth-Century France* (Cambridge, Mass.: Harvard University Press, 1995), 8.

19 Jeffrey D. Sachs and Andrew D. Warner, "Natural Resource Abundance and Economic Growth," working paper no. W5398, National Bureau of Economic Research.

20 Quoted in Bernard Lewis, *A Middle Eastern Mosaic* (New York: Random House, 2000), 225.

21 Land reform is a vast topic, but a spirited, opinionated introduction can be found in Tony Smith, *America's Mission: The United States and the Worldwide Struggle for Democracy in the Twentieth Century* (Princeton: Princeton University Press, 1995). Smith argues persuasively that in countries where the United States has had success in promoting democracy, it has largely been because of land reform. De Soto's book is Hernando de Soto, *The Mystery of Capital* (New York: Basic Books, 2000).

## Chapter 3

1 See Christian Caryl's articles in *Newsweek International*: "Sticking to the Party Line," April 16, 2001; "All Putin All the Time," April 16, 2001; and "Comrade Putin's New Russia," May 7, 2001.

2. Conversation with the author, 1999.

3 Quoted in Joseph Contreras, "Playing Hardball," *Newsweek International*, December 27, 1999, 18.

4 Rachel L. Swarns with Norimitsu Onishi, "Africa Creeps along Path to Democracy," *New York Times*, June 2, 2002.

5 Michael Chege, "Between Africa's Extremes," *Journal of Democracy* 6, no. 1 (1995). Also see Larry Diamond, "Developing Democracy in Africa," Stanford University, available at democracy.stanford.edu/Seminar/DiamondAfrica.htm.

6 Carlotta Gall, "Challenge to Azeri's Iron Ruler," *Financial Times*, February 3, 1998.

7 "A Survey of the New Geopolitics," *Economist*, July 31, 1999.

8 Reprinted in *Asian Age*, January 3, 1998, 12.

9 Arthur Schlesinger, *New Viewpoints in American History* (New York: Macmillan, 1922), 220–40.

10 *Outlook*, November 17, 1997, 22–23.

11 Alvin Rabushka and Kenneth Shepsle, *Politics in Plural Societies: A Theory of Democratic Instability* (Columbus, Ohio: Charles E. Merill, 1972) 62–92.

12 Donald Horowitz, "Democracy in Divided Societies," in Larry Diamond and Mark F. Plattner, eds., *Nationalism, Ethnic Conflict, and Democracy* (Baltimore: Johns Hopkins University Press, 1994), 35–55.

13 Jack Snyder and Edward Mansfield, "Democratization and the Danger of War," *International Security* 20, no. 1 (Summer 1995).

## Chapter 4

1 Elie Kedourie, *Democracy and Arab Political Culture* (Washington, D.C.: Washington Institute for Near East Studies, 1992), 5.

2 Bernard Lewis, *What Went Wrong: Western Impact and Middle Eastern Response* (Oxford: Oxford University Press, 2002), 97.

3 *Sahih Muslim*, book 20, hadith 4533.

4 Quoted in Bernard Lewis, *A Middle East Mosaic* (New York: Random House, 2000), 246.

5 T. E. Lawrence, *Seven Pillars of Wisdom*

6 Quoted in Edward Said, *Orientalism* (New York: Random House, 1978), 38.

7 Bahgat Korany, "Arab Democratization: A Poor Cousin?" *PS: Political Science and Politics* 27, no. 3 (September 1994), 511.

8 Halim Barakat, *The Arab World: Society, Culture, and State* (Berkeley: University of California Press, 1993), 23.

9 Mohammed Heikal, *The Cairo Documents* (Garden City, N.Y.: Doubleday, 1973).

10 Fouad Ajami, "The Sorrows of Egypt," *Foreign Affairs* 74, no. 5 (September/October 1995).

11 World Development Indicators, 2002, World Bank.

12 John Waterbury has demonstrated that, far from being undertaxed, the Middle East is the "most heavily taxed of the developing regions." Using World Bank data from 1975 to 1985, Waterbury showed that "tax revenues as a proportion of GNP averaged 25 percent for Middle Eastern states while Latin America averaged about 12 percent. This reflects not merely the effect of the preponderant weight of captive petroleum corporations in several Middle Eastern countries, which can be easily and heavily taxed. On average 19 percent of total tax revenues in the Middle East came from corporate profits tax, while the corresponding figure for Africa was 20 percent, for Asia 19 percent, and for Latin America 10 percent." But Waterbury errs by neglecting to disaggregate Arab states by type and amount of unearned income. If he had done so, he would have found that the oil-producing states—such as Saudi Arabia and Kuwait—levy few or no taxes, whereas the larger, non–oil producing states such as Egypt and Syria do levy substantial direct and indirect taxes. Although the unearned income that non–oil producing states receive is significant, it is not enough to live on. Most of the unearned income in such states goes straight to the military. So the absence of demands for democracy in the Middle East can be chalked up to two separate factors: mass bribery in the really rich states, and mass repression in the poorer ones. But both are courtesy of income that flows into the government's coffers and requires very little real economic activity.

13 The Pakistani Islamic scholar Abul Ala Maududi argued that the colonial powers could be viewed in the same manner as the pagan tribes at the dawn of Islam. Just as the pagans were fought and resisted by the Prophet, so too should a jihad be waged by Muslims against their colonial oppressors. Qutb adopted Maududi's reasoning and extended it to propose jihad against irreligious Muslim governments. Sayyid Qutb, *Milestones* (Indianapolis, Ind.: American Trust

Publications, 1990). The best introduction to Qutb is Gilles Kepel, *Muslim Extremism in Egypt: The Prophet and Pharaoh* (Berkeley: University of California Press, 1985).

14 On the power of the medieval *ulama*, see Richard W. Bulliet, *Islam: The View from the Edge* (New York: Columbia University Press, 1994).

15 Bernard Lewis, "Islam and Liberal Democracy: A Historical Overview," *Journal of Democracy* 7, no. 2 (1996) 62.

## Chapter 5

1 Bureau of Economic Analysis.

2 Gallup poll data available at www.gallup.com; Harris poll no. 4, January 17, 2001, available at www.pollingreport.com.

3 Between 1964 and 2000, registered voters increased from 65 percent to 76 percent of the voting-age population. During the same period the percentage of the voting-age population that votes dropped from 63 percent to 51 percent. The percentage of registered voters that vote dropped from a stunning 95.8 percent to 67.5 percent.

4 Robert D. Putnam, *Bowling Alone: The Collapse and Revival of American Community* (New York: Simon and Schuster, 2000), 46.

5 Joseph S. Nye, Jr., Philip D. Zelikow, and David C. King, *Why People Don't Trust Government* (Cambridge, Mass.: Harvard University Press, 1997).

6 Edmund Burke, "Speech to the Electors of Bristol," March 11, 1774, in *Select Works of Edmund Burke*, E. J. Payne, ed., vol. 4, (Indianapolis, Ind.: Liberty Fund, 1999).

7 Dale Bumpers, "How the Sunshine Harmed Congress," *New York Times*, January 3, 1999.

8 Glenn Kessler, "2003 Budget Completes Big Jump in Spending," *Washington Post*, April 15, 2002.

9 Quoted in Jonathan Rauch, *Demosclerosis* (New York: Random House, 1994), 135. A new edition of his book is titled *Government's End: Why Washington Stopped Working* (New York: Public Affairs, 1999).

10 A prescient early account of the decline of parties is David Broder's *The Party's Over: The Failure of Politics in America* (New York: Harper and Row, 1972).

11 Adam Nagourney and Janet Elder, "Poll of Delegates Shows Convention Solidly on Right," *New York Times*, July 31, 2000; Adam Clymer and Marjorie Connelly, "Poll Finds Delegates to the Left of Both Party and Public," *New York Times*, August 14, 2000.

12 David Frum, "The Elite Primary," *Atlantic Monthly*, November 1995.

13 Anthony King, "Running Scared," *Atlantic Monthly*, January 1997; also see Anthony King, *Running Scared: Why America's Politicians Campaign Too Much and Govern Too Little* (New York: Free Press, 1999). King's work on American politics is brilliant, informed by a comparative framework that is lacking in most American scholarship on American politics.

14 "The People's Revolution," *San Francisco Chronicle,* May 20, 1998.

15 An exhaustive account of modern-day referendums is David Broder's *Democracy Derailed: Initiative Campaigns and the Power of Money* (New York: Harcourt, 2000).

16 Fred Barnes, "California Doesn't Matter," *Weekly Standard*, July 31, 2000.

17 Susan Fraker, "The Politics of Taxes," *Newsweek*, November 25, 1978.

18 Barnes, "California Doesn't Matter."

19 Peter Schrag, "California's Elected Anarchy: A Government Destroyed by Popular Referendum," *Harper's* 289, no. 1734 (November 1994). Also see his excellent book—*Paradise Lost: California's Experience, America's Future* (Berkeley: University of California Press, 1999)—which should be assigned in political science classes across the country.

20 "Voters' Keep Rejecting Their Towns' Budgets," *New York Times*, September 30, 1990.

## Chapter 6

1 Jean Strouse, *Morgan: American Financier* (New York, Random House), 8.

2 Saul Hansell, "Banking's Big Deal," *New York Times*, September 13, 2000.

3 In writing this section on the change in financial markets, I benefited greatly from a conversation with Donald Marron, until recently the chief executive officer of Paine Webber.

4 Thomas Friedman, *The Lexus and the Olive Tree* (New York: Farrar, Straus and Giroux, 2000), 50.

5 Jerry Falwell, "Our Next Century Vision," July 12, 1998, available at www.trbc.org/sermons.

6 Nicholas Dawidoff, "No Sex, No Drugs, but Rock 'N Roll (Kind Of)," *New York Times Magazine*, February 5, 1995.

7 William E. Schmidt, "TV Minister Calls His Resort 'Bait' for Christianity," *New York Times*, December 24, 1985.

8 Susan Friend Harding, *The Book of Jerry Falwell: Fundamentalist Language and Politics* (Princeton: Princeton University Press, 2000), 260.

9 Jerry Falwell, "Ministers and Marches," March 21, 1965, quoted in Harding, *The Book of Jerry Falwell*, 22.

10 Kimon Howland Sargeant, *Seeker Churches: Promoting Traditional Religion in a Non-Traditional Way* (New Brunswick, N.J.: Rutgers University Press, 2000), 1, 4–5.

11 Janice Radway, *A Feeling for Books: The Book-of-the-Month Club, Literary Taste, and Middle-Class Desire* (Chapel Hill: University of North Carolina Press, 1997), 161.

12 John Seabrook, *Nobrow* (New York: Knopf, 2000), 30. Seabrook uses as an example of the old order *The New Yorker* editor William Shawn and as an example of the new, Shawn's flashiest successor, Tina Brown. I have used examples that I am more comfortable with. I do not think as well of Shawn nor as badly of Brown as he does.

13 Jed Perl, "Welcome to the Funhouse," *New Republic*, June 19, 2000.

14 R. H. Tawney, *The Acquisitive Society* (New York: Harcourt Brace, 1920), 92.

15 See Robert Gordan, "The Ideal and the Actual in Law: Fantasies of New York Lawyers, 1870–1920," in *The New High Priests: Lawyers in Post–Civil War America*, Gerard W. Gawalt, ed. (Westport, Conn.: Greenwood Press, 1984); and Gordan, "Legal Thought and Legal Practice in the Age of American Enterprise, 1870–1920," in *Professions and Professional Ideologies in America*, Gerald L. Geison, ed. (Chapel Hill: University of North Carolina Press, 1983). Also see Anthony T. Kronman, *The Lost Lawyer: Failing Ideals of the Legal Profession* (Cambridge, Mass.: Harvard University Press, 1993).

16 Michael Lewis, *Next: The Future Just Happened* (New York: Norton, 2002), 5. Lewis provides a fascinating account of the democratic effects of the internet, especially on law and finance.

17 Ianthe Jeanne Dugan, "Did You Hear the One about the Accountant?" *Wall Street Journal*, March 14, 2002.

18 John Judis, *The Paradox of American Democracy: Elites, Special Interests, and the Betrayal of the Public Trust* (New York: Random House, 2000), 21.

19 Greg Easterbrook, "Ideas Move Nations," *Atlantic Monthly*, January 1986.

20 See Joseph Alsop with Adam Platt, *I've Seen the Best of It* (New York: Norton, 1992). On Groton, see James Chace, *Acheson: The Secretary of State Who Created the American World* (New York: Simon and Schuster, 1998); and Walter Isaacson and Evan Thomas, *The Wise Men: Six Friends and the World They Made* (New York: Simon and Schuster, 1986).

21 The oft-cited classic is E. Digby Baltzell's *The Protestant Establishment:*

*Aristocracy and Caste in America* (New York: Random House, 1964). His other works are also worth reading, in particular, *Philadelphia Gentlemen: The Making of a National Upper Class* (New Brunswick, N.J.: Transaction Publishers, 1989); and his amusing last work, *Sporting Gentlemen: Men's Tennis from the Age of Honor to the Cult of the Superstar* (New York: Free Press, 1995).

22 The quotation is often attributed to Stanley Baldwin but appears to have been uttered originally by Kipling.

23 Nicholas Lehman, *The Big Test: The Secret History of the American Meritocracy* (New York: Farrar, Straus, and Giroux, 1999), 14.

24 This example is drawn mostly from Wyn Craig Wade, *The Titanic* (New York: Rawson, Wade, 1979). Also see Walter Lord, *A Night to Remember* (New York: Henry Holt, 1955).

## Conclusion

1 Alan Blinder, "Is Government Too Political," *Foreign Affairs*, November/December, 1997.

2 There is a large and interesting literature on this topic. A good starting point would be the overview in United Nations Development Program, *Human Development Report 2002: Deepening Democracy in a Fragmented World* (New York: Oxford University Press, 2002), 56. All the works it cites are worth reading, but in particular see Adam Przeworski, Michael E. Alvarez, Jose Antonio Cheibub, and Fernando Limongi, *Democracy and Development: Political Institutions and Well-Being in the World, 1950–1990* (New York: Cambridge University Press, 2000).

# Acknowledgments

Writing a book while holding down a full-time job requires indulgence and help. I started working on this book while I was at *Foreign Affairs* magazine. James Hoge, the editor, and Leslie Gelb, president of the Council on Foreign Relations, were unfailingly generous, allowing me to take time off to research and write. At *Newsweek*, Mark Whitaker and Rick Smith, the editor and editor in chief, have been similarly understanding, despite the hectic demands of a weekly magazine. I owe, in some ways, an even greater debt to my colleagues at *Foreign Affairs* and *Newsweek* who kept things going while I was working on the book. In particular, my thanks to Gideon Rose, Steven Strasser, and Nisid Hajari. My assistants through these years, Deborah Millan and Ann Coleman, and now Sharon Sullivan and Patricia Huie, have kept my work life from falling apart while I juggled various tasks.

I had invaluable help from two talented young research assistants. Samuel Walsh did the bulk of the research, in particular helping me collate and calculate all the economic data that appears in the book. Sam went on to become chief of staff to a New York City councilman and is now working on a joint degree from the Harvard Law School and the Kennedy School of Government. Joshua Brook began the research for the book when it was quite diffuse and needed focus. After his stint with me he attended the University of Michigan Law School and is now a clerk for a district judge in the Eastern District of New York. In addition, my friend Tarek Masoud helped me mightily with the chapter on Islam. Tarek, who interned at *Foreign Affairs* and then became a reporter at *The NewsHour With Jim Lehrer,* is now working on his Ph.D. at Yale University's political science department.

I imposed on friends to read the manuscript. Thanks to Andrew Moravscik of Harvard, Sheri Berman of New York University, Warren Bass of the Council on Foreign Relations, Zachary Karabell of Fred Alger and Associates, and, as always, Gideon Rose, managing editor of *Foreign Affairs,* who has read my drafts for decades now. Jon Meacham, managing editor of *Newsweek,* read Chapter 6, and gave me some useful suggestions on religion in America.

My literary agent, Tina Bennett, has been a joy to work with, always enthusiastic, persistent, and charming. My editor, Drake McFeely, is that rare editor who is deeply involved in the books he edits. He read the manuscript with great care and made detailed suggestions about structure, tone, and substance, all of which were dead-on. The book is much improved thanks to him. Everyone at W. W. Norton has been pleasant and professional. Thanks in particular to Drake's editorial assistant, Eve Lazovitz, and Traci Nagle, a *Foreign Affairs* veteran, who copyedited the book.

My parents, Rafiq and Fatma Zakaria, have anxiously awaited this book, as they do all achievements—large and small—of their son. I often talked over the book's themes with my father, and he sent me assorted clippings, facts, and insights, from which I have benefited. The discussion of India owes much to our conversations, though I should be clear that they represent my views alone. My brother Arshad has, as always, been a great support. My other brother, Mansoor, gave me one superb suggestion, the book's title, and many others as well. Dan and Joanna Rose have given me and my family the gift of their friendship, for which we are grateful.

Finally, my wife, to whom this book is dedicated. Paula would be much happier on any day reading a novel. Yet she read every word of this book several times, making copious suggestions, at one point diagramming a part of the argument to show me why I had to change it. (She was right.) She's thrilled that the book is done and that I'm at home more often. She can now get back to her novels.

# Index